The
Dream of
Arcady

The
Dream of
Arcady

Place and Time in Southern Literature

Lucinda Hardwick MacKethan

Louisiana State University Press
Baton Rouge and London

Copyright © 1980 by
LOUISIANA STATE UNIVERSITY PRESS

Printed in the United States of America

Design: Robert L. Nance
Typeface: Galliard
Composition: LSU Press
Printing: Thomson-Shore, Inc.
Binding: John H. Dekker & Sons, Inc.

Author and publisher are grateful for permission to reprint material
that previously appeared in these journals:

"To See Things in Their Time: The Act of Focus in Eudora Welty's Fiction,"
American Literature, L (May, 1978).

"Jean Toomer's *Cane*: A Pastoral Problem," *Mississippi Quarterly*, XXVIII
(Fall, 1975).

"Thomas Nelson Page: The Plantation as Arcady," *Virginia Quarterly
Review*, LIV (Spring, 1978).

Library of Congress Cataloging in Publication Data

MacKethan, Lucinda Hardwick.
  The dream of Arcady.

  Bibliography: p.
  CONTENTS: The South as Arcady.—Sidney Lanier.—Thomas Nelson Page. [etc.]
  1. American literature—Southern States—History and criticism. 2. Pastoral
literature, American—Southern States—History and criticism. I. Title.
PS261.M25   810'.9'32   79–16543
ISBN 0–8071–0599–6

To Louis D. Rubin, Jr.

Contents

List of Abbreviations

ONE

The South as Arcady:
Beginnings of a Mode

In 1863 a fifteen-year-old printer's apprentice, living on a quiet plantation in Georgia, published a brief essay on the charms of rural life in his employer's journal, *The Countryman*. The boy was Joel Chandler Harris; the theme of his rather light descriptive piece was one to which he would return in later years with a much more intense recognition of what was at stake. "People who live in crowded cities," wrote the boy, "as a general thing, have no idea of the beautiful stillness of a Sabbath evening in the country, far away from the bustle and turmoil attendant on city life."[1] Harris' simplistic rendering of the differences between country and city involved little more than a fashionable commonplace, to be sure; it is doubtful that his preference for the country was based on much more than pure appreciation for his present circumstances. Turnwold plantation, Harris' home from 1862 to 1866, was a place of peace and comfort, the estate of a gentleman whose slaves were well cared for, his crops well tended, and his library well stocked. Here Joseph Addison Turner had dedicated himself to the occupations of gentleman farmer: "to cultivate corn, cotton, and literature."[2] To Joel Chandler Harris, a poor boy from a nearby village, life in any city could offer little in comparison to the grace and gentility of Turnwold.

1. Julia Collier Harris, *Joel Chandler Harris: Editor and Essayist* (Chapel Hill, 1931), 247.
2. Paul Cousins, *Joel Chandler Harris* (Baton Rouge, 1968), 40.

1

Yet by the summer of 1866 the "beautiful stillness" of Turnwold had been shattered. Turner was bankrupt, the slaves who had worked the land were gone, and the last editorial of *The Countryman* proclaimed that the publication had been "a representative of independent country life, and of the home of the planter. These are gone, and *The Countryman* goes with them."[3] Gone with Harris' source of employment was the world that had made possible the attitudes he described in "Sabbath Evening in the Country." Many years later when he began to re-create the scenes of his youth in his stories, novels, and newspaper features, there would be a different emphasis in his portrayals of country life that had not entered into his first essay—a strong note of nostalgia, a keen sense of loss, and an admittedly romantic vision of the past. Harris would become himself a city-dweller, caught up in all the "bustle" and "toil" of being an editor of the most progressive newspaper of the South. Yet he would always speak of country life in a language of reverence; in 1877 he would write that the plantation "has passed away, but the hand of time . . . has woven about it the sweet suggestions of poetry and romance, memorials that neither death nor decay can destroy."[4]

The figure who became Harris' most successful literary creation was a man who belonged to the world Harris had to leave behind, the aged black Uncle Remus. In the old slave's remembrances of the "laughin' times" before the war, he reflected and became the defender of a whole system of values by which the present could be measured and criticized. The golden atmosphere evoked by Uncle Remus as he told the timeless legends of his race to a white boy of a new era has become, according to social historian Francis Pendleton Gaines, "our chief social idyll of the past, of an Arcadian scheme of existence, less material, less prosaically equalitarian, less futile, richer in picturesqueness, festivity, in realized pleasure that recked not of hope or fear or unrejoicing labor."[5] Gaines is talking here about the Old South, not as it actually existed or perished, but as it has been shaped by artists whose literature spans in time now almost a century during which there has emerged from southern fiction and poetry a complex, compelling image of Arcady.

3. Joseph Addison Turner, *The Countryman*, May 6, 1866. Quoted *ibid.*, 60.
4. Julia Collier Harris, *Editor and Essayist*, 90.
5. Francis Pendleton Gaines, *The Southern Plantation: A Study in the Development and the Accuracy of a Tradition* (New York, 1924), 75.

The popular imagination, tasked with framing a definition of the South, easily translates the actuality into old times in the land of cotton, conjuring up a world committed in both imagery and ideology to the preservation of the simple, good life, to a working respect for nature, and to the practice of neighborliness. The prominence of this idea of the South, employing a landscape certainly of Arcadian dimensions, is due largely to the work of southern writers from the Reconstruction era to the present day who have nurtured in their portrayals of their region some aspect of that ancient pastoral district famed for its rural peace and simplicity. It must be stressed immediately that their Arcadian designs have often come from unquestioning faith or private preference rather than any reasoned exploration or objective perception of the ideal itself as it relates to their images of the South. The easy acceptance, at least at first, on the part of writers and public alike of the idea that the Old South could be portrayed as a dream of Arcady has indeed made for special problems in perception that can be considered part of the challenge as well as the appeal of the works today.

To the extent that many southern writers have developed their images of the South as a dream of Arcady, they seem most often to have retained the trappings of that golden land primarily as a device by which they might expose or rebuke, escape or confront, the complexities of the actual time in which they have lived. And as such purposes, contradictory as they may be, are incorporated into the writers' concepts of the South, their works emerge as clear projections of the literary mode of pastoral. Particularly when we consider the pastoral mode in very broad terms, using for the moment the definition of Frank Kermode who defines pastoral as "any work which concerns itself with the contrast between simple and complicated ways of living,"[6] we can determine many significant analogies between the literary pastorals of other eras and much of the literature of the South. Joel Chandler Harris' Uncle Remus, not unlike Virgil's shepherd, is the device of a comparatively sophisticated poetic mind looking back on a land of dreams threatened with extinction.

The elaborate and often-changed conventions of pastoral literature could never be completely defined or related to southern literature in any examination of reasonable length, yet the patterns of

6. Frank Kermode (ed.), *English Pastoral Poetry* (London, 1952), 13.

similarity, if not perfectly managed in every detail, are certainly clear enough. The emphasis in much southern literature that is most significant in terms of allowing, even necessitating, discussions of it as pastoral is its persistent use of the southern place as a golden agrarian world that is passing or past, always receding farther back into lost time. In addition, southern literature frequently takes as its departure point three specifically pastoral motifs: the urge to celebrate the simplicities of a natural order; the urge to idealize a golden age almost always associated with childhood; and the urge to criticize a contemporary social situation according to an earlier and purer set of standards.

Thus the literature developed by many southern writers over the century that has followed the Civil War belongs in important respects to the pastoral tradition that has its most influential sources in the eclogues of Virgil or the even earlier idylls of Theocritus. Raymond Williams has examined this literary tradition extensively in an early chapter of *The Country and the City*, where he emphasizes the transformation that the form has undergone and the confusion that surrounds present applications of the term "pastoral." Williams makes two points which are central to any discussion relating modern literature to the early, or "classical," pastorals. The first is that, "in classical pastoral and other rural literature . . . there is almost invariably a tension with other kinds of experience: summer with winter; pleasure with loss; harvest with labor; singing with a journey; past or future with the present."[7] Thus in the first of Virgil's *Eclogues*, Meliboeus invokes the lovely view of a rural world at peace, but he goes on to sing of things which demonstrate that this peace "is in explicit contrast to his own condition, as an evicted small farmer."[8] Leo Marx, who in *The Machine in the Garden* studies the traditional forms in relation to pastoral forces in American literature, makes a distinction between "complex" and "sentimental" pastoral by requiring that the complex or "literary" pastoral "manage to qualify, or call into question, or bring irony to bear against the illusion of peace in a green pasture."[9] Certainly the experience of the Civil War as a force disrupting a way of life forever in the South made this element of ten-

7. Raymond Williams, *The Country and the City* (New York, 1973), 18.
8. *Ibid.*, 16.
9. Leo Marx, *The Machine in the Garden* (New York, 1964), 25.

sion not just available but really inevitable for southern literature. Out of the common practice of contrasting the rural "southern way" with the industrial "American way" or the "Old" South with the "New" South have come many ironies of special meaning concerning illusions about the South.

Yet a second point made by Raymond Williams is of more immediate concern—what has happened to the classical pastoral in modern times? As Renaissance writers adapted the classical mode to their own concerns, the "living tensions" of the early work were "excised," says Williams, "and selected images [came to] stand as themselves: not in a living but in an enamelled world."[10] With the "reduction of these primary activities to forms" in the literature of the Renaissance onwards, the pastoral mode became most often not a celebration of simplicity but instead a pretension to simplicity for reasons involving sophisticated political and social alliances. William Empson, in *Some Versions of Pastoral*, goes so far as to interpret pastoralism, in part, as a politically motivated device whereby the artistic or modern upper classes cross the cultural gap which divides them from the common people; he theorizes that "the essential trick of the old pastoral, which was felt to imply a beautiful relationship between rich and poor, was to make simple people express strong feelings . . . in beautiful language."[11]

Williams considers many of the extensions of the pastoral mode into areas of modern thought to be "absurd," and it is important to define carefully and to qualify as specifically as possible what it is that we mean as we use the term "pastoral" in discussing southern literature. Certainly the culture that became a cornerstone for a regional mythology likening the Old South to Arcady pretended simplicity more than it achieved or even wanted to approach the pure state of it. What the ideas and images of the pastoral tradition offer most fruitfully to this study is what Raymond Williams calls "a way of seeing";[12] the pastoralist of any age or environment envisions a particular social structure which becomes a dramatic mechanism for making comparisons between real and ideal worlds, for distinguishing between the artificial and the natural, for examining systems of values for any one of

10. Williams, *The Country and the City*, 18.
11. William Empson, *Some Versions of Pastoral* (Norfolk, Conn., 1950), 11.
12. Williams, *The Country and the City*, 34.

a great variety of purposes, emotional and political as well as artistic. Southern literature in its own clear tradition is associated with strong judgments and a positive system of values—not always the same judgments or even the same system, to be sure, yet a literature that seems to insist on shared standards highly visible and widely articulated. Thus it has been able to speak to the need met by pastorals generally, the need of people in a rapidly changing world to have a vision of an understandable order.

None of the writers examined in this study defined their literary works as "pastorals" or even conceived their landscapes as "Arcadies" with any strict formal sense in mind. When we confer these distinctions, they apply as indications of direction and design taken by certain prominent writers of Reconstruction and modern times. The pastoral patterns exhibited in the works considered here vary greatly and diverge from the basic, conventional forms significantly. Yet the mode of expression is pastoral and the patterns exhibited belong to the tradition in many ways. They have in common a concept of Arcady for which some aspect or image of the South operates (albeit, for some, only ironically) as an idealization of order. And more specifically, we associate with these works, though on different levels and in sometimes even contrasting contexts, certain trademarks of what might be called the "mood" of the pastoral. There is to be seen in them, for instance, a quality of innocence, often embodied in a rural or village personage who serves to emphasize not so much the state of innocence itself but the larger world's loss of it. Then, too, a persistent nostalgia pertains which is, like the innocence, ironic: Arcadia at its most glorious is an entrapment which if never abandoned can never be honestly explored. Two more assumptions of the pastoral mood that we meet frequently are an assertion of the superiority of rural virtues and, more importantly, a reverence for the natural order of nature itself. And lastly, we encounter in all these works the significant oscillation between dream and reality.

What we will find perhaps most intriguing, finally, are the forms these southern dreams of Arcady take, the undercurrents of irony and limitation that sometimes surface without the author's consciousness of them, the striking elaborations that are grafted onto the idealized worlds, the implicit fatalism of the dreams themselves. Sooner or later in all of them the idyllic vision is subjected to the inescapable moment of awakening, to the inevitable pressure of change. And this is the atmosphere that pertains when an approach that we can identify as being pastoral in its mood and implications is brought to bear by the writers in this study.

In dealing with change, the writers here assembled bring a variety of perspectives and solutions; the symbols used to depict change for the South vary as well. Sidney Lanier most often tries to do battle with the commercial spirit that he names "Trade"; Page and Harris can conjure up images of "The War" itself, or of cold-hearted Yankee carpetbaggers, or even of the "Noo-Issue Nigger" to represent the threatening force; for Charles Chesnutt, looking over ostensibly the same plantation field, the white man himself carries the seeds of his world's destruction as he wields the whip on his slaves. Then, as we move into the twentieth century and into a South that has fragmented unalterably into many Souths, the responses and identifications become harder to classify under any unifying vision. Jean Toomer, singing a "swan-song" for the black man's very ambiguously framed Arcadian existence in the rural South, realizes perhaps more fully than any of the other writers included here the artistic possibilities of applying the pastoral mode to the experiences of change that he is charting in *Cane*. The Fugitive-Agrarians might be thought to belong rather easily to a discussion of pastoral, yet their agrarian treatise, *I'll Take My Stand*, is by no means the simple assertion of southern agrarian over northern industrial values that it might seem to be at first glance. As doctrinaire as their preference for the traditional, communal, rural way of life associated with the Old South might look, their measure of their inheritance is taken to meet deeper needs than nostalgia and employs a very complicated sense of what has been lost and what might be gained by the effort. When thinking of the strategy of some of the works of William Faulkner which seem significantly involved in concerns of a pastoral orientation, we find that Faulkner's focus on the moral dilemmas of modern man carries him far beyond the question of how the South itself has changed into the more dramatic problem of the southerner's incapacity for change. Thus the pastoral values that surface in his work tend to turn in directions that threaten the very function of life in time. The work of Eudora Welty provides us, finally, with a celebration of the traditional southern community not as a kind of pastoral fortress, a place of walls built to preserve cherished values and identities belonging to the past, but as a place of windows that must be opened on the wide and mysterious world of the future beyond.

The South is not in the last analysis for all, or even perhaps for any, of these writers fully or simply a dream of Arcady. The Arcadian vision of the South is called into being not as an end in itself but almost always as a frame for artistic and in most cases ideological purposes of a very different order. The complexities involved in dreaming an Arcadian dream of the South are apparent in even the earliest and supposedly the simplest versions we encounter.

In a study of southern writers who deal extensively with the image of the South as Arcady, it is important to note the remarkable conditions through which their literature gained not just credence but formidable influence during and immediately after Reconstruction. Before the war literature dealing with the plantation South had inevitably become associated with the defense of a system which threatened northern interests; however, as Paul Buck says, "A culture which in its life was an anathema to the North, could in its death be honored." [13] Southern writers were quick to take advantage of the opportunity. In the fiction of the postwar South there emerged the vision of a land "where romance of the past still lived, a land where, in short, the nostalgic northerner could escape the wear and tear of expanding industry and growing cities and dwell in a Dixie of the storybooks which had become the Arcady of American tradition." [14] C. Vann Woodward calls it a "freakishly romantic turn of Northern fancy" [15] that wanted to enshrine the Old South as America's golden age, and this tendency of northern readers, when combined with the southern writer's eager impulse to glorify and justify Dixie, produced the grand dream of a southern Arcady and allowed it more attention and respect than it had ever known in antebellum times.

In reality the southerner undergoing Reconstruction was eager to catch up economically with his fellow Americans. Newspaper editorials preached the gospel that "restoration of material prosperity of

13. Paul Buck, *The Road to Reunion, 1865–1900* (Boston, 1937), 208.
14. *Ibid.*, 235.
15. C. Vann Woodward, *Origins of the New South, 1877–1913* (Baton Rouge, 1951), 165.

the South should be the chief object and untiring effort of all her sons."[16] The idea of a New South, committed to progress, to the building of railroads and to attracting northern capital and labor, was being promoted in industrial expositions and through the persuasive oratory of Henry Grady. And southerners were buying the idea. What most of them came to feel, according to John Donald Wade, was that "they were desperately poor, while the North was desperately rich. They wanted to be rich too."[17]

C. Vann Woodward takes note of this parallel development of two conflicting trends: "Along with the glittering vision of a metropolitan and industrial South to come there developed a cult of archaism, a nostalgic vision of the past."[18] Here, in the two conflicting responses to their world that southerners were expressing during the Reconstruction era, we find the conditions which promote the development of pastoral concerns. Here too we should point out that well before the Civil War there were southern writers who celebrated an even earlier South as an agrarian paradise. In the work of John Pendleton Kennedy, William Gilmore Simms, Nathaniel Beverley Tucker, and William Wirt, to name four important examples, a strong element of nostalgia grows out of the recollection of a simpler time. Yet as we think of the development of a regional pastoral consciousness out of which a dominant trend in literature seems to take shape, it is the fact of the Civil War and its destruction of the system through which the South's agrarian economy thrived that provides the impetus for the creation of the particular dream of Arcady that has remained important as a literary motif down to the present time.

At this point we can make some specific assumptions about the conditions out of which the South's dynamic "version of pastoral" has developed. A seemingly simple kind of rural society finds itself being irrevocably set upon a more complex, urban course; it can be seen that in the process much that has always been held to be of spiritual value is being discarded or has already been lost, and in the resulting confusion the cultural aims of the society in question become divided between the pull toward progress and the grip of the past. Frank

16. Quoted in Buck, *Road to Reunion*, 150.
17. John Donald Wade, "What the South Figured, 1865–1914," in *Selected Essays and Other Writings of John Donald Wade* (Athens, Ga., 1966), 85.
18. Woodward, *Origins of the New South*, 154.

Kermode writes that "pastoral flourishes at a particular moment in the urban development, the phase in which the relationship of metropolis and country is still evident."[19] Certainly conditions in the South provided just this "particular moment" when urban development was becoming the inevitable if not the universally preferred course; in the case of the Reconstruction South, a more intense pressure for the writer resulted from the need to vindicate or at least commemorate a mode of "country" life already defeated as well as defamed.

Through the works of writers like Joel Chandler Harris and Thomas Nelson Page, the Old South received new life; the plantation regime was vindicated and its pleasant rural peace held up as an alternative to the confusion of the materialistic New South. In his essay "Social Life in Old Virginia Before the War" Page voiced a nostalgic expression of the pastoral ideal as he envisioned it being practiced in his father's day:

Truly it was a charming life. There was a vast waste; but it was not loss. Every one had food, every one had raiment, every one had peace. There was not wealth in the base sense in which we know it and strive for it and trample down others for it now. But there was wealth in a good sense in which the litany of our fathers used it. There was weal.[20]

The overriding concern of the early versions of the dream of Arcady was for the stability and the maintenance of order and decorum that were felt to be the outstanding attributes of life on the old plantations. The pastoral quest is always basically a search for order. After the Civil War southern writers managed to put the stability in their art that was missing in their lives by formulating neat resolutions to the dilemmas raised by the destruction of the old regime. The most common ending to the plantation romance finds the Yankee soldier marrying the southern belle and thereby saving the old home place from ruin. Such endings symbolize not just the reunion between North and South that was so devoutly to be wished; they represent a restoration of belief in the old order.

Was the planter aristocracy as it was actually established in the an-

19. Kermode, *English Pastoral Poetry*, 15.
20. Thomas Nelson Page, *The Old South* (New York, 1894), 184.

tebellum South worthy of the homage paid so dramatically by northerners as well as southerners after the war? Francis Pendleton Gaines
describes how the post–Civil War plantation fiction elaborates on the
earlier literature: "The scale of life was steadily enlarged, the colors
were made increasingly vivid. Estates swelled in size and mansions
grew proportionately great."[21] And a forceful qualification must be
appended to the image developed in postwar fiction of the planter as
not concerned with money, not materialistic. The eager embrace of
king cotton, the gaudy display of wealth in the fine mansions, the
imported furniture, the finery of costume and carriage—and most
importantly, the exploitation of slave labor to secure these material
gains—act as emphatic refutations of the idea of the planter as Arcadian. And yet the fact that the planter is portrayed as such in order
to complete the pastoral design of the fiction produced after the Civil
War is an indication of the complexities involved in that genre itself.
And the inclusion of the figure of the devoted slave in these works
offers the richest paradox of all.

We have seen how the concept of the South as a unique region grew
into an Arcadian myth through the promotion of the belief that the
plantation provided the last and greatest bastion for the promotion
of the pastoral ideal. Yet the plantation regime was also founded upon
an institution which made the innocence which we associate with a
pastoral way of life impossible. Close to a third of the Old South's
population were slaves, and surely it was a unique kind of Arcadia
which forced human beings to labor in bondage for its support. The
most amazing fact of the matter is not merely that the Negro, associated as he is with the South's guilt and humiliation, is present in the
scheme, but that he is absolutely essential to it. He is the central figure and most often the chief spokesman in post–Civil War portrayals
of the antebellum Arcadia.

The problem of how to deal with the question of the presence of
slaves in Arcady was solved by having the black man plead the cause
of his former master. The case for both rested on the kind of relationship that supposedly thrived in a plantation society. In that simpler world, so the argument went, mutual affection between the races
was the natural state of affairs; black man and white were part of one

21. Gaines, *The Southern Plantation*, 64.

family devoted to maintaining a way of life which joined mansion and cabin together in common endeavors. Thus the most popular narrators of plantation fiction were the slaves or former slaves who reminisced about the good old times before the war, or related the postwar hardships of their owners, and throughout it all demonstrated their loyal support for the regime which, if it kept them in servitude, still provided for their happiness and security.

Francis Pendleton Gaines tells us that "a popular literary device, repeated again and again, was to hand down the legend of splendor and joy through the mouths of the slaves themselves. . . . In spite of proclamations and amendments, the old slave, remembering happier days, wails 'Marse Lincoln gun me freedom. Whar' my Chris'mus?'"[22] Paul Buck makes the additional point in *The Road to Reunion* that, in contrast to antebellum writing, in the Reconstruction stories it is the master who is helpless and often dependent upon his slave's continued loyalty: "Uncle Tom was the martyr of a system, but Uncle Billy [the faithful family retainer in a story by T. N. Page] was as he himself stated the 'chief 'pendence uv Meh Lady.'"[23]

What resulted from the device of having the Negro narrator to tell the tales of the old plantation was that "subtly and with great felicity a persuasive dogma of defense was inculcated in this literature."[24] The Negro character was invaluable for establishing the picturesque mood of the plantation. In the city he was the helpless tool of corrupt politicians, blundering do-gooders, and thieves masquerading as reformers, but on the plantation he was welcomed as a venerable member of the family to whom the children of the new age were brought in order that he might instill in them a sense of pride in their heritage.

As a romantic rustic, therefore, the "darky" was a personage of great importance to southern literature. However, the judgment of a later day is that he was "primarily a device by which a white philosophy of race relations was advanced."[25] After the Civil War the great northern magazines began catering to the new national curiosity concerning different sectional habits and traditions. The Negro was the most

---

22. *Ibid.*, 63.
23. Buck, *Road to Reunion*, 210.
24. *Ibid.*, 209.
25. *Ibid.*, 210.

picturesque and popular figure brought forward by southern local colorists answering the call for such fiction, and they found themselves enabled, through the interest of the North, to combine the two motives closest to their hearts. They made names for themselves as writers by satisfying the reading public's demand for delineations of the quaint and romantic qualities of plantation life; the Negro was characterized for the most part as the childlike, comic recipient of the white planter's benevolent guidance. In this way the North was presented with the southerners' racial philosophy couched in the most attractive terms possible: the southerner best "understood" the Negro through his long and typically benign association with him; he was therefore the best judge of how to handle race relations and should be given control over policies dealing with the freedman's assimilation into the national life. Writing in 1888 on "The South as a Field for Fiction," even the great abolitionist Albion Tourgée was forced to admit defeat. "Our literature," he said in surrender, "has become not only Southern in type but distinctly Confederate in sympathy."[26]

C. Vann Woodward has commented that "the [fictional] outpourings of the eighties were not alien to the spirit of the New South." By offering to the nation a picture of the South as a region basically hospitable to the best ideals of America, the fiction of this period helped immensely to hasten the process of reconciliation and also the process of Negro disfranchisement. "Embarrassing race conflict dissolved in liquid dialect,"[27] Woodward reports, for a northern public tired of abolitionist frenzies and eager to get on with other things was content generally to accept the South's new image.

The charge that plantation literature during and after the Reconstruction era was chiefly written as propaganda to establish a national policy of white supremacy has often been overstated. Still, it is important to attempt to determine the motives of the men who glorified the Old South and gave to a civilization founded on slavery and racial prejudice the romantic appeal of pastoral idyll. If their stories are primarily southern propaganda, what is their relation to genuine pastoral?

The first thing to consider is that the pastoral as a literary form has

---

26. Albion Tourgée, "The South as a Field for Fiction," *Forum*, VI (February, 1888), 405.

27. Woodward, *Origins of the New South*, 167.

in modern times frequently been used as a vehicle for advancing political preferences. However, when a writer deliberately distorts certain aspects of the past in order to promote his own special interests, the literature he creates is actually working at cross-purposes with the legitimate aims of the pastoral genre. In all pastoral there is some amount of idealization of the past; seen from the vantage point of a troubled technological present, the rural order of an earlier era takes on a rosy glow. Harris and Page both admitted that their view of the Old South was "idealized by the haze of time." The writer makes use of the human tendency to idealize the past in order to dramatize his concern for the discrepancies he observes "between rural and urban, country and courtly, simple and complex, natural and artificial,"[28] as Walter Greg says. The problem is to determine when such idealizations are being used not to make some significant comparison between two different ways of life but to engage the active sympathy of the reader for special causes by exploiting his nostalgic longings and his desire to escape from reality.

There is no question but that the romantic idealizations of plantation life perpetuated by writers of the decades immediately following the Civil War resulted in frequent and glaring distortions of the real Old South. Between the popular conception of the plantation and the actual conditions on actual plantations there exist great discrepancies, as Gaines capably demonstrates in *The Southern Plantation*. Yet, whereas some of the plantation literature of the post-Reconstruction era without a doubt misrepresented realities of the Old South in order to promote a narrow sectional viewpoint, the best work of the period nevertheless has qualities which have helped to give it a broad basis of appeal. In some cases it is because the characterizations ring true to human nature in spite of the romanticized settings, in others because the stories contain the lyric intensity of elegy or the enduring charm of fable. Always in the serious art there is the mark of genuine concern for the values behind the manners and the splendor.

This is not to say that this literature is good simply because it is sincere. The writer's love of his subject matter is one of the most obvious features of plantation literature. However, it is also obvious in these works that the writer seldom has a full understanding of that subject matter. He is almost always too involved in justifying his material to be able to judge it with anything like artistic detachment.

28. Walter W. Greg, *Pastoral Poetry and Pastoral Drama* (New York, 1959), 5.

Thus his creations often remain in the realm of the sentimental romance. They are naïve, sometimes heavy with special pleading, usually lacking in the sense of distance necessary to convey the ironies involved.

It is Richard Weaver's judgment in *The Southern Tradition at Bay* that "Southern literature became mature when it first became capable of irony." Thus he contends that "the early Reconstruction writers who undertook to defend the antebellum South by picturing it without fault were making a mistake," because "only when the impulse to justify is replaced by the impulse to see the thing in the round does something like an enduring justification become possible." Justification all too often superseded the artistic desire to see the Old South clearly or see it whole in the first important postwar fiction. Yet Weaver admits that this early literature had significance: "Whatever diverse aims the authors had in mind, they contributed to the vindication of the South by making it a concrete reality, a part of the stubborn fact of the world, against which political delusions must always break."[29]

Weaver's assessment of the literature dealing with the Old South is important to this study, because the prevailing concern of his book definitely involves the image of the Old South as Arcadia. A promoter of the southern agrarian movements of the 1930s, Weaver voiced the belief that when the "victims of the confusion and frustration of our own time" began to study the Old South, they would find there the roots of *"the last non-materialist civilization in the Western World"*; thus he felt that the modern South offered a challenge to the nation, the "challenge to save the human spirit by re-creating a non-materialist society."[30] This challenge has been the preoccupation of many southern writers. The writers of the last decades before the twentieth century, with varying capacities for critical awareness, recognized the many uses, political as well as literary, that the creation of images of the South as Arcadia could have. The fact that Weaver himself believes that the South has clung "more or less unashamedly to the primitive way of life" is an indication of the persuasiveness of the dogmas that found an attractive setting in post-Reconstruction fiction. Yet as we turn to literature of the modern southern renascence, it is the ironies and negations connected with Weaver's own

29. Richard Weaver, *The Southern Tradition at Bay* (New York, 1968), 340–41.
30. *Ibid.*, 391.

idea of the South as "the last non-materialist civilization in the Western World" that often have made the modern works a compelling commentary on, instead of simply an extension of, the earlier works.

A study of post-Reconstruction southern literature properly begins with a look at the status of life and art in the South at the close of the Civil War. The writer whose experience best reflects how the impulse to simplify might naturally grow out of the conditions that prevailed in the South immediately following the war is Sidney Lanier. Through his writings we become aware of the problems that any southern writer would face whose love of the old world was counterbalanced by the motivation to make his way in a totally new and alien one. Lanier formulated the design of his art from the tensions that operated so forcefully in his own life. In his work an urgent need for peace and quiet and a sense of the South's moral superiorities are pitted against other compelling and contradictory needs, in particular those of succeeding in an urban, industrialized society and of having to acknowledge the economic deficiencies that led to the South's defeat.

Yet Lanier's version of the pastoral reflects, for southern literature, the road not taken. His work bypassed the plantation myth with its rich—though often distorted and morally ambiguous—suggestions of a simple, glorified past; instead Lanier located his idea of pastoral value in the myth of a yeoman South peopled by small independent farmers who would reflect the Jeffersonian dedication to self-sufficiency and simplicity. In a study of southern literature Lanier's position is instructive of the options as well as the problems facing a writer emerging from the devastations, cultural as well as economic, wrought by the war. The question of the direction his work might have taken had he lived into the period dominated by the plantation writers is also important to consider.

Thomas Nelson Page and Joel Chandler Harris offer the most complex as well as the most popular examples in post-Reconstruction literature of how the pretension to simplicity could be made to seem a genuine principle of the old plantation South. The impulse "to see the thing in the round" as Weaver put it might often be missing from their evocations of the old order, yet their response to contemporary times represents an important evaluation of the only region in America that ever ideologically identified itself as a rural Arcadia.

We must look to the work of Page and Harris, in studying Arcadian motifs in southern literature, to find a significant element of any pastoral design—the simple rustic spokesman. By making the loyal black slave function in the capacity of apologist for the plantation's golden age, Page and Harris created literature that becomes for us enriched by a sense of paradox that often escaped the writers themselves. Through the inclusion of slave characters the plantation idylls of Page and Harris deny, at the same time that they attempt to promote, the ethical superiority of the southern system.

The work of a black writer of the same era can be used to counterbalance the versions of the South as heaven and haven that we encounter in the plantation writings of Page and Harris. In Charles Chesnutt's stories and novels we come upon a design in which the standardized features of the plantation are twisted into grotesque contradictions of the true ideal. Chesnutt's work might be read as commentary or even satire on the pastoral assumptions of the white southerner of the post-Reconstruction period. In this context it is not only his collection of conjure stories, *The Conjure Woman*, which explodes with irony upon the dream of Arcady but also the bitter portrayal in his last published novel, *The Colonel's Dream*, of a benevolent "New South" white southerner who has a vision of redeeming his neighbors from a tragic sort of mock-pastoral existence.

Thus in the first part of this study we trace the development of southern literature through four writers who lived and wrote in a period which witnessed the transposition of the South's "feudal fantasy" from shaky actuality into enduring myth. The writers themselves came from widely divergent backgrounds and differed in their visions of what the South could or should represent to the world after the Civil War. Yet their works attest—even in their variety—to the utility of the image of the South as a simple rural world. For Lanier, Page, Harris, and even Chesnutt, the image offered pertinent possibilities as a way of seeing and a way of evaluating the losses and gains they themselves experienced as they entered the new world that emerged from the Civil War. And it is largely their involvement in the development or the critical examination of some facet of this image that enabled them to contribute to the literary flowering in the twentieth century of more complex dreams and metaphors for the South as America's most alluring and most ambiguous Arcadia.

TWO

Sidney Lanier:
The Scythe of Time,
The Trowel of Trade

So is your pastoral life whirled past and away." This was Henry David Thoreau's reaction as he watched a cattle train roar through the woods near Walden Pond. The "ear-rending" sound of the train occurs many times in Thoreau's essay, always interrupting, always disturbing the beauty and serenity of his life in the woods. Thoreau was conducting an experiment in nature and also an exercise in the formation and use of images. In *Walden* train and pond are matched, opposed, and reconciled through Thoreau's intricate artistry, and one of the many revelations that emerges is that, except in art, the day when a pastoral life could be lived was gone, or soon would be.

The southerner, picking up the pieces of his world after the Civil War, was forced like Thoreau to look upon a pastoral life being "whirled past and away" by the hurricane force of a great industrial power. His ordeal was at once more intensely and more romantically defined by him as he witnessed literally a scene that Thoreau only prophesied largely in symbolic terms, the destruction of a whole way of life. Sidney Lanier, who fought in the war and returned to Georgia to see both economic and artistic aspirations crushed, wrote a painfully personal version of Thoreau's elegy to Arcady in a letter to a northern friend in May of 1866: "I can scarcely discern any sight or sound of those old peaceful days that you and I passed on the

'Sacred soil of M[idway]'—The sweet, half-pastoral tones that should come from out that golden time, float to me mixed with battle-cries and groans."[1]

A world that had been cultivated to be or appear to be a showcase of pastoral values had disappeared in the space of the years of war, and in its place was a chaos so complete that even memories of "that golden time" were hopelessly marred. When the South began to function again, there was total confusion concerning priorities, programs, possibilities. The struggle for all at first was the sheer business of survival in a land almost completely devastated in terms of wealth, manpower, and leadership. Lanier was to write of this period that "with us of the younger generation of the South, since the war, pretty much the whole of life has been merely not dying."[2]

For the southern artist the economic woes were compounded by aesthetic ones. Lanier could remark that "whereas I *used* to live wholly to make beautiful things, I now live half-ly to make money: and I hate all half-way things."[3] An artist who interpreted his past—as Lanier obviously did—as a kind of pastoral playground had an especially difficult conflict to resolve. There was no hope of restoring the Arcadian atmosphere which had existed as much (if not more) as a staple of the imagination as a part of reality. To be an artist in the immediate postwar South was to be aware of both the new realities and the need to find a new language for the imagination. If pastoral inclinations could survive the holocaust (and they did for most, it seems) then the major task for the artist would be to find valid metaphors to use in bringing the pastoral ideology into some kind of dynamic alignment with the inescapable forces of contemporary history.

Lanier did not look to the plantation past for such a metaphor. He seldom chose to make use of the powerful images that a plantation setting could provide, and in particular he ignored almost completely the Negro as character and symbol of the Old South. The few

1. Sidney Lanier to Milton H. Northrup, May 12, 1866, in Sidney Lanier, *Letters, 1857–1868*, ed. Charles R. Anderson and Aubrey Starke, Vol. VII of *Centennial Edition of the Works of Sidney Lanier* (Baltimore, 1945), 221.

2. Sidney Lanier to Bayard Taylor, August 7, 1875, in Sidney Lanier, *Letters, 1874–1877*, ed. Anderson and Starke, Vol. IX of *Centennial Edition*, 230.

3. Sidney Lanier to Harriet Fulton, January 22, 1866, in *Letters, 1857–1868*, p. 211.

Negro dialect poems that he wrote as a young man evidently only embarrassed him, for he wrote once to ask a friend, "Tell me, ought one to be a little ashamed of writing a dialect poem?"[4]

It becomes instructive, therefore, to view Lanier as one of the first southern writers of pastoral intent yet also one of the very few such writers before the twentieth century who did not exploit the plantation tradition to develop and convey his major themes. When his youthful novel *Tiger-Lilies* (1867) was published, one reviewer wrote that Lanier had "a genuine feeling for Southern character," and added that "there is every element of romance in the life of the South, and he has a clear field before him."[5] Yet Lanier chose to leave the field of the plantation romance for others to till.

There are many reasons we might suggest for Lanier's lack of interest in the metaphors we associate with what he himself had called the South's "golden time." First, his own family background did not include any personal involvement in plantation society. He grew up in Macon, Georgia, a bustling little city, and while his letters tell of his presence at the kind of parties that are a staple of plantation fiction, he seems to have had little personal stake in the demise of this part of the antebellum scheme. In some of his poetry he goes so far as to attack what he saw as a materialistic bias behind the farming operations conducted on the large plantations. Secondly, Lanier came of age as an artist a little too early to capitalize on the northerner's fetish of curiosity about the South or to feel, as a primary impulse, the Union's new indulgence in nostalgia for things past. These two encouragements to plantation fiction began to be felt in publishing circles in the 1870s, but Lanier was already condemning, by 1868, "the habit of regarding our literature as Southern literature, our poetry as Southern poetry, our pictures as Southern pictures."[6] He wanted to "sing for the ear of the whole world," and the South seemed to offer by itself few subjects for song. As Lanier put it to a northern friend soon after the war had ended, "You are all so alive, up there, and we

4. Sidney Lanier to Charlotte Cushman, June 17, 1875, in *Letters, 1874–1877*, p. 208.
5. Review of *Tiger-Lilies, Atlantic Monthly,* XXI (1868), 382.
6. Sidney Lanier, "Furlow College Address," in Sidney Lanier, *Tiger-Lilies and Southern Prose,* ed. Garland Greever, Vol. V of *Centennial Edition,* 260–61.

are all so dead, down here. . . . There's not enough attrition of mind on mind, here, to bring out any sparks in a man."[7]

Lanier, then, did not seem to have had the sense of a usable past within the South to draw on for images to voice his artistic concerns. As a young writer he turned to his readings of the English and German romantics and to Emerson for his symbols as well as for tone and theme; in addition, he came to lean heavily on medieval sources for his ideals and images, and while he might have developed parallels between the antebellum South and feudal Europe, his concepts of such ideals as chivalry and social grace were largely shaped by literary sources and not enriched by any of his own insights into similarities between his region and the earlier culture he so admired. In the best of his mature poetry, Lanier relied on a very private religious response to nature for his inspiration and his landscapes. And in his last years, when he was writing his marshland verses, he seemed to have been moving into new areas of concern that were even less specifically southern than his early interests. His late reading of Whitman, for instance, indicated an important direction to him. While he told Whitman, in a letter dated May 5, 1878, "I entirely disagree with you in all points connected with artistic form," he added his praise for Whitman's concern for "the absolute personality of the person, the sufficiency of the man's manhood to the man."[8]

Lanier's direction as a writer, if judged by his usual sources of inspiration, might seem to have few connections with the pastoral mode, which relies in large measure on the creation of a concretely realized social environment to symbolize the tensions threatening man in time. Yet Lanier offers a good starting point for a study of pastoral strategies as they function in southern literature precisely because his works attempt to deal with these tensions without utilizing the Old South's "peculiar" communal structure to symbolize a threatened Arcady. Lanier visualized all life—his own, his region's, his nation's—in terms of the kinds of dichotomies that are the basis of pastoral writing:

7. Sidney Lanier to Milton H. Northrup, June 11, 1866, in *Letters, 1857–1868*, p. 228.

8. Sidney Lanier to Walt Whitman, May 5, 1878, in *Letters, 1878–1891*, ed. Anderson and Starke, Vol. X of *Centennial Edition*, 40.

simplicity versus complexity, the artistic spirit (which he usually allied with "Chivalry") versus the commercial spirit (usually termed "trade"), the debilitating pressures of modern society versus the healing power of nature.

The circumstances of his own life gave Lanier his most vivid experience of these dichotomies. Returning a permanent half-invalid to Macon after being imprisoned at Point Lookout during the Civil War, he saw that for himself, as for his region, there would no longer be enough time or money for the simple life. He despised the business world, yet he saw no other hope than to become involved in the North's vision of the future, at least to some extent. The simple, natural world of rural Georgia held out health, truth, peace, but Lanier was determined to succeed in the modern world, which meant he must be increasingly involved in money matters and the thing he called fame, which always eluded him. Although he was deeply concerned for the dilemmas facing the South during Reconstruction, his emotional temperament, added to the desperate state of his own physical and economic situation, led him, in his literary work, to construct his imagery most often out of his private vision. The world beyond seems to have been useful not for giving him a larger stage on which to develop his conflicts, but only insofar as it could be assimilated into his highly subjective expression of his inner needs.

John Lynen, in defining the setting most common to pastoral art, describes it as "a unique little world in itself, separate from ordinary experience, yet it still displays the familiar reality. . . . The remoteness of the pastoral Arcadia is counterbalanced by its closeness to nature and hence to the physical reality underlying all life."[9] In much of Lanier's work, from *Tiger-Lilies* through his poetry, there is little convincing physical reality to counterbalance the remoteness of his pastoral landscape. This is not to say that Lanier's poems contain no concrete imagery; physical details appear in abundance, and his most compelling scenes are, in fact, rather vivid renderings of southern, or at least rural, locations: there are homesteads, corn and cotton fields, rivers and meadows and woodlands, and lastly, the beautifully evocative marshlands of the Georgia seacoast. Yet in so many cases, the value of the physical object for Lanier seems to be its use as a kind of fuel

9. John F. Lynen, *The Pastoral Art of Robert Frost* (New Haven, Conn., 1960), 20n.

for exercises in transcendentalizing the natural into the philosophical: the stalk of corn becomes a "poet-soul," a southern mountain retreat becomes a musical castle-in-the-air. In his poem "Symphony" the whole of nature becomes locked into identifications with musical instruments and symphonic structure. The flute speaks, for instance, "for each no-tongued tree / That, spring by spring, doth nobler be." The identity of the tree disappears, and with it goes our sense of familiar reality.

The early novel *Tiger-Lilies*, which Lanier himself came to view as valuable only as "the genuine and almost spontaneous utterance of a developing mind,"[10] indicates how much Lanier's work needed the kind of counterbalancing that Lynen discusses. Remoteness is certainly the word for the settings of the novel; the characters live within an ideal little world that seems to find the "real" itself sordid. Consider this description of Thalberg, the mountain resort where the heroes and heroines gather at the beginning of the story:

This house does not bandy civilities with the mountains but presents to them a simple, reverential form; somehow the stables and outer offices, though well-built, are cunningly hid; and rightly, for here in the high presence of the primary intrinsically-beautiful, no mere secondary economically-beautiful should obtrude itself.[11]

Thalberg is idealized to the point that it belongs only superficially to any particular region or society. It represents Lanier's concept of a pastoral paradise, hazily southern in its concern for manners, its gentlemanly pastimes of hunting and drawing-room debate, and in the sketch of its owner, host John Sterling, a man of honor and culture who loves nature and scorns money. Still, Thalberg is not immune to threats from a more "real" world, and what interest the novel engenders comes from Lanier's inclusion of the concept that the threats come from within the pastoral confines of Thalberg itself as well as from without.

Philip Sterling, returning to his home at the beginning of the novel, is refreshed and encouraged by a morning ramble along the moun-

10. Sidney Lanier to Robert S. Lanier, July 13, 1866, in *Letters, 1857–1868*, p. 233.
11. Sidney Lanier, *Tiger-Lilies*, in *Tiger-Lilies and Southern Prose*, ed. Garland Greever, Vol. V of *Centennial Edition*, 24.

tain trails. Yet, after "communing" awhile with nature as he stands Byronesquely on a mountain top, the young lord of the manor muses: "But I wish I were down in the cities; I'm ready for work, and it's all a dream and a play up here in the mountains" (TL, 13). Thalberg is a retreat from "cities whose commerce perplexes religion," but Philip Sterling, with whom Lanier obviously identifies himself, feels prepared to meet the challenge of a more complex world. Consequently, there is no indication that Thalberg symbolizes any permanent way of life; there are foreshadowings throughout Book I of the novel that the idyllic life enjoyed here is only a pause, perfect but also precarious, in the lives of the characters.

The threat from without that comes to Thalberg in Book II is, quite naturally, the Civil War, and by the novel's close both Thalberg and Richmond have gone up in flames. No attempt is made to reconstruct the dream of the past, although in an amazingly unreal climax all Lanier's pairs of beautiful lovers are ecstatically reunited in a park in Richmond against a backdrop of the burning city; they make plans for "nest-building," and the novel ends incredibly with a prayer, "may love line them soft and warm, and may the storms be kind to them!" (TL, 193).

Garland Greever gently states the case against *Tiger-Lilies* when he says that "nobody ever read it through for the fiction's sake."[12] Lanier in his preface to the work voiced some fears about "enriching reality at the expense of truth,"[13] yet this was to be the very least of his worries. His major characters almost never become real for us because Lanier is much more interested in using them to voice his vague transcendental theories than in developing them as individuals with personalities of their own. The one exception is his portrait of the Smallin brothers, Gorm and Cain, mountain rustics whose appearance marks an exquisite touch of realism for the novel. The story of Cain's reaction to his brother's desertion from the army becomes a separate piece both in style and in the dramatic intensity that Lanier achieves with it. Unfortunately, Lanier made very limited use of the potential that is recognizable in his treatment of Cain, yet the mountaineer stands out as an example of what might be done in southern literature with a pastoral figure who commands respect because of his

---

12. Garland Greever (ed.), "Introduction" to Sidney Lanier, *Tiger-Lilies and Southern Prose*, xix.
13. Lanier, *Tiger-Lilies and Southern Prose*, 6.

simple and dignified response to a complex and corrupt civilization.

One early poem that, like the sketches of the mountaineers in his novel, indicates Lanier's awareness of the potential of the rural character is the dialect work "Thar's More in the Man Than Thar Is in the Land." The poem dates from the same period as *Tiger-Lilies* and carries the message that the subsistence farmer, diligently sowing his corn and wheat in the old red Georgia land, might be happy and prosperous, "so fat," in fact, "that he wouldn't weigh." Lanier manages a comic contrast between Jones, who "couldn't make nuthin' but yallerish cotton," and Brown, who bought the land from Jones, "rooted it up and plowed it down," and in five years has the satisfaction of asking the impoverished Jones to come in for dinner and a sermon: "whether men's land was rich or poor / Thar was more in the man than thar was in the land." This imaging of a pastoral way of life in concrete terms works for this poem because Lanier is sufficiently caught up in the situation to allow it to develop in its own terms. His own voice is successfully submerged in the perspective of a narrator who belongs totally to "them old red hills and stones." It was not, evidently, a perspective with which Lanier felt very comfortable, yet it was one which might have given his concern for pastoral values an effective medium had he chosen to pursue it.

Lanier concentrated on poetry and music in the years following the publication of *Tiger-Lilies*, but his lack of money, his failing health, and his growing family left little time for these favorite pursuits. Yet in 1873 he gave up all attempts to practice law, accepting instead the position of flauto primo in the Peabody Symphony Orchestra in Baltimore, a profession which would hardly allow him to support himself, much less his wife and children. He devoted the rest of his brief life to his music and to writing poetry, only grudgingly looking to the increasingly difficult business of physical survival. So he became not unlike the romantic John Sterling of *Tiger-Lilies* who, given a choice between a good fire and good music, stated unequivocally that men had a much greater need for the music.

Although Lanier made his break with the business world through his music, it was his poetry, and his dream of fusing poetry and music in the poem, that absorbed most of his creative energies until his death in 1881. In this area he was, in his best efforts, a "nature poet," concerned to show man's relation to and need for the natural world. Lanier's concern for nature reflected his own situation in the post–Civil

War world. Caught up of necessity in the materialistic spirit of the age he wished to address, he was also confirmed in a belief that only in the simpler realm of farm and forest could man find the answers he needed to live fully in any age. Thus pastoral promptings inevitably found their way into most of his poetry. As in *Tiger-Lilies*, however, the problem for Lanier in his poems would be to find a way to display the tensions involved in his world view through some credible living environment.

In an essay published in 1872, Lanier defined his favorite image, the "nature-metaphor," as one which would effect "a union of human nature and physical nature . . . a beautiful eternal bridal of spirit and matter, in which the immortality of the former gains the form of the latter."[14] This definition indicates Lanier's blind spot as a poet: he had great difficulty in retaining a sense of his "matter" when he was exploring the questions of "spirit" that were of deep personal concern to him. Too often his poems, despite long passages of physical description, do indeed offer very little feeling for a concrete world. The importance of the details as images is sacrificed to their function as symbols. In his finest work, the ideas grow out of visual experiences which he does not abandon once the symbolic connections are set.

Lanier's first major poem, entitled "Corn," indicates the drawbacks in his concept of the nature image as a "bridal of spirit and matter"; a later poem about corn, "The Waving of the Corn," proves that he could overcome the didacticism that often smothers his imagery with ideas. The poem "Corn" is the more "southern" of the two in terms of the situation that inspired the writing of it; "The Waving of the Corn" works better, however, in establishing a pastoral sense of tension through a consistently concrete environment.

"Corn" was the first of Lanier's work to bring him any important critical response. It was written after Lanier had spent his first winter in Baltimore in 1874 and was returning to Georgia with new eyes for his native region. The poem contains three very distinct sections, the first a stage-setting piece in which the poet "loses" himself in nature, the second a song in praise of corn and its benefits to the land, the third a lament for a wasted cotton plantation. William Dean How-

14. *Ibid.*, 308–309.

ells, in rejecting the poem for the *Atlantic Monthly*, pointed out the difference in tone between the first and last sections and wrote that neither was "striking enough to stand alone."[15] Lanier did not mean them to stand alone; he led his narrative gradually to a contemplation of the cotton planter in an attempt to show a contrasting side to his ideal of the southern farm.

"Corn" begins casually as a description by the poet of a walk he takes through a wood; he wanders, seemingly without other purpose beyond the enjoyment of nature, until he comes upon an enclosed corn field where "one tall corn-captain stands" above the rest. To this "lustrous stalk" he addresses the rest of the poem, remarking on its many virtues and finally contrasting the beauty of this locale to the barrenness of an "old deserted Georgian hill" nearby which has been abandoned by "restless-hearted children." It is this comparison which recalls to him the plight of one such "child," an acquaintance who "nursed his cotton, cursed his grain," and who thus brought about the waste that the old hill symbolizes.

Up to this point, the unity of the poem has been superficially preserved because everything has been addressed to the tall "corn-captain" by the lover of nature. Only in the last verse does Lanier turn his attention completely to the hill; his personification of it as a "gashed and hairy Lear" who has been left "discrowned, undaughtered, and alone" is overwrought and stands out awkwardly in the poem, since for the most part the imagery that has come before grows out of the situation and the surroundings of the poet. The narrative of the planter is nonetheless essential to Lanier's scheme; the idyllic landscape of the first section needs to be opposed by the harsh reality of the barren hill making its testament to the waste brought on by the plantation system. The poem's chief weakness is not that it contains the different sections, but that Lanier lost his hold on the realities of his landscape as he became more immersed in his "cause," the plea for diversified farming and a return to the life-giving land.

The chief concern in "Corn" is dramatized by the contrast in scenery between the cornfield and the barren hill, yet the only effective imagery in the poem is in the introduction, where Lanier displays his deep feeling for nature as he describes his stroll through the woods.

15. William Dean Howells to M. M. Hurd, quoted in Aubrey Harrison Starke, *Sidney Lanier: A Biographical and Critical Study* (Chapel Hill, 1933), 188.

From this elegiac mood, Lanier's tone grows into indignant commentary on the waste brought on by Trade, yet he is at his artistic best before he begins to preach and while he is calmly absorbed in the sights and sounds of the forest. The "old companies of Oaks," the "matted miracles of grass," the "hickories breathing deep and long" are what catch his imagination and result in the poem's best images as well as the poet's best grasp of tone.

One might say that in terms of effective contrast between pastoral and nonpastoral landscapes, Lanier's late poem, "Song of the Chatahoochee," accomplishes through control of tone what "Corn" fails to do. The river leaves the serene mountain and valley counties to follow the course prescribed by duty, "Downward, to toil and be mixed with the main." The mill wheels of the plain, the commerce of the city, must be supported if only reluctantly; the pure experience of environments untouched by man's economic instruments must give way. Thus in this poem the river through its song expresses the inevitable sense of counterforce that must enter at some point into a viable pastoral vision.

Lanier's other corn poem, "The Waving of the Corn," while it lacks the drama of the earlier one, succeeds much better in sustaining a unified presentation of a pastoral atmosphere. Lanier had originally ended "The Waving of the Corn" with a querulous, didactic stanza, but fortunately this part was omitted when Bayard Taylor advised Lanier that it "forces a moral where none is needed," and clashed with the "feeling of peace and blissful pastoral seclusion" of the rest.[16] This poem was written in the summer of 1876, when Lanier had settled his family in West Chester, Pennsylvania, with the hope of having enough income from his writing to establish a permanent home there. His hope had been premature, and Charles Anderson relates how, during that summer, "stranded penniless . . . with lingering resentment of the abuse meted out to his [centennial] Cantata, depression of spirit followed as he brooded over the plight of the artist."[17]

The plight of the artist as Lanier visualized it in the poem involved the encroachment of the "terrible towns" upon a rural scene which has offered the poet a temporary release from his enervating toils in

16. Bayard Taylor to Sidney Lanier, September 23, 1876, quoted in Sidney Lanier, *Letters, 1874–1877*, p. 400, n. 140.
17. Charles Anderson (ed.), "Introduction" to Sidney Lanier, *Poems and Poem Outlines*, Vol. I of *Centennial Edition*, xxxix.

the city. Here we are given the classical pastoral situation. Raymond Williams explains that "the contrast within Virgilian pastoral is between the pleasures of rural settlement and the threat of loss or eviction," and Lanier's poem succeeds in developing this contrast between the moods of pleasure and threat through one fully realized landscape.[18] He establishes a real world which retains its evocative function throughout the poem, so that when the threat comes, it means something; it is measured in terms of an actual distance from an actual place whose enchantments are deeply yet simply felt.

In the first stanza of "The Waving of the Corn" Lanier thanks the ploughman who left a tree ringed with clover in his cornfield. It is to this spot that the poet comes daily for solace, and all of his responses are to sights and sounds that belong to this particular vantage point. In the second stanza he listens to a farmer's boy whistling, to a cricket and a bee, and to a dove:

> Far down the wood, a one-desiring dove
> Times me the beating of the heart of love:
> And these be all the sounds that mix, each morn,
> With waving of the corn.

Not until the final stanza, as he continues to measure his distance from various sounds, does the poet bring himself to acknowledge, first with a sense of security, that "Trade ends where yon far clover ridges swell." Yet then a prayer, expressive of a deep-seated doubt, comes spontaneously to mind. The prayer is worked unobtrusively into the natural framework of the poem and into the natural setting as well, which is what accounts for the poem's success as a pastoral expression:

> Ye terrible Towns, ne'er claim the trembling soul
> That, craftless all to buy or hoard or sell,
> From out your deadly complex stole
> To company with large amiable trees,
> Suck honey summer with unjealous bees,   .
> And take time's strokes as softly as this morn
> Takes waving of the corn.

Lanier's mode and method here are definitively pastoral in the

18. Williams, *The Country and the City*, 17.

classical sense: his appreciation of the rural scene absolutely and yet ironically depends upon his awareness that he has come from the more complex and less attractive city world and that this world threatens a core of simplicity that is rooted in himself more deeply than in any outer world. More importantly, perhaps, his struggle with the threat of the "terrible town" brings him to a comprehension of what it is that ultimately threatens the ideal he embodies in his rural scene—time itself. And it is as he contemplates the corn's soft taking of time's strokes that the poet finds strength within himself to deal with its effects on his own life and dreams.

Lanier moved from the rural South to a northern city in order to be where the intellectual and economic opportunities abounded, but in "The Waving of the Corn" he demonstrated the price he had to pay. Without money, contacts, or physical strength to do battle in a highly competitive atmosphere, he found himself longing to be free forever from the bruising existence of the city. In another poem of the same summer, "Clover," he argued that "the artist's market is the heart of man." The poem gives voice to Lanier's longings as pastoral artist for a world founded on higher values than the present one afforded. Lanier felt that one of his missions as a poet was to reawaken people to the possibilities of such a world, yet his poems seldom give a concrete vision of it, and if he has any particular period in mind, it is the Middle Ages to which he turns and not to the prewar South.

Not often was Lanier able to extend his sense of his "enemy" to a recognition of the diminishments caused by the strokes of time itself in any real place. Usually "Trade" was Lanier's villain, in essays, poems, and letters both early and late. In a letter written in 1872 to Paul Hamilton Hayne, before he had clearly formulated his determination to leave business for good, Lanier had complained, "Trade, Trade, Trade: pah, are we not all sick? A man cannot walk down a green alley of woods, in these days, without unawares getting his mouth and nose and eyes covered with some web or other that Trade has stretched across, to catch some gain or other."[19] And in 1875 Lanier constructed his intricate poem "Symphony" around the same idea. It was not until 1876, as he perhaps felt his own death approaching, that Lanier got beyond Trade, as he did in "The Waving of the Corn," to

19. Sidney Lanier to Paul Hamilton Hayne, April 17, 1872, in Sidney Lanier, *Letters, 1869–1873*, ed. Anderson and Starke, Vol. VIII of *Centennial Edition*, 224.

see the final, fatal threat of time to his own personal dream of Arcady.

In 1877 Lanier suffered so severely in health that doctors prescribed a trip to Florida as offering his only hope of survival. "The Marshes of Glynn," his masterpiece, owes its greatness to the period of reflection and spiritual growth that the Florida sojourn allowed him. The poem records a process by which the poet discovers nature to be the foundation of his religious belief, not through any mystical sensations of purgation and ecstasy, but through the conscious use of all the senses to go beyond concrete forms into the heart of spiritual reality. This is Lanier's answer to materialism and to time—a love of nature so complete that it triumphs over all.

The question arises as to whether Lanier was sounding a retreat in "The Marshes of Glynn," using this pastoral setting to make his escape from conditions in the real world that were finally too much for him to handle. A close study of the poem indicates that he was not abandoning any of his former interests but had instead found a new focus and a new source of strength to use in dealing with them. Lanier recorded how his soul, having all day "drunken the soul of the oak," found the will at sunset to rest at ease, no longer badgered by thoughts of "the scythe of time and the trowel of trade." Here where the live oaks seemed proof of the permanence of nature's beauty and serenity, for once "belief overmasters doubt," and Lanier was no longer afraid of his world.

Sustained by the spirit of the live oak, the poet speaking in "The Marshes of Glynn" has the courage to take a step beyond nature as he has always known it and to "stand / on the firm-packed sand, free / by a world of marsh that borders a world of sea." He resolves to be like the marsh hen, who has faith enough in nature's goodness to build her nest on the "watery sod": he vows, "Behold I will build me a nest on the greatness of God." As he makes his commitment, the sea pours in over the marshland in a symbolic baptism of the poet's soul, through which he at last witnesses God transcendent and immanent in all creation.

The poet compares his absorption in the realm of the spirit to a state of sleep. He realizes that he has, at the same time, not been able to grasp the full meaning of his experience. It has been a dream of the senses, not quite complete, and the poem ends on a note which suggests that this has been only an initiation and that the quest has just begun: "And would I could know what swimmeth below when the / tide comes in / on the length and the breadth of the marvellous marshes of Glynn."

In Lanier's earlier poem "Symphony," the manner in which the horn, speaking for the chivalrous knight, undertakes to do battle with "cheapening" trade is one of bravado; the tone is that of a reckless boy who has heard tales of the glories of war but knows none of its realities. In "The Marshes of Glynn" the voice speaking is consistently that of a man who knows the world as it is, admits his doubts, and seeks the marshland not as escape but from a religious need to know a new level of experience. Thus the marshes represent a pastoral landscape that adheres to a familiar reality. The poet receives strength as he centers himself in the natural world, intimately and tangibly felt, until he can reckon with the force that threatens this world and can experience an infusion of the stability that it represents.

Once having discovered the symbolic value of the marshland for his poetry, Lanier never abandoned it. Although "The Marshes of Glynn" appeared anonymously in an anthology entitled *A Masque of Poets* in 1878 and thus earned little acclaim for Lanier, he planned to use it as the cornerstone for a series of "hymns" to the marshes. One of these, "Sunrise," is an extension of the mood and message of the earlier marsh poem. It is not so much a poem of seeking as its companion piece. For "Sunrise" starts, rather than ends, with night and with questions, while it ends with a triumphant anthem of praise to the sun as life giver. Lanier praises the sun as symbol of all his most cherished ideals—art, honor, simplicity, peace. And although he recognizes that his struggle with adversity will continue ("the worker must pass to his work in the terrible town"), his faith in the greatness of his endeavors has been transfixed in the benediction that comes from "my Lord the Sun." "I am lit with the sun," says Lanier, and thus his victory in the "dark race" with life as it must be lived each day in the real world is assured. Shining through "the seas of traffic" and the "hell-colored smoke of the factories" is the face of the sun, revealing to Lanier that his vision of a better world has been upheld and approved.

To attempt to evaluate Lanier as a writer of southern pastoral is at once to be forced to acknowledge his weaknesses as a poet. In his vision of life there was an emotionalism that too often amounted to pure sentimentality. There was also a lack of realism, a preference for melodrama over controlled appraisal. Frequently Lanier counted on abstractions and musical effect to get across his ideals, and his portrayals of rural settings were overburdened with allegorical inferences. What Robert Penn Warren denounced as his "passion for synthesis" sometimes led him to solutions which do not really confront but merely attempt to transcend the conflicts involved.

At the beginning of a period of surging interest in southern local color, Lanier was striving to make his work entirely nonsectional in its appeal. Although Cain Smallin in *Tiger-Lilies* and the cracker and Negro dialect poems show what Lanier might have accomplished in this field, he preferred to experiment more with new musical effects than with dialects. He wanted to be a national poet, and he often criticized the South for its backward attitude toward intellectual and cultural responsibilities. When all of this has been admitted, however, it must still be granted that Lanier's imagination and idealism led him to look to the South for the metaphors and morals that he used in portraying his fictional worlds. The marshlands and Georgia hills, the cotton flowers, cornfields, and green pines, the orange groves and sands of Florida are all given a memorial in his poetry. To the important degree that his art was influenced by the contradictory feelings of deep love and also great frustration concerning his southern heritage, Lanier bears a resemblance worth noting to two southern writers of a later generation, Jean Toomer and Thomas Wolfe.

Lanier's own life seems a contradiction: he loved the rural life but ambition took him to the "terrible towns"; he championed the ideals of an earlier time but believed devoutly in progress; he bemoaned the "scythe of time" and the "trowel of trade" yet had great faith in science. Thus the opposing urges that adhere to the pastoral point of view were expressed in his life as well as in his art, and it seems that with his visionary habit of mind, he looked for solutions to his personal as well as his artistic problems in a dream of an ideal future.

For his dream of Arcady Lanier looked past the plantation South that loomed in his own native background and located his vision of Arcadia in an earlier setting—Jefferson's scheme of a nation united in a belief in the land as life giver and in farming as the purest form of labor for mankind. In this respect Lanier anticipated the Nashville

Agrarians, who despite many similarities have usually looked disparagingly on Lanier's efforts both as philosopher and poet. Their reasons for denying Lanier as an early disciple of the kind of program they defined in *I'll Take My Stand* seem to stem mostly from a distaste for his artistic failings—his sentimentality and often unorganized obsession with abstractions. They objected, too, to his naïveté about economics and to his praise, however vague, of the ideal of a nation united in its pursuit of a better life. Yet certainly in his articulation of his objectives and concerns as a writer, Lanier displayed a love of agrarian traditions and an indictment of materialism that are kindred to the principles of the Nashville group. And we find in the artistic framework of Lanier's best poetry the tensions and longings that are at the heart of the pastoral spirit of agrarianism itself.

In 1880, near the end of his life, Lanier published an essay entitled "The New South" in which he looked with pleasure on the trend that he saw in the South toward the development of small farms. The idea of a "New South" meant decidedly something else at this time to those like Atlanta orator Henry Grady, who in his famous address in 1886 used the term "New South" to define the hope of many southerners that their region would revitalize its economy along national, industrial lines. Lanier, for all his praise of national spirit, was glad to see that the South in its agriculture was going in a different direction from the Midwest, which he felt was involved not in farming but in "mining for wheat" in huge commercial ventures.[20] Lanier saw the independent small farmer as the South's greatest asset, and his idea of the southern yeoman, while certainly it avoided the reality of sharecropping and rural poverty that would become staples of the southern countryside, indicates at least that in hoping for something "new" for the South, Lanier hardly allied himself with those who wanted to exchange old values for the North's materialism.

In his literature and in his life, Lanier illustrates for us one artist's search for an imagery that might adequately express the struggle between a materialism that critics could easily identify with the North and a humanism that, ironically, would come to be associated with a region that had used human chattel to sustain its way of life. Lanier, always looking ahead to a united nation, would hardly have wanted

20. Sidney Lanier, "The New South," in *Tiger-Lilies and Southern Prose*, 336.

to have had a hand in the making of the regional myth that would sweep the entire nation's interest into the southern writer's grasp. The phenomenon of the Old South's resurrection in literature was to belong to a younger generation of writers who shaped their visions of the plantation into a dream of Arcady to captivate a country well on its way to worldwide industrial prominence. The April, 1884, issue of the popular northern periodical *Century* used a portrait of Lanier as its frontispiece and contained a tribute to his life and work. Yet in terms of the future of southern literature that issue contained something of much greater significance that had very little to do with Lanier, for in its pages was a story written by a young Virginian, Thomas Nelson Page. "Marse Chan" would become the classic story of plantation life and remains today the starting point for any study of the imagery of the Old South.

THREE

Thomas Nelson Page:
The Plantation as Arcady

Thomas Nelson Page, like Sidney Lanier, located Arcady in a dream of the past for which chivalry and simplicity served as cornerstones. Yet in all other respects, Lanier's pastoral landscapes seem very different from Page's. Lanier often looked to feudal England as a model environment, and when he did turn to the southern scene as a location of values, it was to the Jeffersonian ideal of the small farm that he paid his tribute. The passionate, personal idealism of Lanier was seldom channeled into the framework of social structure and class concern that is characteristic of most pastoral, whereas the political problems that so engrossed Page found very suitable expression in pastoral forms. Page's pastorals closely reflect not the Jeffersonian ideal but an approximation of what Jefferson himself had in reality—the gracious homeplace, the habits of aristocracy as well as agriculture, and the labor of black slaves to sustain the ideal. And it was Page's version of Arcady that commanded the attention of the literary world in the decade that followed Lanier's death in 1881. Serving up short stories of the time "jus' fo' de folks wuz set free," Page wrote of the right place with the right point of view to capture a reading audience ready for a new kind of fiction and a new perspective on the South and slavery.

The phenomenon known as "local color" became a dominant interest on the American literary scene as the 1880s began. Local color writing blended, often in incongruous combinations, a fairly realis-

36

tic concern for fidelity to physical setting and particularity of detail with a definitely romantic emphasis on the picturesque local legend and the quaint eccentricities of regional manners and mores. The reasons for the rise of local color are diverse and complex, but chiefly we can say that it seemed to feed the burgeoning awareness of a reconciled nation concerning sectional differences that needed new study and reinforced tolerance. As Robert Bone explains, "In the legitimation of cultural diversity the local-color movement played a vital role. During a time of transition, when national loyalties were still tenuous, a regional literature offered a viable alternative."[1] Whatever the reasons, for the South and particularly for the South's post–Civil War generation of writers, the timing had great significance.

As the South in the 1880s emerged from the darkest hours of Reconstruction, her apologists found that literature, particularly local-color fiction, could do what those glorious men in gray had not done— it could win the war of ideals over the value system of the plantation. As Edmund Wilson puts it, "Having devastated the feudal South, the Northerners wanted to be told of its glamor, of its old-time courtesy and grace."[2] Another reason for the North's new interest is more closely related to matters of pastoral mood. Again, Wilson's assessment states the case: "A rush of industrial development had come at the end of the war, and the cities of the North and West, now the scene of so much energetic enterprise which rendered them uglier and harsher, were losing their old amenities."[3] Writers like Thomas Nelson Page, Joel Chandler Harris, Irwin Russell, and at times George Washington Cable could spread out before the admiring eyes of northerner and westerner the simple beauties of the Old South, playing up the elements which their audiences of other regions most missed in their own lives—graciousness and class distinctions, scorn for material values, and free enjoyment of a rural environment, a slow pace, and a strict code of honor.

The names of Thomas Nelson Page and Joel Chandler Harris are almost always linked in discussions of southern local-color writing and

---

1. Robert Bone, *Down Home: A History of Afro-American Short Fiction from Its Beginnings to the End of the Harlem Renaissance* (New York, 1975), 9.
2. Edmund Wilson, *Patriotic Gore: Studies in the Literature of the American Civil War* (New York, 1962), 605.
3. *Ibid.*

particularly the most potent form of it often labeled the work of a "plantation school." In the following studies of Page and Harris we will see some of the forms that their revival of the plantation legend took. Certainly a magnificent dream of the Old South as Arcady took shape under their penmanship; the staples of the most powerful myth of the region were furnished in their stories of Old Virginia and Uncle Remus. Yet going beyond the top layer of mammies and magnolias, porticoes and corn pone, we find that as we turn from Page to Harris we will see very different modes of vision as well as very different critical capacities in these two writers' versions of Old South pastoral. We find, moreover, that their dreams turned in rather unpredictable directions, the implications of them growing beyond their conscious purposes. It is strange to see what happens when Page allows a young black sharecropper to have his own dream of a better future; it is stranger still to see what happens when Uncle Remus, telling his stories of the dreamlike folk hero Brer Rabbit, puts the plantation version of Arcady down in the middle of the briar patch.

Thomas Nelson Page, the son of a Virginia aristocrat living on a gracious plantation, could watch with pride as his father rode out in bright uniform and flowing cape to defend the Confederacy. Yet in later years he would remember his father's homecoming even better than his grand departure. What was most vivid to his memory was the image of "his hand over his face, and his groan, 'I never expected to come home so.'"[4] Out of such recollections, out of his sense of the discontinuity between life before and after the Civil War, Page was to fashion for the South a definitive version of the dream of Arcady. The cornerstone of Page's vision would be his dual focus of pride and loss; the strength of his fictional re-creations of the Old South as Arcady would rest primarily in his ability to balance his belief in his idealizations with his awareness of threat and inevitable doom facing them. Nostalgia might win out over fatalism, yet the feeling that this golden world cast its glow from the center of impending peril is what makes its charm effective.

Growing up during the Civil War on a Virginia plantation, Page

4. Page, *Old South*, 33.

was quite naturally drawn to evaluating the quality of life before and after the war. That he would idealize the past was an inevitable consequence of the experiences which made up the most impressionable years of his life. Before the war he was the proud son of a slaveowning planter, taught by conservative parents to respect the old and suspect the new. His childhood was, by all accounts, remarkably carefree until the war intervened. He seems to have been provided with the opportunity to know all the pleasures of rural life while avoiding its hardships.

Page's fictionalized account of his own youthful adventures during the Civil War, recorded in the popular boys' book *Two Little Confederates*, provides an intriguing glimpse of the atmosphere that was to mold Page's later concerns as a writer. The tale deals with the exploits of two youngsters, who, like Thomas Nelson Page and his younger brother Rosewell, lived out the Civil War on a tidewater plantation. From idyllic pursuits of fishing, possum hunting, and squirrel shooting, the boys' energies are turned during the war to searching for deserters, hiding family heirlooms and Confederate officers from the Yankees, and, finally, to aiding their mother in the matter of sheer day-to-day survival as food supplies diminish and the defeat of the glorious Confederacy becomes an inevitability.

Page, in this nostalgic review of the war years that changed his own life so drastically, shows the two little Confederates' romantic acceptance of the war as a kind of boys' King Arthur world offering adventure and fame. Still, the effects of the defeat are not glossed over. Page recalls again his father's return from service after the fall of Richmond: "It seemed like a funeral. The boys were near the steps, and their mother stood on the portico with her forehead resting against a pillar. . . . It *was* a funeral—the Confederacy was dead." The father's final gesture in this scene is worth special note. He turns to his last remaining slave, his body servant Ralph, gives him his last dollar, and tells him he is free: "Ralph stood where he was for some minutes without moving a muscle. His eyes blinked mechanically. Then he looked at the door and at the windows above him. Suddenly he seemed to come to himself. Turning slowly, he walked solemnly out of the yard."[5]

5. Thomas Nelson Page, *Two Little Confederates* (New York, 1916), 178, 179.

From what we learn of Page's early experiences through *Two Little Confederates*, we can grasp the artistic potential of his situation; he was in a very sensitive position to measure the impact of the destruction of the old world and the violent advent of the new. His imagination was steeped in experiences that he had shared or had heard recounted by old soldiers and old slaves. Yet without the pressure of upheaval that was provided by the war, it is doubtful that Page would have had the impetus to produce what has become the classic fictional account of the plantation myth. The war and its aftermath emphasized for Page the values of the old world just at the moment that they were disappearing, leaving him with a sense that the regime that had been destroyed had a tragic grandeur and his childhood memories a special importance that might serve as instruction for posterity.

It is this zeal to project a mode of the past onto present existence that most distinguishes Page from antebellum writers of the plantation school, whose work often carries overtones of pastoral feeling. For instance John Pendleton Kennedy's *Swallow Barn*, written in 1832, has an aura of nostalgia about it that sometimes grows into pure melancholy. Kennedy's preface to an 1851 edition of the novel contains remarks similar to dozens of Page's commentaries about the superiorities of plantation life. "*Swallow Barn*," Kennedy intoned, "exhibits a picture of country life as it existed in the first quarter of the present century. Between that period and the present day, time and what is called 'progress' have made many innovations therein." There follows a list of qualities that the Old Dominion was in danger of losing, and it is a list that Page might easily have copied: good fellowship, sunny luxuriance, overflowing hospitality, etc., etc.[6] This concept of an Old South that is a vanished society pertains to many works written well before the Civil War. Yet Page differs in that he watched, at a most impressionable age, the actual demise of that sunny civilization and found, as he began writing in the aftermath of its destruction, an opportunity not just to commemorate or to express a sense of loss but to measure, to rebuke, and actually to have some effect on the shape of the present. The pastoral impulse could gain a positive, assertive direction in such an atmosphere, and this is exactly what Page hoped to do with his plantation Arcadies. After the

6. John Pendleton Kennedy, *Swallow Barn: A Sojourn in the Old Dominion*, ed. Jay B. Hubbell (New York, 1929), 8–10.

war Page was poor, not as poor as many in the South, but poor enough to lack the privileges and comforts to which he felt that he and his family were entitled. His ancestors had been wealthy and prominent men, and although his own father was never very prosperous, Page had a pride of class causing him to attach great importance to his forebears' accomplishments. Money was more important than lineage in many social circles after the war, and Page, who had so much of the latter and so little of the former, came to see his ancestors, perhaps somewhat defensively, as heroic embodiments of a golden age. In several of Page's essays on life in Virginia before the war, he included remarks on the status and honors accorded to Pages and Nelsons of earlier generations. This was a mechanism by which he connected himself to his past and made himself a part of the glories which seemed unavailable in the present.

Lacking the funds to go to law school, Page became a tutor for cousins in Kentucky after attending Washington College for a short time, and he finally earned enough money there to enable him to return to studies at the University of Virginia. In November of 1874 he successfully passed examinations entitling him to practice law, the traditionally favored profession for southern gentlemen. Yet he also began, around this time, to write. In April, 1877, his first important piece, a Negro dialect poem, was published. "Uncle Gabe's White Folks" depicted an old black servant recalling the glories of his master's life before the war. It was ten years later, with the publication of *In Ole Virginia* in 1887, that Page was established as an influential authority on the Old South.

This first collection of his stories was his masterpiece, an achievement never duplicated in his many other works, which seldom sustain the unique blend of nostalgia, romance, and local color that is the highlight of the stories of *In Ole Virginia*. Yet the works which followed continued to gain a large and fairly sympathetic audience. In a collection of essays entitled *The Old South*, Page wrote an eloquent if also chauvinistic "history" of plantation civilization as it could be viewed only through the eyes of a Virginia aristocrat. When he turned to the novel form, he dealt best with cavalier heroes who had to make the transition to the modern world but who survived actually because they remained attached to the old values. During the last ten years of his life Page devoted himself almost completely to public affairs, notably as United States ambassador to Italy, but his major achievement remained his early fictional evocations of the special world that was the South in enchanted times "befo' de wah."

Page revered the past and let its haze overshadow the present in the fictional worlds he created. However, he was not turning his back on the postwar South, even though he balked at calling it new. His reasons for evoking the vision of an idealized Old South had very much to do with current affairs. Grace King wrote in her memoirs that "it is hard to explain in simple terms what Thomas Nelson Page meant to us in the South at that time. He was the first Southern writer to appear in print as a Southerner, and his stories . . . showed us with ineffable grace that although we were sore bereft, politically, we had now a chance in literature at last."[7] Remarking that the South had lost the Civil War as much by its failure to explain itself in print as anything else, Page took it upon himself, while admonishing others to do the same, to show the world what the South could do in print. His purpose, as he explained in the Plantation Edition of his works, was not to campaign for a return to the old order; instead his claim was that he had "never wittingly written a line which he did not hope might bring about a better understanding between the North and South, and finally lead to a more perfect Union."[8]

I

The three aspects of the antebellum world which Page turned into staples of his Arcadia were the plantation locale itself with the great house at the center; the image of the southern gentleman; and most important, the "old time" Negro, the slave or "servant" as Page calls him, through whose voice the Old South achieves mythic status. Taking up these points as they appear in Page's major works, we begin, as almost all of his descriptions of plantation life begin, with the planter's home, which was for Page the hub of the universe. It is of interest to note that most of Page's stories and novels, and the essays dealing with southern culture as well, contain, near their beginning, a fairly thorough account of the home occupied by the hero or hero-

7. Grace King, *Memoirs of a Southern Woman of Letters* (New York, 1932), 377.
8. Thomas Nelson Page, *The Novels, Stories, Sketches, and Poems of Thomas Nelson Page*. The Plantation Edition (New York, 1906), I, xi.

ine, and at any time in the stories the threat of the loss of that home portends a tragedy of major proportions.

Guy Cardwell, in a study of the use of the plantation house in southern literature, makes some comments about its importance as a symbol. His explanation is helpful in showing why the house is such a central image for Page. For many, Cardwell says, the plantation house represented an "idea of agrarian orderliness and the redemption of a turbulent society." It was "the natural basis for a social order, the natural support for a moral order," and came increasingly to be seen as "a little world, a way of life, an epitomizing of cherished values that were to be defended at all costs."[9] The great house, with its simple and stately facade, its ordered arrangement of buildings and gardens and fields, its aura of serenity and grace, was easily equated with the southerner's idea of what Eden must have been, and so it seemed to Page.

One of Page's most lyrical panegyrics to the Old South, an essay entitled "Social Life in Old Virginia Before the War," begins with a description of Oakland, his own boyhood home. With few alterations, Oakland could serve as the setting for almost all of Page's plantation stories. The striking quality of his description of the house is his orderly arrangement of the picturesque scene into a composite that contains all the elements which he cherished about the Old South. "Oakland" is notable for the plainness of its construction; there is a quaintness in its design, a "manliness" about its offices and quarters, a special dignity in the way it is set among historic oaks, and a feminine grace showing through the orchards and gardens that flourish on the grounds. Thus by careful selection of detail, Page makes his concept of the plantation house reflect all the virtues that he felt the aristocrats of the Old South possessed. For him the plantation exuded an aura that encouraged the best behavior; even in the back "office," where the men relax and trade tales, bits of gossip are "veiled in chaste language . . . to meet the higher truth that no gentleman would use foul language."[10]

Page quotes the words of George W. Bagby in order to evoke the

9. Guy Cardwell, "The Plantation House, An Analogical Image," *Southern Literary Journal*, II (Fall, 1969), 7, 15–16.
10. Page, *Old South*, 172–73.

emotional quality of the plantation: "'Sorrows and care were there overall—where do they not penetrate? But, oh! dear God, one day in those sweet tranquil homes outweighed a fevered lifetime in the gayest cities of the globe.'"[11] There is a sense in Page's essay that enclosed in this world are all the worthwhile opportunities and experiences that a man could wish for. It is a self-sustaining world, with the typical pastoral stress on the nonmaterial and on the idea that only in such a rural locale could a man really know what life was all about. The estate managed by the southern aristocrat, as Page acknowledges by his treatment of his own home, was much more than a fine dwelling place. It was intended to be a symbol of the quality of the man who lived in it, testifying to his virtue, his isolation from the common, and his kinship with the land he had conquered.

When we come to Page's stories, then, we are made aware that the locations that Page depicts are charged with special significance. Every story contains reference, often extended, to the homes of the leading characters. In discussing these, Page is establishing the credentials of his heroes—if they come from a fine plantation, they are almost invariably of high moral quality and deserve universal admiration. A study of the stories in Page's first volume, *In Ole Virginia*, reveals that the plantation homes described are uniformly designed to be outward and visible signs of the spirit of the people who settled the southern region and created an aristocratic utopia out of a wilderness. In these early stories, the preservation of the old estates represents for those involved in it an effort to maintain the nation's only remaining stronghold of nonmaterial values.

In Page's first story, "Marse Chan," the white narrator, a stranger to the southern locale he is visiting, is struck immediately by the atmosphere surrounding the "once splendid mansions" which seem to him, in their "proud seclusion," to indicate that "distance was nothing to this people; time was of no consequence to them. They desired but a level path in life, and that they had, though the way was longer, and the outer world strode by them as they dreamed."[12] The outer world is always somewhere beyond the settings that Page uses for the stories in *In Ole Virginia*. The pertinent action in most of them takes place before the Civil War, so that the serenity of the scene is not

11. *Ibid.*, 177–78.
12. Thomas Nelson Page, *In Ole Virginia* (Chapel Hill, 1969), 1.

disturbed, although the sense of impending destruction is always present. It is of this world that Page's most famous narrative spokesman, the venerable Unc' Sam of "Marse Chan," says: "Dem wuz good ole times, marster—de bes' Sam ever see! Dey wuz, in fac'! Niggers didn' hed nothin' 't all to do—jes' hed to 'ten' to de feedin' an' cleanin' de hosses an' doin' what de marster tell 'em to do. . . . Dyar warn' no trouble nor nothin" (IOV, 10). This, of course, is the most important testament of all to the beneficent effect of the plantation setting on its inhabitants; the old slave, who would know better than anyone else all facets of life on the plantation, gives his wholehearted endorsement to its "good ole times."

In the story "Meh Lady" the sense of place is the strong motivating force, in which a young Virginia belle and her faithful retainers struggle to maintain a home constantly threatened by Yankees or carpetbaggers. To leave the plantation, it is implied, would be death. After the war Meh Lady's estate stands as a small, embattled island where the old values and sense of pride are being defended against the rude forces of change.

The story in *In Ole Virginia* which least meets with Page's idea of normal conditions of plantation life is "No Haid Pawn." The plantation with the weird name "No Haid Pawn" is the antithesis of Oakland and the estates described in Page's other stories. Page wants to show here what happens to the plantation ideal when unworthy beings attempt to imitate its concepts. No Haid Pawn was built by strangers to the area, men of Creole blood who "never made it their permanent home. Thus, no ties either of blood or friendship were formed with their neighbors, who were certainly open-hearted enough to overcome anything but the most persistent unneighborliness" (IOV, 166). An unhealthy atmosphere surrounds this mansion, which is totally out of keeping with what was expected from the true plantation house, and eventually, in what was probably an attempt to copy the fate of Poe's House of Usher, Page allows nature to reclaim what the evil Creoles forfeited by their lack of morality and their disdain for the customs of the community. In this respect, the story offers some interesting parallels to Faulkner's treatment of "Sutpen's Hundred" in *Absalom, Absalom!* In "No Haid Pawn," Page experimented with a new kind of atmosphere and setting, yet he ended by reemphasizing a cardinal principle applied to all his plantations; that is, the place reflects its owner and thus the true plantation will symbolize and proclaim the ethical superiority of its inhabitants.

Page's most successful novel, *Red Rock*, contains interesting treatment of the kind of values that the plantation represented for him. "Red Rock" is the name of a southern estate which, like Page's own Oakland, is full of the history, memories, and the pride of its owners. In *Red Rock* Page tells the standard southern version of Reconstruction as he chronicles his heroes' loss of their homes to scalawags and carpetbaggers. Thrown into a world in which money is the new standard of power and influence, the southern gentry are almost completely helpless. Their plantations, Page would have us believe, were never operated for profit, but only for the purpose of upholding the lifestyle of the gentlemen who maintained them. The plot of *Red Rock* tells how several old Virginia plantations were lost after the Civil War through the virtuous naïveté of their owners, and how eventually right conquers might, so that the plantations are restored to the only people who deserve them.

The real threat to Red Rock and other places like it is defined by Page's chief spokesman in the novel, Dr. Cary, who points out that the enemy is not just the Yankee. "We are at war now," he tells the townspeople, "with the greatest power on earth: the power of universal progress. It is not the North we shall have to fight, but the world."[13] Dr. Cary announces the South's last stand but recognizes that the battle is a hopeless one. "From having been one of the most quiet, peaceful and conservative corners of the universe," Red Rock's county becomes, at the mere rumor of hostilities, a scene of "almost metropolitan activity" (RR, 42), and the old world can never be the same again.

In *Red Rock* the devastation to the old order is total, and the "gentle families," so "wealthy" at the first, have nothing to fall back on but their pride. In the end Red Rock is returned to the Gray family, but the happy resolutions that Page devises for his heroes are hardly satisfactory, for he has too conclusively demonstrated in the course of the novel that the old world is gone forever. Red Rock remains intact only as a symbol of the kind of wealth that was the Old South's greatest asset. Yet in a present given over to the pursuit of "mere riches"

13. Thomas Nelson Page, *Red Rock: A Chronicle of Reconstruction* (Ridgewood, N.J., 1967), 41.

it gains an additional kind of force as Page's rebuke to all that the new world represents.

Gordon Keith (1903) appeared five years after *Red Rock* and was Page's rambling attempt to juxtapose and compare in fiction the environments of the plantation South and the urban North. The novel contrasts three settings representing opposing value systems. Page opens, as usual, with a vignette of plantation life. From here the hero, young Gordon Keith, moves on to areas beyond the ideal world of his youth, first to a small mining town in the mountains. After this "initiation" into life organized around purely materialistic motives, he faces the ultimate test of his moral fiber, the city of New York, which reflects the amorality, greed, and selfishness of those who live there.

Gordon Keith is naturally superior to the alien society that he must meet beyond the friendly boundaries of the plantation. His first and only true home supplies the only credible setting of the three dealt with by Page in the novel. The Keiths' plantation, Elphinstone, is of the same type as Red Rock: "Elphinstone was, indeed, a world to itself; a long, rambling house, set on a hill, with white-pillared verandahs, closed on the side toward the evening sun by green Venetian blinds, and on the other side looking away through the lawn trees over wide fields, brown with fallow, or green with cattle-dotted pasture-land and waving grain, to the dark rim of woods beyond." [14] Page never deviates from his idealized mental picture—all of his descriptions of southern estates point up the self-sufficiency, the "proud seclusion," and the symmetry of plantation life.

Page does not manage his other settings with anything like the flair or conviction that makes his plantations real for the reader. The mining town has some realistic touches, but New York, the main battleground for Keith, is totally unreal. Page wants to make it show all that is wrong with modern life, but the result is mechanical and relies on all of the clichés traditionally applied to urban environments. There are only trite impressions offered, such as this one:

Business was the watchword, the trademark. It buzzed everywhere, from the Battery to the Park. It thronged the streets, pulsating through the outlets and inlets at ferries and railway stations and crossings, and through the

14. Thomas Nelson Page, *Gordon Keith* (New York, 1903), 4.

great buildings that were already beginning to tower in the business sections. (GK, 223)

Gordon Keith's response to all of this is first awe, then envy, and finally, of course, disdain.

In *Gordon Keith* industrialism is shown as having corrupted a whole society, and Keith himself has to make repeated returns to the country in order to keep from yielding to the temptations that the "glitter and gayety" of the city make so attractive. Page endows his pastoral environment with the only moral force present in the novel as he describes how Keith conquers the urge to become like his city acquaintances:

When the temptation grew too overpowering he left his office and went down into the country. It always did him good to go there. . . . He had been so long in the turmoil and strife of the struggle for success—for wealth; had been so wholly surrounded by those who strove, tearing and trampling and rending those who were in their way, that he had almost lost sight of the life that lay outside of the dust and din of that arena. He had almost forgotten that life held other rewards than riches. He had forgotten the calm and tranquil region that stretched beyond the moil and anguish of the strife for gain. (GK, 515)

In attempting to create tension in *Gordon Keith* by his contrast of the atmospheres of city and country, Page lays too heavy a hand on the southern side of the scale, and the novel suffers badly because of his inability to let both worlds speak for themselves dramatically.

II

The plantation, for Page, was the breeding ground for heroes. It provided the cornerstone "of a civilization so pure, so noble, that the world to-day holds nothing equal to it."[15] All of Page's major characters exhibit the traits of feudal lords, and all of them are involved in a crusade to preserve an ideal way of life against the forces of inevitable change. Their threatened plantation homes are a symbol of their struggle, and perhaps of its futility. In any case, Page's planta-

15. Page, *Old South*, 51.

tion settings provide much more than mere scenery; they supply motivation and meaning for the works as a whole and are at the center of Page's design.

The southern plantation owner's attitude toward his home resembles that of a feudal lord toward his domain. Two things are of utmost importance to this figure as Page presents him—his land and his honor. Both are sacred, and both are the exclusive possessions of a particular kind of human being whom Page names reverently "the Virginia gentleman." It is a title which he does not lightly bestow, for it belongs only to his small group of embattled chivalric heroes who try to maintain the virtues of the Old South while the rest of the nation is being given over to materialism. In his home state before the war, Page declared, "to be a Virginia gentleman was the first duty."[16]

In Ole Virginia, *Red Rock*, and *Gordon Keith* contain many representatives of the "gentleman" type. Among the heroes that are portrayed in these works, there are two types: the old gentlemen who are conservative fathers, often stubborn authoritarians, gracious to ladies and guests but unbending in their opposition to anything that threatens the status quo, and the young gentlemen who must meet new challenges posed by a changing technological society.

In the stories that make up *In Ole Virginia*, there is not too much distinction made between what is expected of the young and of the old; fathers and sons alike are involved simply and wholeheartedly in exemplifying the charm and chivalry that characterized life in the Old South. Because few of the stories deal with the question of what behavior should be in a defeated "new" South, the gentlemen both old and young in the stories of Page's first collection live out their roles in a kind of King Arthur's court that has many intriguing aspects but does not often try to treat the problems facing different generations of "gentlemen" after the Civil War.

Dr. Cary in *Red Rock* and General Keith, the hero's father in *Gordon Keith*, are patrician types whom Page uses to proclaim his philosophy of gentlemen in postbellum situations. They are allowed to survive the war in order to show the great disparity between the Old and New South and to emphasize how much has been lost. In *Red Rock*, Dr. Cary speaks always for propriety and good manners. Money

16. *Ibid.*, 189.

means nothing to him; name and honor, everything. The war takes everything from him except his knowledge of and abiding faith in who he is. To his nearly destitute family he says, "We have each other . . . and we have—the land. It's as much as our forefathers began with" (RR, 59). His struggle to deal with a new breed of businessmen according to the old code of gentlemen makes him pathetic but no less proud, and in his death it seems to his community that "the foundations were falling out—as though the old life had passed away with him" (RR, 557).

General Keith is in many ways a more satisfying creation than Dr. Cary, largely because Page does not even try to make him seem real. Dr. Cary is far too good to be true as he goes through life doing his innumerable acts of selfless charity. General Keith, on the other hand, appears more like the spirit of gentlemanly behavior than a real person. Page tells us at the beginning that "he knew the Past and lived in it; the Present he did not understand, and the Future he did not know." After the war General Keith watches the end come to a whole way of life, yet he manages to remain himself "unchanged, unmoved, unmarred, an antique memorial of the life of which he was a relic" (GK, 3). We are given no real picture of his personal tragedy, so he takes on the status of a pure symbol of the permanence of certain values inherent in the Old South.

Page's young aristocrats differ from their elders in breadth of experience, but not in substance. From Marse Chan to Gordon Keith, they form a neat chain of similar young heroes waiting to put the code they have been taught to the tests that will prove them true Virginia gentlemen. In the plantation stories of *In Ole Virginia*, the young man usually dies in the course of performing some act connected with the ritual of earning this title. He will be remembered by a former slave who was his childhood companion and who sees "young marster's" death as a blessing which saved the hero from having to cope with the postbellum world.

In *Red Rock* the youthful heroes are not spared the trauma of facing life in a new kind of world. It is their task to rebuild the South as near to the image of the old as is possible. Yet one episode in *Red Rock* provides a particularly interesting idea of Page's real ideal of a gentleman farmer. It occurs when Steven Allen attempts to do his part to keep Red Rock going by working in the fields himself. Page tells us that Allen has been "moved by the grassy appearance of the once beautifully cultivated fields" of Red Rock to take up his "bucolic operations." His idea of the romance of such labors comes to an end, however, when he is insulted by Red Rock's former overseer. His reaction: "That's the last time I'll ever touch a hoe as long as I live. I've brains enough to make my living by them, and if I haven't I mean to starve" (RR, 93, 95). There is no stronger proof than this that the pastoral world so cherished by the Grays and Carys and Page's other aristocrats depended for its continuance on the labor force that was freed at the end of the war. The code of the southern gentry held such menial tasks to be degrading, and while he loved basking in the atmosphere of simplicity that plantation life afforded, the southern gentleman as conceived by Page is incapable of participating in that life at its most elemental level. He might "commune" with nature but it is his slaves who work in it to maintain his paradise.

It must also be noted that when Jacquelin Gray finally succeeds in recovering Red Rock, it is not because his gentlemanly approach to things has served him to such good use. Instead, Page must rely on a series of scarcely credible coincidences, such as a powerful northern senator turning out to be a college chum of Dr. Cary's, in order to make things work out well. Actually, the gentlemen of the novel have to depend for their survival on many factors not related to their ideals, and this is the weakest aspect of the novel.

In *Red Rock* the superiority of the type represented by Jacquelin Gray and Steven Allen is never questioned, even by their many enemies, who envy their status in society even more than their possessions. In *Gordon Keith*, the young hero has to prove this superiority to an alien world and is, in fact, immediately rejected by the mother of his first love. Although he comes from "the best blood of two continents," the girl's mother disapproves of him because he cannot afford to give her daughter the "best advantages." When pressed to say if by "best advantages" she means money, the lady replies, "Why, not in the way in which you put it; but what money stands for—comforts, luxuries, position" (GK, 115).

Gordon Keith's task throughout the novel is to show that the things "money stands for" are worthless when compared to the values of his region. It is up to him to prove by getting a fortune that fortunes without honor are worthless. In the course of converting his northern materialist friends to his point of view, he delivers numerous sermons like the following: "Fashion is a temporary and shifting thing, sometimes caused by accident and sometimes made by tradesmen, but . . . good manners are the same to-day that they were hundreds of years ago. . . . The basis is always the same, being kindness and gentility" (GK, 122). Adhering to such principles is what enables Keith to defeat unscrupulous businessmen and to come to the financial aid of unfortunate friends. In the end a sophisticated city slicker pays him the highest tribute by saying, "He made you live in Arthur's court, because he lived there himself" (GK, 236).

Page argues in *Gordon Keith* that twentieth-century urban society, as represented in the novel by New York City, is "the most corroding life on earth," and money the most sordid kind of wealth. His hero reaffirms the ideal world from which he came by using its values to beat modern materialists at their own game. The trouble with the novel's tactics, however, is that its hero, while professing great disdain for money, must even so depend on it to get where he wants to be in life.

Page had great difficulty in making any of his young aristocratic southerners believable. While characterizing them as the worthy representatives of all that the Old South stood for, he still wanted to be able to show that they could function successfully as heroes in a materialistic age. Part of his problem, particularly in his novels, was that he was preaching a "creed outworn" to a generation increasingly interested in other things, but his inability to produce believable characters in much of his fiction was due to more than this. What we get in his gentlemanly portrayals in his novels are products of an environment rather than people with individual emotions or spontaneous ideas. Marse Chan and Marse George, in the stories of *In Ole Virginia*, generate a great deal more interest than Page's later heroes. However, this is not really because they are portrayed with more flexibility, but because they are seen through the eyes of Page's Negro narrators, who speak with much greater originality and more warmth of feeling than does the stiff, omniscient gentleman-narrator of the novels.

III

The Negroes of *In Ole Virginia* are the most important figures that Page produced in his fiction. Not only are they more lifelike than the white heroes he created, but also they carry the chief responsibility for making and proving his arguments about the benevolence of race relations in the Old South. This is not to say that the Negro as Page presents him is not a stereotype, but only that Page, in conceptualizing the Old South darky, felt free to be more imaginative and less dogmatic than he was with his Old South gentlemen, and the result is that his black men usually have much greater appeal than his whites. Page lost some of his inhibitions when he used the voice of the Negro to tell his tales. They still preach his personal philosophy, but they do so in a way that enlarges and to some degree changes our vision of the world that he wanted us to see.

Sam, the old black freedman who was companion and servant to Page's Marse Chan, expresses the crux of southern race relations in refreshing terms; speaking to his master's dog, he says, "Yo' so sp'ilt yo' kyahn hardly walk. . . . Jus' like white folks—think 'cuz you's white and I's black, I got to wait on yo' all de time" (IOV, 3). The old servant's pointed remark, however, is meant to be more of a joke on himself than a criticism of white attitudes, as his subsequent actions show. The dog is treated with all the respect and favor due a monarch, simply because he once belonged, as did Sam himself, to the beloved Marse Chan. The fact that Sam was, by the sheer fact of his black skin, a slave, does not bother him at all. Actually he longs pitifully for the time when "Niggers didn' hed nothin' 't all to do—jes' hed to 'ten to de feedin' an' cleanin' de hosses, an' doin' what marster tell 'em to do."

In like manner do most of Page's Negro narrators dispose of the so-called "Negro question." His strategy was simple but effective. The supposed victims of the plantation system linger on after its demise to tell of its glories and to express their confusion and dismay at the sordidness of their new position in life. This method fulfills William Empson's analysis of the pastoral as implying "a beautiful relationship between rich and poor" by making "simple people express strong feelings . . . in learned and fashionable language."[17] Page's Negroes, by proclaiming in quaint dialect the superiority of their masters and their happiness with their lot, were certainly being used for this kind of purpose. They gave testimony to an idyllic relationship between themselves and their masters, and by speaking soothingly to the con-

17. Empson, *Some Versions of Pastoral*, 1.

sciences of a white society, they reestablished for northerners and southerners alike a sense that the old system supported a feeling of solidarity between races that was sadly lacking in the present.

The Negro, Page believed, was "the Southerner's problem." This is the title of a book he devoted to the subject, in which he found a very simple solution. It was based on the principle of "the absolute and unchangeable superiority of the white race" and on the belief that the Negro's "true interest lies in maintaining amity with the Southern white." The Negro needed to recognize that his best friends were his former owners, who had before the war "found him a savage and a cannibal and in two hundred years gave seven millions of his race a civilization, the only civilization it has had since the dawn of history."[18]

Page's fiction was designed to dramatize his racial views, and his stories became in fact his most effective tool for displaying what he felt was the true case concerning the relationship between whites and blacks which had once existed and could again exist in the South. Francis Pendleton Gaines points out that Page's Negroes feel a "not incongruous dignity" at being included as members of the plantation family.[19] Page's argument was that the slave enjoyed a secure place in life and a certain sense of status through his bondage. Only by being a slave could he participate in the exclusive world of the planter, yet his gratitude for the opportunity was nevertheless unbounded.

Such is the case with Sam when he is given to his young master in "Marse Chan." Sam relates with great pride what was for him the greatest moment in his life, when "ole marster" singled him out: "An den he sez: 'Now Sam, from dis time you belong to yo' young Marse Channin'; I want you to tek keer on im ez long ez he lives. You are to be his boy from dis time. . . .' An from dat time I was tooken in de house to be Marse Channin's body servant" (IOV, 6).

Page was trying to make the point in "Marse Chan" that it would have been better for Sam if slavery had never ended, but for the modern reader Sam's description of all the wonders of the old time cannot disguise the fact that his present misery is the direct result of his having been made, at birth, totally dependent on a way of life which

18. Thomas Nelson Page, *The Negro: The Southerner's Problem* (New York, 1904), 292, 285.
19. Gaines, *Southern Plantation*, 78.

could not save either him or itself from destruction. Of course, Sam sees nothing of this, and his account of his existence before the war is meant to be an uncritical defense of the old regime, one that would put to rout the image left by Harriet Beecher Stowe's Uncle Tom. This it managed to do more effectively than even Page could have hoped, as witnessed by the reported spectacle of the great abolitionist Thomas Wentworth Higginson weeping over Sam's description of Marse Chan's untimely death.

Two incidents mar the aura of pastoral serenity that Sam works hard to establish. One is an account of how Colonel Chamberlin sells a number of his slaves, including one named Maria, to pay off some of his debts. Old Mr. Channing attempts to buy Maria, because she is married to one of his slaves. He is successful, but Chamberlin, out of spite, brings a lawsuit to keep Channing from having her, and the matter is in court, Sam tells us, "off an' on, fur some years, till at lars' de co't decided dat M'ria belonged to ole marster" (IOV, 11–12). Another incident whose symbolic overtones were apparently not intended by Page is the blinding of Mr. Channing as he heroically enters a burning barn to save a slave. The slave had been sent into the flames to save the horses, and Page must have meant for the incident to show a master's willingness to risk his own life for his slaves. For the modern reader, however, this motive hardly disguises the fact that it was the "blind" master who unthinkingly exposed his slave to the danger in the first place.

The Arcadia that Page defined for the Old South thus was a very beautiful but also very ambiguous paradise which definitely contained the seeds of its own destruction. The heroic qualities of Sam's master—his fairness, his dislike of violence, his courage—are not enough to keep his region from its inevitable collision with the outer world and the force of progress. There is more pathos in Marse Chan's death than simply the fact that it keeps him from being reconciled with his true love. He dies in a war that he opposed in order to defend a system already doomed. And in spite of his brotherly regard for Sam, and Sam's undying loyalty to him, he is unable to provide for his slave's future. The result is a pathetic figure whom Page devised in order to praise the Old South, but who also reveals, all unconsciously, the plantation's inherent weaknesses.

The situation of Unc' Billy in "Meh Lady" is not as pathetic as that of the other Negro narrators in *In Ole Virginia*. For him, the old world manages to be retained on his plantation through the auspices of a former northern soldier (with Virginia ancestors, Page hastens to inform us) who returns after the war to win the hand of Meh Lady and restore her home to its earlier elegance. Viewing the reconciled pair of lovers, who represented for Page's readers an idyllic reunion of North and South, Unc' Billy sits with "de moon sort o' meltin' over de yard," and thinks "hit 'pear like de plantation 'live once mo', an' de ain' no mo' scufflin', an' de ole times done come back ag'in" (IOV, 138).

Billy plays a much more dynamic role in his story than Sam does in "Marse Chan." He is the only male figure in the story besides the southernized Yankee officer, and he is free to act with much more independence and individuality. Of course, his concerns are made identical to those of his white mistresses, yet he is allowed to interact with them as a mature, responsible adult, and his emotions as he masters the disruptions and disorder of his life are on the whole well conceived. He and his wife are the two forceful characters in the story, exhibiting a will to survive that is much more credible than their mistresses' noble but futile and fairly feeble efforts.

It is fitting that, at the wedding of Meh Lady and her lover, Billy takes the responsibility unasked when the minister requests someone to give the bride away. His reasoning is simple and yet full of dignity: "an' I don' know huccome 'twuz, but I think 'bout Marse Jeems an' Mistis when he ax me dat, an' Marse Phil, whar all dead, an' all de scufflin' we done been th 'oo, an' how de chile ain' got nobody to teck her part now 'se' jes' me; an' . . . I 'bleeged to speak up, I jes' step for'ard an' say: 'Old Billy'" (IOV, 137–38). Although Billy achieves a great deal of stature in this scene, his explanation nevertheless borders on being an apology for his presumption, and Page is quick to put him back in his place as simple darky.

There is one story in *In Ole Virginia* that differs from the rest in its focus and its message. Although not told from a Negro's point of view, the central character is a Negro whose tragic situation is not minimized by any of Page's usual propaganda of white benevolence. Ole 'Stracted, in the story of that title, is a former slave who had been sold many years before to help to pay off his master's debts. His wife and child were sold elsewhere, and the old black man lives only to be reunited with his master, who had promised to buy him back with his family. Though he has no memory of anything that has happened to him since the sale, he has made his way back to his plantation, which is now in ruins and is owned by "po' white trash." The old man's only identity is bound up in his belief that his master is coming for him. Thus he spends his time dreaming "of a great plantation, and fine carriages and horses, and a house with his wife and the boy" (IOV, 154).

Ole 'Stracted's hopeless fantasy is matched by the far more compelling dream of a young neighbor who turns out to be the old black man's son. Ephraim is a freedman trying with great dignity against impossible odds to make a good living for his wife and family. In spite of the new sort of potential here, there are still some of the standard biases. It is a poor white and certainly not a southern gentleman who victimizes Ephraim, and Ole 'Stracted never considers freedom a favorable alternative to the idyllic conditions he knew as a slave—the point is never made that the plantation system was responsible for separating him from his family in the first place. But Ephraim is a different kind of Negro from those whom Page had treated sympathetically in his other stories.

Ephraim's dream, like his father's, is of a southern Arcady, but his is based on a future which holds dignity and self-sufficiency for his family, while Ole 'Stracted's is based on his memories of a time when his master provided for him. Ephraim has a recurring vision "in which he saw corn stand so high and rank over his land that he could scarcely distinguish the stalk, and a stable and barn and a mule . . . and two cows which his wife would milk, and a green wagon driven by his boys" (IOV, 149–50), in which, in short, he would be a prosperous farmer sustaining himself and his family through his own labors on his own land.

This dream is a simple one which involves all of Ephraim's energy and keeps his hopes alive. It is one which Page lets us feel he has every right to realize, and this is what makes "Ole 'Stracted" so different from the other stories of his first collection. Page's usual attitude toward the freedman is one of scorn concerning the "new issue nigger" who does not have the proper respect for the old values. He frequently advised that the freedman should turn to his master for guidance and remain dependent on the white man until some vague future time when his race might finally "deserve" to govern itself. In this one story, however, he seems to admit the justice of a plan whereby the Negro could take his life into his own hands through owning and working his land.

Page's story, despite the sympathy it gives to Ephraim's dream, finally demonstrates that the young freedman's hopes are as futile as his father's belief that his master will find him. Ephraim and his wife do not own their land, and never in a lifetime of sweating in the fields and taking in washing could they hope to earn enough to buy it. Everything they can possibly raise goes to pay their rent to the white man who lives on the hill. Page has sympathy, but in the story, as well as in the essays he devoted to solving the "Negro question," he has few practical ideas as to how the Negro could maintain his self-respect and achieve his dreams in a white man's world.

Ephraim's wife, when she realizes the hopelessness of their situation, "instinctively" thinks of her former master: "I wonder whar Marse Johnny is? . . . He wouldn' let him turn we all out" (IOV, 148). But Marse Johnny is gone, just as Ole 'Stracted's master was gone when he was most needed by those whom Page's "benevolent" institution had put in his keeping. Page evidently could not bear the indictment of the old world that his story implied, so he got himself off the hook through a fortuitous, if improbable, coincidence of the kind that he used to resolve most of the potentially tragic situations in his works. The money that Ole 'Stracted has saved to buy back his wife and son goes at his death to Ephraim, who discovers just in time that the feeble-minded old man is his father. Thus he can buy his land and make his dream come true.

Page's conclusion is not a solution but an evasion of the implications of his story. The most disturbing element about "Ole 'Stracted" is that it appears in the same volume with "Marse Chan" and "Meh Lady," stories in which the Negroes themselves sing the praises of the system that causes all of the suffering in "Ole 'Stracted." Even Ole 'Stracted longs for the past, however; his energies have always been fixed on the idea that his master will save him, so he is incapable of doing anything to save himself.

The situation of the black man in Page's pastoral kingdom is ambiguous at best, though it was clearly the author's intention to depict plantation life as the ideal mode of existence for both master and slave.

His black spokesmen are meant to illustrate that Negroes and whites, in the old and better world, were united in their pursuits and purposes. In making this stand, Page carves an image of the white man as the hero of Arcady, dedicated to preserving a civilization perfect in its innocence and magnificent in its program for the good life. His Negroes, however, remain his most compelling creations, as characters lost in a new world and from their longings creating the myth of a world which fulfills their need for an identity and a sense of purpose.

That Page never consciously explored the flaws of the Old South, that he failed to see the ambiguities of his own re-creations of the plantation as an ideal world, is only too clear a fact. His intention was not to hide the sins of the past, for indeed, he was blind to them himself. What he hoped to accomplish was to challenge the practices of the present by comparing them in art to the customs of a simpler, more natural time. Thus his stories have the force of what was for him a dream. Page created out of his own deep convictions a romantic world whose charm at times overshadows the realist's demand for a counterbalancing acknowledgment of truths based purely on fact. We return from Page's fiction to the real world very much aware that his vision was marred, yet also aware that, as dreams go, the one Page fashioned for the Old South was convincing enough to give force to a myth that has itself shaped many realities and outlasted many others.

Truth wears many guises in art, and a genre like the pastoral, which usually begins with deceptive expressions of preference for simplicity and progresses through contemplations of opposing kinds of values, might very well end by raising more riddles than it solves about the nature of reality. The case of Joel Chandler Harris is more dramatic in this respect than even that of Page. In light of our perspective, we would not expect that the realities of plantation life, particularly for the black slave, could find acceptable expression in the sentimental renderings of white southerners whose culture and experience placed the black man in a position of inferiority. And indeed it is easy to find the lies, the blind spots, in such portrayals. Yet the important thing is that truth is there, though it is often ironically hidden as we have seen by dissecting the interpretations of the slave mind offered by Page. A study of Harris' Uncle Remus collections reveals a mode of truth that transcends the need to unveil ironies that the writer himself did not understand.

In the folktales that Uncle Remus tells, and in the responses to these tales that Harris allows his storyteller persona to display, truth wears the costume of the subversive Brer Rabbit. The stark clarity of the folktale form, the winning simplicity of the old black man who tells the tales, the reputed naïveté of the man who made the teller of the tales, all these combine to produce an effect which is anything but simple. Through the structure of a dream within a dream, the stories recorded and in some measure crafted by Harris offer us the truth of both the despairs and the hopes of the black man locked in the white man's Arcady.

FOUR

Joel Chandler Harris:
Speculating on the Past

Joel Chandler Harris, editor of the Atlanta *Constitution*, creator of Uncle Remus, and author of more than thirty books, considered himself to be a simple man. In his later years he liked to call himself "the farmer," and from the start to the finish of his remarkable literary career he insisted that he was only "accidentally" an author. The idea of achieving simplicity in his life seems to have been a goal of religious magnitude for him; he fled from banquets held in his honor, called his home in a fashionable suburb of Atlanta alternately "the Wren's Nest" or "Snap Bean Farm," and wrote, only four months before his death, "We are all extremely ignorant with respect to some of the most important things in this world, and before our knowledge can be deeper we shall have to become as little children; we shall have to drown our egoism in a perfect deluge of simplicity."[1]

The ideal of the simple life that Harris imposed upon his thinking about both his own life and his region's identity was never to be a reality for him in the post–Civil War South to which he loyally proclaimed allegiance. His region was far more complex than he cared to admit for factual or fictional purposes, just as he himself was never as simple as he tried to pretend. The reminiscences of Walter Hines Page concerning his first meeting with Harris confirm the discrepancy that is notable between what Harris was to the world and what

---

1. Julia Collier Harris, *Editor and Essayist*, 265.

he thought of himself: "It was impossible to believe that the man realized what he had done. I afterwards discovered that his most appreciative friends held the same opinion—that Joe Harris does not appreciate Joel Chandler Harris."[2]

There is one indication, at least, that Harris recognized the complexities of his personality as well as any of his friends. In a letter to one of his daughters, dated March 19, 1898, he remarked, "You know all of us have two entities, or personalities," adding that he himself had an "other fellow" inside him, somewhat contemptuous of plain Joe Harris and "hard to understand." He excused his creative abilities by saying that "when night comes, I take up my pen, surrender unconditionally to my 'other fellow,' and out comes the story."[3]

Harris' letter represents a rather facile attempt to explain away a problem that was noted often even during his own lifetime; that is, neither the life nor the art of Joel Chandler Harris is simple and both exhibit certain perplexing, even contradictory urges which make it difficult to come to any final analysis of his genius as a writer or his motivations as a man. Biographical studies portray Harris alternately as a jolly humorist who always appreciated a good joke and a sensitive recluse who was often depressed and despised having any attention directed his way. It is somewhat hard to see why a man so painfully shy never considered any career other than that of newspaperman, a job in which he was constantly facing public exposure. Again, Harris professed to hate politics or controversy of any kind, yet he wrote very strong editorials on some of the hottest political issues of his time and allowed them to appear in the leading publications of the nation. He has been labeled both a white racist and an unusually perceptive interpreter of the Negro and is mentioned in the same breath with both Henry Grady, the New South's most eloquent spokesman, and Thomas Nelson Page, the Old South's most ardent literary defender.

The relationship between Harris' personal beliefs about the South and the Negro and what he produced in his fiction presents the most fascinating and crucial problems of all. He wrote editorials on the beautiful relationships that only the plantation system could make possible, but he also wrote stories about forced separations of hus-

2. Walter Hines Page, "The New South," Boston *Post*, September 28, 1881, quoted in Julia Collier Harris, *The Life and Letters of Joel Chandler Harris* (Boston, 1918), 178.
3. Julia Collier Harris, *Life and Letters*, 384–86.

bands from wives and mothers from children, about cruel overseers and incompetent masters. White southerners could read his books and find justification for the way of life they had gone to war to defend. White northerners could read his books and believe that the white southerners were thoroughly reconstructed and should be given control over their own affairs, particularly the affairs that related to the future of the black man in the South. But black men could also read Harris' books, as Charles Chesnutt read them to his children, and could find in them not just stereotypes of the contented darky and faithful black family retainer but also, as Louis D. Rubin points out, black characters who "in their humanity and strength strike at the very foundations of race prejudice."[4]

So where did Harris himself actually stand on the question of race? Even his greatest creation, black Uncle Remus, seems to contradict himself in different stories. When he is placed in his Atlanta setting, and sometimes when he is talking about trivial matters back on "Miss Sally's" plantation, he is essentially the comic, obsequious, old-time darky that the plantation myth has perpetuated down to the present time. Yet the Uncle Remus who projects himself into the stories of the fabulous rabbit, re-creating for a small white boy a fantasy world where animals are people and the weakest always win, is a human being of great depth and special dignity who certainly transcends the traditional stereotypes.

All that can be said with assurance is that Harris was a white southerner who shared, not surprisingly, the racial attitudes of the majority of the whites of his region. It can be added that he was no doubt aware of the propaganda value of his stories and quite agreeable to the opportunity of exploiting the public's sympathetic curiosity about the good old days in the plantation South. As Paul Buck says, Uncle Remus and the Negro characters of other southern local color writers were "the answer of the Southern genius of the eighties to the Yankee genius of the fifties." But the significant point, which Buck is quick to add, is that "Harris alone, perhaps, created in Uncle Remus a Negro character which had existence in life independent of traditional types."[5] Harris at his best as a writer could get beyond even his own ways of thinking to give originality and credibility to a hu-

4. Louis D. Rubin, Jr., "Southern Local Color and the Black Man," *Southern Review*, VI (Autumn, 1970), 1017.
5. Buck, *Road to Reunion*, 211.

man being of another race and ostensibly an entirely different psychology from his own.

Where did Harris stand on the question of the South's goals and possibilities after the Civil War? He sat beside Henry Grady at a desk in the offices of the South's most progressive newspaper and even took Grady home with him to his rural birthplace of Eatonton to let his old friends hear the great orator preach the new gospel of diversified farms and factories for the South. Yet Harris himself hated cities, decried the materialistic instinct that seemed to be spurring the South's progress, and spoke yearningly of the old times on the plantation as being "the brightest and pleasantest of all the dreams we have."[6] And while he praised and probably envied Grady for being "the embodiment" of a "smiling faith in the future,"[7] his own preferences turned out to be decidedly different.

Among the many contradictions that appear in both the life and works of Harris, these two—his attitude toward the black man's place in the South and his approach to the concept of material progress—are the ones that seem most often to cause critical comment and confusion. Harris' creation of Uncle Remus reflects his own answers to these problems. Through the voice and imagination of a black slave, Harris confronted issues about which he had a lifelong concern. The story of how the famous Atlanta author-editor came to identify his deepest longings with those of a being ostensibly his opposite must begin with his early exposure to the actual plantation world that would become, in Remus' tales, a very topsy-turvy version of Arcady.

Harris was born in December of 1848 in the small, middle Georgia town of Eatonton, but as he was to recall later in several autobiographical accounts, life really began for him in March of 1862. It was in that year that he undertook his "most important journey," as he came to view it, a journey consisting of a wagon ride to a plantation called Turnwold, not very far from his hometown. Here he would work for the next four years as a compositor for a weekly newspaper published on the plantation grounds.

The newspaper whose "staff" Harris joined at the age of thirteen was called *The Countryman* and was the unique venture of its equally

6. Julia Collier Harris, *Editor and Essayist*, 115.
7. Joel Chandler Harris, *Life of Henry Grady, Including His Writings and Speeches* (New York, 1890), 60.

unique owner and editor, a lawyer-scholar-gentleman planter named Joseph Addison Turner. His influence on Joe Harris lasted much longer than the four years the boy spent on his plantation. Harris' own father had deserted his mother shortly after his birth, so it is probable that he found in Turner the only strong male authority figure he was ever to know. Although in Eatonton the community seems to have taken a paternal interest in Mary Harris and her son, it is likely that the circumstances of his birth and parentage made it impossible for him ever to feel completely secure there. At Turnwold he was evidently made to understand that he belonged. The acceptance that he found at the Turner home was no doubt an indispensable factor in providing him with the confidence he needed to pursue the kind of life he was to choose later.

Turner was more than a father figure for young Harris. He gave his apprentice, among other things, a very thorough training in all aspects of newspaper writing and publishing. It was probably Turner who introduced his apprentice to the tradition of middle Georgia humor established by such writers as Augustus Baldwin Longstreet, William Tappan Thompson, Richard Malcolm Johnson, and Bill Arp. Turner was himself a writer, of poems as well as news articles, but of added significance for Harris, he was an ardent promoter of southern literature. He encouraged Harris' efforts at writing and opened his large library to him. Yet his most important contribution to Harris' career was the very lifestyle he maintained at Turnwold and the access Harris was given there to the lore of the slaves with whom he seems to have had many close associations. Writing years later about slavery as he had witnessed its operation at Turnwold, he said that "under the best and happiest conditions" the "realities" of a slavocracy "possess a romantic beauty and tenderness all their own."[8] Perhaps because of the circumstances of his birth and his position at Turnwold, Harris saw the paternalistic aspect of the white owner's relationship to his slaves as a quality of the old world that operated to his own advantage.

It is instrumental at this point to compare Harris' boyhood with that of Thomas Nelson Page, the writer with whom his name is most often linked as a fellow chronicler of the old plantation South. Page

8. Julia Collier Harris, *Editor and Essayist*, 117, 129.

grew up the son of a plantation owner, descended from a well-established line of Virginia aristocrats. Thus he enjoyed throughout his youth a sense of well-being and status founded upon the sure knowledge of his birth and family heritage. The plantation culture belonged to him in a way that it could never belong to Harris. Perhaps the Georgia author's keener insights and fresher responses to that way of life, then, are due in part to the distance forced upon him by his awareness that he participated in its blessings not by blood and birth but only circumstance and charity. He more than likely was able to be more critical and more freely imaginative in his treatment of the plantation because he had no reason to feel, as Page doubtless did feel, a directly personal sense of responsibility for its destiny.

In one respect, however, Page and Harris are very much alike. The Civil War caused the end of the most idyllic period of both of their lives, and for both the abruptness with which the plantation regime was destroyed caused their memories to be colored with more romance than realism, more nostalgia than fact. Page left home and heritage to accept a position as tutor to cousins in Kentucky; Harris left Turnwold with even more uncertain prospects. In 1866 Turner gave up trying to publish *The Countryman.* His farewell edition stated proudly that his paper had been "a representative of independent country life and of the home of the planter," but added mournfully that "these are gone, and *The Countryman* goes with them."[9] Harris was out of a job, yet years later he could romanticize about the event: "A larger world beckoned to Joe, and he went out into it."[10]

The "larger world" Joe Harris entered was to include Macon and Forsyth, Georgia, New Orleans, and Savannah, all within four years' time. By 1870, when Harris made his move from the small, weekly *Monroe Advertiser* in Forsyth to the Savannah *Morning News,* he was experienced in many areas of writing and editing and was ready to take the responsibility for turning out a daily humor column based on current regional affairs. Yet despite his successes in the journalistic arena, he seems to have often been very depressed during this period. It is probable that circumstances which would have no reason

9. Joseph Addison Turner, *The Countryman,* May 8, 1866, quoted in Cousins, *Joel Chandler Harris,* 60.
10. Joel Chandler Harris, *On the Plantation,* quoted in Julia Collier Harris, *Life and Letters,* 52.

to plague him while he was at Turnwold—his illegitimacy, his lack of
formal education, his rather odd physical appearance—began to give
him serious doubts about himself once he was out in the world.

Thus it seems that it must have been during the years immediately
following his departure from Turnwold that Harris developed not only
his bent for humor but also his lifelong dread of strangers and strange
situations. Each new job brought new misery, until we find him
writing, in letters to a friend, such brooding comments as: "I have
an absolute horror of strangers"; "I am morbidly sensitive"; "the best
part of my life is made up of small things"; "I am never more lonely
than when in a crowd."[11] Throughout his life, Harris was to be
plagued by a feeling that he was different and inferior, a feeling which
seemed, he once wrote, "the result of some abnormal quality of the
mind." At the height of his fame he would still be calling himself a
scribbler; he would steadfastly refuse to give speeches or even to read
his stories to children; there are suggestions that he often drank heavily.

Yet Harris sought and attained the kind of fame that was bound to
place him in the limelight. In one of the same letters in which he writes
of his great shyness, he also states that "the main point is success and
advancement," and he talks of moving on "towards that shining Sodom
called New York." He achieved great popularity as a humorist while
writing for the Savannah *Morning News*, and after six years there he
accepted an editorial position with the South's leading newspaper, the
Atlanta *Constitution*.

When Harris joined the staff of the *Constitution* he was only twenty-
seven years old, but he already had fourteen years of practical newspaper experience. The short humorous paragraphs that he turned out
daily for the *Morning News* were reprinted all over the state, so he was
well qualified for the advancement signified by his new job. By associating himself with the *Constitution*, Harris committed himself to
a city that was fast becoming an urban metropolis and to a newspaper that was to rise, during his time there, "to supremacy as the
South's leading advocate of business enterprise and of friendship with
the North," in Paul Buck's words.[12] The feelings that Harris had nurtured since his boyhood at Turnwold—his love of peace and simplicity, his distaste for city life, his belief in plantation ideals—all had to

11. Julia Collier Harris, *Life and Letters*, 83–84, 90.
12. Buck, *Road to Reunion*, 186.

be forced into the background of his conscious life in order for him to become an active participant in the world that was pushing its way into Atlanta in 1876. Harris seems to have made the transition from "cornfield journalist" to big city editor with few preliminary qualms, but as his fiction and the essays of his later years show, the sentiments that he cultivated at Turnwold were not completely routed by the New South fever that raged in the offices of the *Constitution*.

As an active spokesman for his progressive newspaper, Harris editorialized on some topics close to his heart, such as the "Negro question" and the need for a southern literature free from sectional bias. By 1879 he had tried his own hand at writing fiction, producing one very weak novel and several very popular humor sketches about an old black "uncle" named Remus, who lived a "scufflin'" life in busy Atlanta. In that year Harris had Uncle Remus tell his first folktale against the background setting of an old plantation. In 1880 the first collection of Uncle Remus stories was published as *Uncle Remus: His Songs and His Sayings*, and Harris' career as a fiction writer was established.

The first Uncle Remus volume and all the ones which followed presented an idyllic world as seen through the eyes of an old black rustic whose loyalties centered upon his memories of life before the war. It has often been noted how Harris, in his published collection, even changed the ending of one story that had earlier appeared in the *Constitution* so that he would avoid any possibility of stirring up old sectional rivalries. In the newspaper version Uncle Remus kills a Union soldier who was aiming a rifle at his master. In the book version Uncle Remus only wounds the soldier, who is nursed back to health and eventually marries "Miss Sally" in a classic example of the reconciliation motif.

Harris' creation of Uncle Remus caused him to be accepted during his lifetime as an authority on "the Negro." His fictional treatment of the black man suggested to northerners and southerners alike that he had an exceptional understanding of the black race. Uncle Remus had a quality of reality about him, a personality so richly yet artlessly detailed, that he was seen from the first as an accurate portrayal of what the Negro of his time and place must have been like.

In his introduction to the first Uncle Remus book, *Uncle Remus: His Songs and His Sayings*, Harris fostered the impression himself that he sought to present a Negro character who would give a true picture of his race. Reproducing genuine Negro dialect was an important aspect in creating this impression, but Harris also issued a warning concerning the dialect that he worked so hard to verify: "If the language of Uncle Remus fails to give vivid hints of the really poetic imagination of the Negro; if it fails to embody the quaint and homely humor which was his most prominent characteristic; if it does not suggest a certain picturesque sensitiveness—a curious exaltation of the mind and the temperament not to be defined by words—then . . . my attempt may be accounted a failure." He trusted that he was presenting in his book a "new and by no means unattractive phase of Negro character," one which would "supplement" Mrs. Stowe's picture, he added pointedly.[13]

Harris' introduction tells of certain fables that are seen as being "thoroughly characteristic of the Negro"; in pointing out this aspect of the tales themselves, Harris showed that he was well aware that the stories had a psychological importance that outstripped their purely humorous value. Harris understood, though he never emphasized, that what went on in the tales about the animals was inherently related to the Negro storyteller's feelings and attitudes. "It needs no scientific investigation," he pointed out, "to show why he selects as his hero the weakest and most harmless of all animals, and brings him out victorious in contests with the bear, the wolf, and the fox. It is not virtue that triumphs, but helplessness; it is not malice, but mischievousness."[14]

Harris was stressing in his early commentary the importance of Uncle Remus' relationship as storyteller to the material he is given to tell. Yet many of Harris' most prominent critics have overlooked this aspect of the Remus works. Mark Twain, for instance, once wrote to Harris concerning the folklore tales that "in reality the stories are only alligator pears—one eats them merely for the sake of the dressing," or, in other words, only to get on to the enjoyment of Harris' delightful, nostalgic backdrops.[15] Too often the outer frameworks,

13. Joel Chandler Harris, *Uncle Remus: His Songs and His Sayings* (New York, 1908), viii.

14. *Ibid.*, xiv.

15. Mark Twain to Joel Chandler Harris, August 10, 1881, quoted in Julia Collier Harris, *Life and Letters*, 169–70.

rather than the tales themselves, as Uncle Remus tells them, are ana-lyzed to determine Harris' attitudes toward race and the Old South as well as to evaluate his merits as an artist. Yet the tales themselves and Uncle Remus' feeling for them actually reveal more about Har-ris' insights and artistry than do his carefully conceived frameworks or his authorial intrusions and asides.

What Harris allowed Uncle Remus to do in his capacity as teller of folktales was to construct a black slave's dream of Arcady—a dream which manages to undercut the white society he served so charm-ingly in the framework sketches. Uncle Remus' Arcady centers on Brer Rabbit, an unlikely but strikingly effective hero figure who reverses the rules which must be followed in Remus' real life while he paro-dies the white society that exerts all the pressures. The paradise that results is no traditional Arcadia to be sure; however, it is important to recognize that what was going on for Harris as he shaped the tell-ing of the folktales was an artistic purpose that has much in common with the shaping of most pastoral literature; the ultimate issue is the same: a man from a troubling, complex world is creating, with the aid of a rustic persona, a world of deceptive simplicity which em-bodies some of his own contradictory urges.

The first thing that Uncle Remus wants to make clear to his young listener concerning his stories is that they are not about mere ani-mals. "In dem days," he explains, "creeturs had lots mo' sense den dey got now; let 'lone dat, dey had sense same like folks."[16] His creatures exhibit all the foibles of human nature—slyness and selfishness, pride and greed, jealousy and hypocrisy. They are, of course, people: "Folks put me in min' er de creeturs" (CT, 191) says Uncle Remus, and there is no question but that the things that go on in his animal kingdom represent a sampling of the kind of human actions with which he most identifies himself and his situation.

The animals have recognizable social patterns; they are, for all their individuality, members of a community which provides in a primi-tive sense for group needs. They acknowledge some social and moral rules (almost always in order to break them at the first opportunity) which yet help to define and regulate their activities and abilities. So-cially they are all potential equals. If they choose not to associate with

16. Joel Chandler Harris, *The Complete Tales of Uncle Remus* (Boston, 1955), 14.

one another, it is not because they acknowledge any gradations based on cliques or classes, but because they are so naturally and highly competitive. At the center of their social framework is "Miss Meadows" and her "gals," who are never clearly defined. Whether Miss Meadows is an animal, a lady, perhaps even Mother Nature herself is never explained, but she and her retinue function as the genteel and civilizing influence among the animals who seek her approval, vie for her praise, and bow to her judgment. To miss one of Miss Meadows' "affairs" is a fate too awful to contemplate.

Although the animals must survive on their own individual merits and wits, there is one figure looming large in the background of their lives who does not seem to be bound by the limitations they have to accept. This is Mr. Man, who is a kind of half-god figure for the animals. Seldom do they take him on as a rival without disastrous results. Despite many warnings, Mr. Lion decides one time to find Mr. Man and give him a "larrupin'" that will show the animal community who is boss; of course he is tricked by his own pride and gets "frailed" into submission by Mr. Man (CT, 141). There are rare occasions when Mr. Rabbit is able to outwit Mr. Man, as when he talks Mr. Man's daughter into freeing him from her father's trap in order to see him dance (CT, 126). Yet most often the animals steer clear of all humans, recognizing, as Uncle Remus puts it, that "Mr. Man got w'at lots er folks ain't got—good luck, long head, quick eye, and slick fingers" (CT, 339).

Mr. Man's presence in Brer Rabbit's world more than likely represents an intrusion of the white master's influence into the dream from which the Negro legends are constructed. He is the only figure whose superiority is granted automatically, and he is the only one who is shown using the other creatures to do his labor for him. The story "Why Mr. Dog is Tame" contains an image of Mr. Man and a lesson which a slave on a white man's plantation would find especially meaningful. Through the legend Uncle Remus is explaining why the dog is Mr. Man's domestic servant while the other animals are free. At one time, Uncle Remus relates, Brer Dog "galloped wid Brer Fox, an' 'loped wid Brer Wolf, an' cantered wid Brer Coon." After a particularly hard winter, though, he is persuaded by Brer Wolf to attempt to borrow a chunk of fire from Mr. Man. Brer Dog's "'umble-come-tumble" appearance saves him from Mr. Man's gun, and when the man discovers that the dog can be useful to him, he puts a collar on the animal and makes him a part of the household. When Brer Dog meets Brer Wolf later and is asked why he never returned to the woods, Brer Dog's response has subtle significance; he merely points to his collar and says, "You see dis? Well, it'll tell you lots better dan what I kin'" (CT, 698).

The great irony of the story is that Brer Wolf envies Brer Dog's new situation, since the latter is now fat and well cared for. Brer Wolf tries to ingratiate himself with Mr. Man, but Mr. Man misunderstands the wolf's "perliteness" (which consists of showing all his teeth) and shoots him. In the story the dog's condition of dependence and servitude is made to seem desirable, and in this manner, perhaps, a slave could mock his own low station in life.

It seems reasonable to assume that the Mr. Man of the tales stands for the authority figure who dominates the slave storyteller's own life—the white plantation owner. Mr. Man wields great power, he enjoys security and comfort, and he owns land and domestic animals. Uncle Remus never specifies whether or not his Mr. Man is black or white. When the little boy demands to know the skin color of the man in one story, Uncle Remus seems completely indifferent to this particular detail: "De man mought er bin ez w'ite ez de driven snow, er he mought er bin de blackes' Affikin er de whole kit en b'ilin'" (CT, 459).

Uncle Remus is not as totally uninterested in skin colors as some of his casual remarks would indicate, as we see in another story in which he explains to the white boy that "niggers is niggers now, but de time wuz w'en we 'uz all niggers tergedder" (CT, 110). His theory of how the different races came into being gives all men black skins at the beginning of time. Only when people discovered a pond in which "dey'd be wash off nice en w'ite" if they jumped into it, did the situation change. All of the people, of course, wanted to be made white, but the magical pond water was used up before everyone could get in, the result being that some came out "w'ite ez a town gal," some became the color of "murlatters," and the Negro race, the last folks to get to the pond, whitened only their palms and the soles of their feet. Here a rather surprising reversal of acceptable orders puts the Negro first, if only for a little while.

Mr. Man, whether black or white, is not morally judged by the animals, for a prominent feature of their world is its almost total lack of emphasis on the rightness or wrongness of any action. Justice is of a most primitive kind, and violence is accepted usually without comment or complaint. The only rule that seems to hold true regularly is "Do before it is done to you." Brer Rabbit kills off numerous Brer Foxes and Brer Wolves with grisly effectiveness and no compunction whatsoever. Uncle Remus says only that the creatures "dunno right fum wrong. Dey see what dey want, en dey git it ef dey kin, by hook en by crook. Dey don't ax who it b'longs ter, ner wharbouts it come fum" (CT, 560).

In the opinion of Uncle Remus, tales about human beings are far less satisfactory than tales about animals, since "folks can't play no tricks, ner git even wid der neighbors, widout hurtin' somebody's feelin's, er breakin' some law er nudder, er gwine 'g'inst what de preacher say" (CT, 563). The slave's own life has been narrowly circumscribed by the laws of a white society that stress submission and instant obedience; no civilization could have been more code-conscious than the plantation South. Consequently it is little wonder that in the imaginary society created for the rabbit moral codes exist only to be ignored or ridiculed, particularly by Brer Rabbit himself.

In one of Uncle Remus' stories, the kind of code his masters might design is given parodic treatment by the animals, then completely overturned by Brer Rabbit. The result is a violent reversal of the sort of values upheld in Uncle Remus' plantation world. The tale is "Mr. Rabbit Nibbles Up the Butter," in which we see, at the beginning, a rare display of harmony and good will being put on by the animals. They have become so friendly that they are even storing their provisions in the same place and working together in the fields. The picture is one of idyllic peace, which is soon to be destroyed by Brer Rabbit.

Brer Rabbit cannot resist sneaking off to have a "nip" of Brer Fox's butter at frequent intervals, until finally he empties the whole bucket. Each time he leaves the field to have his snack, he returns with news of his wife's supposedly grave illness, until after the last foray he brings word that she has died. To comfort Brer Rabbit, the fox and possum set a dinner for him at which they plan, of course, to serve the butter which has long since disappeared. To learn the identity of the butter thief, Brer Possum devises a test which will prove who is the culprit. The animals are each to jump over a brush heap set afire; the one who falls in must be the guilty party, for they all believe that the truth will "out." All believe, that is, except the rabbit, who is the first to jump and clears the fire, giggling all the while. It is the innocent possum who cannot make it across and so perishes for his ideal.

The little white boy is appalled by this violent example of injustice, but Uncle Remus remains unmoved. His only explanation is that "in dis worl', lots er folks is gotter suffer fer udder folks sins. Looks like hit's mighty onwrong, but hit's des dat away" (CT, 57). Brer Rabbit disrupts the peace that has sprung up in the community, he accepts sympathy and generosity from those whom he has wronged, and he mocks the ideals of honor, truth, and justice. Yet Uncle Remus, with a lifetime of resignation behind him, accepts no moral to the tale other than that innocent people often pay.

The moral pretensions of a civilization which thrives on slavery are questioned subtly in another tale, in which Brer Rabbit and Brer Wolf make a bargain to sell their "ole mammies" in order to buy provisions to stave off famine. The two take Brer Wolf's mother first, and after selling her, they head back home "wid a wagon-load of vittles." On the way, however, Brer Rabbit tricks Brer Wolf into leaving for a while and then manages to make him believe that the horses and provisions have all sunk in quicksand. The wolf finally leaves the scene in despair, whereupon Brer Rabbit recovers the wagonload of goods from its hiding place and takes the full share home. Uncle Remus' only comment is to say, admiringly, that Brer Rabbit "druv de hosses home en git all de vittles, en he ain't hatter sell he ole mammy n'er. Dat he ain't" (CT, 289).

Brer Rabbit's world is a world without moral standards or social classifications, a world, therefore, that is just the opposite of Uncle Remus' in which code and class are primary considerations. In the animal society, all that counts is survival, a feat often accomplished only through violence or knavery. Here one can at least determine fairly easily where he stands in relation to his fellow creatures. There is, moreover, in the nature of things, provision for a primitive kind of balance of power which keeps any one creature from being able to subjugate others for any length of time.

In Uncle Remus' dream world a crawfish can cause a deluge in order to get revenge on an elephant; a terrapin can beat a bear at a game of tug o' war, and Brer Rabbit, of course, can challenge lions, tigers, wolves, bears, and foxes and come out on top. Uncle Remus finds this aspect of his legends most consoling. He often points out with pride that, where the rabbit dwells, "tain't de biggest en de strongest dat does de mostest in dis world" (CT, 529). For all the violence and upheaval in the tales, there is still at the heart of the rabbit's civilization an order which gives the weak protection against the strong. As Uncle Remus explains, "De littler de creeturs is, de mo' sense dey got, kaze dey bleedged ter have it. You hear folks say dat Brer Rabbit is full er tricks. . . . What folks calls tricks is creetur sense. Ef ole Brer Lion had as much sense ez Brer Rabbit, what de name er goodness would de balance er de creeturs do? Dey wouldn't be none un um lef' by dis time" (CT, 548).

In Uncle Remus' own world, the balance is lacking. The rich white man stays rich and powerful; the black slave remains helpless, and his "creetur sense" does him little good. Harris recognized that this could be a primary factor in the way the Negro structured his legends to make his hero "the weakest and most harmless of all animals." Through the telling of stories about a mythical place where not virtue, nor strength, nor status triumphs, but only helplessness, a counterforce is brought to bear on the plantation world that Remus inhabits. The legends could provide a slave with compensation for his inferior position and at the same time allow him, using pastoral strategy, to judge the society that makes him inferior.

There are many kinds of exploits depicted in the legends which could serve to illustrate the special sense of fulfillment a black slave might feel as he related them. Of these we can point to three major categories based on the typical action taking place in the story: the tales of getting free, the tales of outdoing, and the tales of exploitation. In each of these three kinds of activity, there is depicted an urge or motive to which a black storyteller could respond in a particularly personal way. Brer Rabbit is often caught, but he always gets away; he has ways of outclassing and showing up his neighbors; he uses others without ever being used by them. Freedom, pride, and power are the three things Brer Rabbit has a precarious hold on that a slave would be most aware that he himself lacked entirely.

Among the stories of getting free, the tale of the magnificent tar-baby provides the classic example of the rabbit's ability to escape. Here, as in so many of the tales, it is pride which causes the rabbit to get caught and his understanding of another creature's pride which allows him to get loose again. Insulted by the tar-baby's refusal to speak to him, Brer Rabbit attacks the fox's trap doll until he is stuck fast to it. Brer Fox is certain that he has got his victim this time, but the rabbit tricks him into throwing him into a briar patch; this, he says, would hurt more than any other torture. Reading the story one can almost feel the strains of hilarity and exultation in the voice of Uncle Remus as he relates the rabbit's parting words to Brer Fox: "Bred en bawn in a briar-patch, Brer Fox—bred and bawn in a briar-patch" (CT, 14).

For Uncle Remus, of course, the attraction of the tales does not lie in learning *if* the rabbit will escape but in sharing the news of *how* he manages to do it every time. In the first folklore tale he ever published, Harris has the old man tell his young listener, with an assurance amounting to religious faith, that "Brer Fox ain't never cotch 'im yit, en w'at's mo' honey, he ain't gwine ter" (CT, 6). What is particularly enjoyable to Uncle Remus is the versatility and cleverness employed by Brer Rabbit to extricate himself from the clutches of his foes.

There are several stories in which Brer Rabbit manages not only to free himself but to trick one of his enemies into taking his place in captivity. Thus when he gets caught in a trap Brer Fox has set in his pea patch, all he has to do is to convince Brer B'ar that he is being paid a dollar a minute to guard Brer Fox's peas. Brer B'ar eagerly takes his place and is left to face the wrath of the fox (CT, 74). Such a feat would be doubly satisfying to a storyteller who personally knew so little of freedom, much less of control over others.

The many legends which show Brer Rabbit exploiting his neighbors point to an interesting aspect of the slave's own existence. Through a double reversal of values the Negro's hero, lowliest of animals, uses his cleverness to make himself stronger than the fiercest animals around him; then he uses his unique strength to force others into the humiliating positions that he is supposed to occupy. Not only is the rabbit not a victim, but others become his victims, which suggests on the part of the slave storyteller a desire not only for freedom but for dominance of the kind so often exercised over him.

Brer Rabbit in one story tricks Mr. Lion into letting himself be tied up by the rabbit, who tells him that by doing so he will save himself from being blown away by a terrible "harrycane" that is coming. Not content merely with tying the lion, Brer Rabbit stays around to witness the lion's discomfiture when he realizes there is to be no hurricane. Brer Rabbit just sits confronting the increasingly uneasy lion, washing his face and paws and enjoying a tremendous sense of smugness. When other animals show up to find out the cause of the lion's bellowing, Brer Rabbit "tuck n' gun ter talk biggity un strut 'roun'" (CT, 354). His obvious self-satisfaction, one cannot help but feel, is being shared by the narrator.

In a like manner does Brer Rabbit victimize most of the bigger and supposedly better animals of the kingdom. He even uses his wiles on poor Miss Cow, tricking her into getting her horns stuck in a persimmon tree and then bringing his family to the spot to milk her dry (CT, 28). But probably the most satisfying story of exploitation, at any rate one which Uncle Remus takes more than the usual delight in telling, is the tale of how Brer Rabbit rides Brer Fox to a party at Miss Meadows' (CT, 17). Brer Rabbit has bragged to the gals that Brer Fox was once his father's riding horse. Naturally Brer Fox is eager to make Brer Rabbit recant in front of Miss Meadows, so eager that he even consents to carry the rabbit to her home. Through a series of deceptions, Brer Rabbit gets the fox to don saddle, bridle, and blinders, and when they are close enough to Miss Meadows', he sticks spurs into Brer Fox's sides, and the two go flying through her gate. Brer Fox, tied to the "hoss-rack," has never been so thoroughly vanquished, while the rabbit, sitting with the gals and "smokin' his seeygar same ez a town man," revels in his heightened position of power and prestige.

A third group of stories, those of "outdoing," show Brer Rabbit in adventures which could easily fulfill the Negro's need to achieve recognition in a world which has made him an outcast. Brer Rabbit does not have an established social place in his world any more than the slave did on the plantation, but in the rabbit's case, it is because he doesn't want one. He can never stand to get along with his neighbors for long, but he does want their admiration and seeks it through numerous exploits designed to highlight his talents. The only times his show-off schemes seem to backfire are when he challenges an even weaker, more pitiful creature than himself. The story of his race with Brer Terrypin is the classic example.

The animals in Uncle Remus' make-believe world are so often stymied by Brer Rabbit that they wonder if he has perhaps been given some supernatural powers: "Brer B'ar, he up'n low, he did, dat he boun' Brer Rabbit is a nat'al bawn witch; Brer Wolf say, sezee, dat he 'speck Brer Rabbit des in cahoots wid a witch; en Brer Fox, he vow dat Brer Rabbit got mo' luck dan smartness" (CT, 241). Uncle Remus, with a good deal of pride, tells a tale about the time Brer Rabbit actually does seek to get some kind of magic from Mammy-Bammy-Big-Money, the Witch-Rabbit. Brer Rabbit has begun to feel "monstous humblyfied" by all his close calls, so he asks Mammy-Bammy for some additional brain power with which to outwit his foes. The old witch puts him through a series of difficult tests which he completes so well that she refuses his request, saying, "Ef you git any mo' sense, Son Riley, you'll be de ruination uv de whole settlement" (CT, 264–68). Uncle Remus shows his pleasure at this assessment of his hero's abilities by adding, "Bless yo' soul, honey, Brer Rabbit mought er bin kinder fibble in de legs, but he wa'n't no ways cripple und' de hat."

It is actually fairly important that Brer Rabbit accomplish his feats without the aid of magic. For the Negro storyteller, the fact that only the rabbit's mental dexterity keeps him out of harm would be a comforting feature of his heroism. There is, for example, one story of a supposedly "astonishing prank" of Brer Rabbit's which consists of no more than a simple, even accidental ruse. The rabbit manages to scare Brer Fox and Brer Wolf almost to death, not because of magical powers but simply because he has fallen into Brer B'ar's honey pot and then become covered all over with leaves, so that he looks like "de gran'daddy er all de boogers" (CT, 134). Another time he breaks up a party to which he was not invited just by beating on a set of drums (CT, 161). One of the best stories of this type involves Brer Rabbit's campaign to get all of the animals to leave him alone in a mansion that they have all, except for him, worked very hard to build. He accomplishes his aim by using simple psychology and a few well-chosen stage props. Excusing himself from the house-warming party, he takes upstairs with him a gun, a cannon, and a bucket of slop water. Then he gets the animals to believe that the noise of the gun being shot is his sitting down; the cannon going off is his sneeze; the pail of slop water, rolling down the stairs at them, is his tobacco spit, and this is enough to convince them that he is, despite appearances, a very big man who makes a very poor house companion.

The great appeal of stories like these is the simplicity of the ruses employed by Brer Rabbit to confound the other animals. It takes no supernatural powers, but only a mind that can make the very humblest of circumstances and devices work to his advantage. With only the crudest of means—with things that a slave would know well—Brer Rabbit ends up having an elegant mansion all to himself, where, Uncle Remus says, enviously, "he sleep like a man w'at ain't owe nobody nothin'" (CT, 141). Not to owe anything to anyone, always to be able to escape oppression when it threatens, never to have to beg, and sometimes to be able even to lord it over others a little—these are humble enough wishes which the rabbit makes into magnificent accomplishments through sheer inventiveness.

John Herbert Nelson wrote in one of the earliest serious studies of Harris that "Brer Rabbit represents the ideal hero of their [the black race's] primitive dream world—an individual capable, through craft and downright trickery, to get the better of a master class seemingly unbeatable."[17] When words like *god* and *hero* are used to describe the Negro's relationship to Brer Rabbit, an important point to remember is that the rabbit's prowess as a deity is severely limited by the circumstances and situation of the narrator who worshipfully tells of his escapades. If Brer Rabbit comes out on top, he is still always very near to being on the bottom; if he always manages to escape, he is also always perilously close to getting caught. Thus if he qualifies as a hero figure, he must certainly be classified as one of the picaresque mold. No idealist could have created such a god, whose feats involve neither high principles nor idyllic resolutions.

Uncle Remus points out the difference between his hero and the white child's standardized conception of one when he compares the "Cinderella" tale to his own legends. Commenting on "Cinderella," he declares, "It's so purty dat you dunner whedder ter b'lieve it er not." Uncle Remus finds a "purty tale" very difficult to identify with. His own world is like that of his animals; of them he says, "Now de creeturs never had no god-m'ers; dey des hatter scuffle an' scramble an' git 'long de bes' way dey kin" (CT, 614). The race of men whose imaginations were fired by the kind of adventures Brer Rabbit could have consisted of people who combined a brand of broad humor with a definitely unromantic sense of what one needed to survive in a world much more congenial to wolves than fairy godmothers.

How far Harris himself could go in understanding and perhaps even

17. John Herbert Nelson, *The Negro Character in American Literature* (Lawrence, Kansas, 1926), 116.

participating in the Negro's motives for identifying with Brer Rabbit is a matter for speculation only. As Louis Rubin makes clear in his study of the relations of Harris, Remus, and Brer Rabbit, Harris most certainly was *not* embarked on any program "whereby slyly he strove in his Uncle Remus stories to counter the policies of white supremacy" that were a part of his own world. Rubin's point is that Harris' identification with Uncle Remus was instinctive, fostered by his "powerful sympathy for the underprivileged, the discriminated against"; this quality in Harris is what enabled him to "reach out in imagination to comprehend the situation of the black man in a society made up, so far as he was concerned, of foxes and wolves who possessed all the money, the education, the power, the advantages."[18]

Thus, while it cannot be proven that Harris consciously perceived the intricacies involved in his black narrator's relationship to the rabbit-hero, a definite case can be made for assuming that Harris' own situations and concerns drew him to the legends and helped to make his dramatizations of them so successful. His terrible shyness, his "umble-come-tumble" appearance, his unjustifiably low opinion of his background and capabilities made life often a painful affair for him; however, these things also enabled him to involve himself artistically in the plight of a group which seemed the opposite of himself in every respect except that they were outcasts and underdogs—like himself, he would add.

The Uncle Remus who tells the stories of Brer Rabbit creates a fantasy that stresses the elemental over the artificial. The brutality of this dreamworld is a brutality that parallels the laws of nature instead of the arbitrary and self-serving distinctions of a ruling class. In the neighborhood of the briar patch, pretensions and hypocrisy are easily unmasked. Certainly Joel Chandler Harris, who came to feel some guilt for his role in bringing progress to a New South, could find these aspects of the rabbit's realm very attractive.

When we trace Harris' conscious direction of the character of Uncle Remus through the major collections of his stories, we see that one of the main issues of the framework sketches was Harris' increasing concern for his own world's loss of innocence. Uncle Remus' name for Atlanta is "Lantatantarum," a label which signifies for him its

---

18. Rubin, "Southern Local Color and the Black Man," 1020, 1021.

confusing bustle and impersonality. The little boy to whom he tells his stories comes increasingly into contact with city ways and values so that an additional drama in the Remus books involves the old man's attempts to enchant the child with the charms of simple rural life. Particularly in the last Remus volume, *Told by Uncle Remus*, Remus' nostalgia has a bitter cast which indicates that the need to escape the present has become especially intense but more and more difficult for the old storyteller to accomplish.

The first two Remus collections are given old plantation settings which exude an atmosphere of idyllic peace and security. Uncle Remus' listener is a very young white child who has not yet learned to distinguish fact and fantasy and who is given all the sheltering love and attention by the old uncle that Harris' own childhood must have lacked. Thus the plantation world that is displayed in *Uncle Remus: His Songs and His Sayings* (1880) and *Nights with Uncle Remus* (1883) contains the features that Harris probably coveted most during his stay at Turnwold.

Most of the material in the first collection was taken from contributions Harris wrote for the *Constitution* from 1876 to 1880. This was the time during which the *Constitution* became the South's most progressive paper, a time when Henry Grady's faith in the future must have lit every corner of every office. Certainly there is no dissatisfaction with the times to be discerned in the brief background sketches attached to the tales published in Harris' first book. Uncle Remus lives a carefree life in a cabin near Miss Sally's "big house." There exists between him and the child who visits the cabin to hear the legends a mutual affection and trust that unites them completely in unquestioning acceptance of Brer Rabbit's adventures. The background sketches to the tales are usually short, establishing quickly a sense of good will and well-being, often in just a sentence or two.

In *Nights with Uncle Remus*, the introductory sketches are not simply prologues to the action of each legend but contain detailed drama themselves. This second collection is made up entirely of folklore stories told in an antebellum setting that is as carefully and extensively delineated as the tales themselves. Uncle Remus shares storytelling honors with three other slaves, all of whom relate tales appropriate to their personalities and interests. Continuing drama is provided by the courtship of two of these characters, Sis Tildy and

Daddy Jack, who are married in a traditional slave ceremony at the end of the book.

There is an aura of golden nostalgia in *Nights with Uncle Remus*, but it can hardly be construed as an overt declaration of preference for old times and values. The most notable feature of the plantation scenes depicted in this book is the view they give of antebellum life as it was lived not in the big house but in the slave quarters; the romance concerns not a gentleman and belle, but a "house gal" and an "old coast" Negro. Harris felt at home treating this aspect of the plantation, in which the characters reflect his own humble position. It is still a happy vision, with no hint of discontent. Only rarely does Uncle Remus seem to project himself into a postwar era through comments reflecting Harris' growing perception of the change coming over the South: "Dey ain't no dancin' 'deze days," complains the old man; "folks shoes too tight, en dey ain't got dey limbersomeness in de hips w'at dey useter is."[19]

Harris meant the third Uncle Remus book, *Uncle Remus and His Friends* (1892), to be the last. He seems to have been afraid that Brer Rabbit and Co. might be wearing out their welcome with the reading public. The little boy is older now, he asks more questions, demands more facts, and Uncle Remus is easily irritated by his doubts. Seriously to question the truth of the tales amounts, for him, to a kind of heresy. There is the feeling given that the boy is growing away from the friend of his early childhood, an inevitable occurrence but also a tragic one from the old man's point of view. When the not-so-little child looks skeptical about a detail in a particular tale, Uncle Remus says, "Well . . . ef you gwine ter 'spute dat, you des ez well ter stan' up en face me down 'bout de whole tale."[20] He then provides the factual explanation that the boy wants, but it obviously grieves him to have to do so.

The magic charm of the tales, and the secret of Uncle Remus' own charm, depends, as he knows, to a large extent on the capacity for imaginative belief that only a child can sustain. If the stories are worth hearing at all, Remus frequently implies in this volume, they are worth entering into without expecting logical reasons or utilitarian pur-

19. Joel Chandler Harris, *Nights with Uncle Remus* (Boston, 1883), 51.
20. Joel Chandler Harris, *Uncle Remus and His Friends: Old Plantation Stories, Songs, and Ballads with Sketches of Negro Character* (Boston, 1892), 175.

poses. That Harris' respect for the progressive standards of his day was dwindling is suggested by Uncle Remus' problems with his young listener, and also by the old man's criticisms of the materialism he sees around him: "Hit's money, honey, de worl' over," he remarks. "Go whar you will . . . en you'll fin' folks huntin' atter money—mornin' en eve-nin', day en night."[21]

If in Harris' third Uncle Remus volume there are intimations of his changing attitude, then in the fourth and last major book devoted to the old man's stories there is no longer any doubt that the conclu-sions Harris had reached about the New South were not satisfying ones. The simple nostalgia, the enjoyment of memories of an old and simpler time, have become a different thing. In *Told by Uncle Remus* (1905) the emphasis is not on the goodness of the old days and ways but on the badness of the new. The little boy in the last book is the son of the first little boy. He has been sent down to the plantation, now a postwar plantation, from Atlanta, where his health had not been very good. We are told that "the little boy was not like the other little boy; he was more like a girl in his refinement; all the boyishness had been taken out of him."[22] Uncle Remus, for the first time in a very long life, has to enlist the boy's interest in the tales, for this boy had had it drilled into him that "A is always A." The child is literal-minded and priggish, a product of a modern city upbringing which Uncle Remus can only deplore. He is not very successful in his attempt to change this new little boy, who comes to love Uncle Remus but never completely to trust him.

Told by Uncle Remus is a lament for childhood and a plea for chil-dren to be left to grow up in their own good time. The old man continually compares this little boy to his father, who as a child was stronger, more imaginative, and happier than his son. The main dif-ference that Uncle Remus sees is that the son, product of a New South, very seldom laughs. Uncle Remus tells him, "Yo pa' useter set right whar you settin' an laugh twel he can't laugh no mo'. But dem wuz laughin' times, an' it looks like dey ain't never comin' back."[23] This last Uncle Remus wants no part in the future; he says, "You may think

21. *Ibid.*, 130.
22. Joel Chandler Harris, *Told by Uncle Remus: New Stories of the Old Plantation* (New York, 1905), 5.
23. *Ibid.*, 59.

dat dez times is de bes'; well, den, you kin have um ef you'll des gi' me de ol' times."[24]

In a letter to James Whitcomb Riley, written around the same time as these Uncle Remus tales, Harris said that he intended to keep on writing about "old times, and the old timey people. And if anybody doesn't like it, why he can just go ahead speculating in futures, and I'll speculate on the past."[25] Uncle Remus in the last volume devoted to his stories speaks more directly for Harris than did any of the earlier uncles, and he speaks as one who knows that the kind of existence he represents is becoming difficult to visualize.

Uncle Remus, in his ultimate role as a character, provided Harris' last word for concerns that are at the heart of any concept of "the good life." The South was opting for a civilization which would be, in Henry Grady's prophecy, less "splendid" yet "stronger," better equipped to fit into the industrialized nation that it had once chosen to defy. Through all the different Uncle Remuses that he created over the years, Harris refused that modern option. His stereotyped, old-time darky Uncle Remus provided propaganda for the Old South, while the Uncle Remus who told the stories of Brer Rabbit inverted the ideals of the traditional southern version of Arcady to render shrewd assessments of the realities of the plantation. Yet the image of Uncle Remus has endured as an individual who explained his own world in his own terms and as a character in whom the human element stands higher than any doctrine.

The relationship of Uncle Remus, as Harris' creation, to the world of Brer Rabbit cannot be assessed with any full degree of certainty concerning Harris' understood control as artist in this area. Yet another writer of Harris' time would recognize fully the possibilities of manipulation within the device of having a black narrator tell slave folktales within a larger, "framework" kind of setting using the trappings of plantation life. Charles Chesnutt, America's first truly gifted black fiction writer, used the Uncle Remus tales, as structured by Harris, as a model for the fictional framework of his own collection of folktales, *The Conjure Woman*. This powerfully satiric work, according to Robert Bone, "constitutes a devastating parody of Southern pastoral."[26] As such, it might seem to mock everything that Har-

---

24. *Ibid.*, 39.
25. Julia Collier Harris, *Life and Letters*, 466.
26. Bone, *Down Home*, 75

ris had in mind with Uncle Remus. Certainly the black narrator of Chesnutt's tales, Uncle Julius, demonstrates a keen awareness of his powers of subversion and judgment that Uncle Remus never even vaguely suggests and Harris himself might never have had even remotely in mind. Yet the fact remains that Harris, with an artist's sensitivity about his Uncle Remus stories, provided a more complex and satisfying use of pastoral forms than can be found in the work of any other white writer of plantation fiction. And even more striking is the fact that he was able to recognize and adapt with skill a strategy that had been one of the black slave's, and would be one of the black writer's, most important weapons: the mask of irony that Uncle Remus wears on occasion is the same device that would allow black storytellers from Charles Chesnutt forward to gain an entrance into a white racist world whose values could then be twisted from within with some stunning consequences.

FIVE

Charles Chesnutt's Southern World: Portraits of a Bad Dream

Charles Chesnutt grew up in a time and place that encouraged, and actually necessitated, his cultivation of a sense of irony. As a black man who chose to write fiction during the Reconstruction era, he discovered that there was a ready market for litanies to the plantation and the "old times" of massa, mistress, and mammy. About the same years that Joel Chandler Harris was editorializing on the plantation past as "the brightest and pleasantest of all the dreams we have," Chesnutt, looking forward instead of backward, was contemplating moving away from the South, commenting, "I shudder to think of exposing my children to the social and intellectual proscription to which I have been a victim."[1] How could Chesnutt as writer treat the highly popular dream of an Old South that was, to his own people, a nightmare? The answer he developed was irony, and the plan that he incorporated in his fiction allowed him to render an account of the plantation that stripped away its Arcadian guise and revealed the hellishness of black slavery in the midst of the white man's paradise.

As Blyden Jackson pointed out in his essay "The Negro's Image of the Universe as Reflected in His Fiction," irony has been an ever-present factor in the way that the black man looks at his universe and in the way he presents that universe in his work. Ironic dissimulation, "the concealing of superior knowledge on the part of the iron-

1. Julia Collier Harris, *Editor and Essayist*, 115; Helen M. Chesnutt, *Charles W. Chesnutt: Pioneer of the Color Line* (Chapel Hill, 1952), 31.

ist," is, as Jackson noted, a special skill not only of Socrates but of "a long line of Uncle Toms."[2] It is the particular irony of living without true liberty in a country devoted "officially and otherwise" to democracy that has played such a large role in determining the Negro's perspective in his art, according to Jackson, and Chesnutt's perspective was certainly no exception.

When Chesnutt pondered his course of action as a writer, he recognized immediately that his fiction, if it were to do anything toward expressing the needs and aiding the cause of his people, would have to employ the subtlety of irony. When he was not quite twenty-two he described in his journal a carefully wrought scheme for fiction writing that sounds more like a battle plan. The object of his fiction, he said, would be "not so much the elevation of the colored people as the elevation of the whites." His method—"Not a fierce indiscriminate onset, not an appeal to force, for this is something that force can but slightly affect." Instead, Chesnutt reasoned, "the subtle almost indefinable feeling of repulsion toward the Negro" was a position which "must be mined, and we will find ourselves in their midst before they think it." His ultimate aim—"recognition and equality" for the Negro, a goal which he felt the "province of literature" could best accomplish, since through it one could "lead people out, imperceptibly, unconsciously, step by step, to the desired state of feeling."[3] Although this last statement seems to indicate Chesnutt's defense of the use of art for propaganda, it is perhaps even more a recognition of his own desire to create something more permanent and more valuable than mere propaganda.

It is of interest to note that, as part of his "plan," Chesnutt chose not to find a different regional base for his fiction but, on the contrary, to use the South itself and the popular motifs developed by white writers to describe the southern way of life as his own arena. While Thomas Nelson Page's old darkies and Joel Chandler Harris' Uncle Remus were making their popular fictional escapes back to the haven of the southern plantation, Chesnutt himself was escaping from Fayetteville, North Carolina, to Cleveland, Ohio, where he found

2. Blyden Jackson, "The Negro's Image of the Universe as Reflected in His Fiction," in Abraham Chapman (ed.), *Black Voices: An Anthology of Afro-American Literature* (New York, 1968), 626.
3. Helen M. Chesnutt, *Charles W. Chesnutt*, 21.

employment, a permanent residence for his family, and the resources that enabled him to become increasingly successful as a writer. Yet in his fiction he almost always returned to the South he had known in his youth and to the knowledge he had acquired in his early years of the many incongruities life held there. His physical distance did not keep him from a fine perception of the way in which the lives of southerners—both white and black, removed to northern havens or set squarely within southern challenges—were influenced and usually controlled by the unique force that the plantation past managed to exert. He himself was never free from the influence of the past, as his literary career and its products have demonstrated.

Chesnutt, after reading Albion Tourgée's *A Fool's Errand* in 1880, contended that he, as "a colored man, who has lived among colored people all his life," and who had moreover grown up in the South as a keen observer of its people, could write just as good a book about the South as Tourgée had done. Before he had a chance to prove his point, he served as principal of the Normal School in Fayetteville for two years, taught himself stenography and law, established himself and his family in Cleveland, and only in spare moments found time to write stories. Most of his first efforts as a writer were about "conjuring" among southern slaves. By 1893 three of his stories on this theme had been published by the *Atlantic Monthly*, and Chesnutt added five others to a collection which he sent to Houghton Mifflin. The book he proposed to them would, he said, have a "special distinction" as being "the first contribution by an American of acknowledged African descent to purely imaginative literature." The chief merit of his work, he added, was perhaps just this "new point of view" that he was able to give the treatment of Negroes in fiction. [4]

Houghton Mifflin rejected Chesnutt's first attempt, but he continued writing stories for seven more years, sending them to editor Walter Hines Page, and proposing collections of his material until finally, in 1898, the publishing company agreed to bring out, as "an experiment," a collection of his conjure stories. It had been nearly twelve years since the *Atlantic Monthly* had published "The Goophered Grapevine," but at long last Chesnutt had arrived.

Chesnutt's *The Conjure Woman*, appearing in March of 1899, was

4. *Ibid.*, 68.

more successful than either he or his publishers had dared to hope. So promising did the future look that in September of the same year, Chesnutt decided to give up his law practice in order to devote himself full-time to the business of authorship. Reviews of *The Conjure Woman* had been highly favorable; Houghton Mifflin was preparing a second collection of his stories, which appeared later in the year as *The Wife of His Youth*; he had completed a life of Frederick Douglass for the Beacon Biography Series. There was no reason not to believe that, at the age of forty-one, he might not go on to become a major American fiction writer. Had not the great William Dean Howells himself spoken of him in the same breath as "Mr. James" and "Miss Jewett," and said of him, "If he has it in him to go forward on the way he has traced for himself . . . one of the places at the top is open to him"?[5]

In spite of these rosy predictions, the future did not yield the expected fruits. Six years after he had abandoned his law practice in order to pursue a literary career, Chesnutt published his last novel, *The Colonel's Dream*. *The Colonel's Dream*, and before it *The House Behind the Cedars* (1900) and *The Marrow of Tradition* (1901), dealt much more openly and directly with the issue of race prejudice than did *The Conjure Woman*, which on the surface looked enough like the benign plantation stories of Page and Harris to pass for another nostalgic collection about the quaint ways of colored folk "befo' de wah."

Certainly *The Conjure Woman*, for all its surface good nature, was in substance as firmly committed as the later novels to "leading people out" from attitudes of racial bias. Yet its message is delivered through multiple levels of irony which allow the reader to go no further than he wants to go in involving himself in the realities that are being exposed. Reading at the shallowest level, William Dean Howells could write a review of the collection which would affirm that "whatever is primitive and sylvan or campestral in the reader's heart is touched by the spells thrown on the simple black lives in these enchanting tales."[6] It would be impossible for anyone, even Howells, to ignore the stern messages of Chesnutt's later works in like manner. Reading *The Marrow of Tradition*, Howells would find himself compelled to

5. William Dean Howells, "Mr. Charles W. Chesnutt's Stories," *Atlantic Monthly* LXXV (May, 1900), 700.
6. *Ibid.*

call it "bitter, bitter."[7] And to his publisher Chesnutt would write rather despondently after this, "Mr. Howells . . . has remarked several times that there is no color line in literature. On that point I take issue with him. I am pretty fairly convinced that the color line runs everywhere so far as the United States is concerned."[8]

Although in his last novel Chesnutt greatly modified the violent, melodramatic picture of race relations that so incensed southern readers of *The Marrow of Tradition*, still *The Colonel's Dream* was judged to be more of a zealot's tract than an "objective" work of fiction. One reviewer wrote, "The book is a bitter, passionate arraignment of the white people of the South."[9] Yet *The Colonel's Dream* reveals an artistic power which has long been ignored since the book's classification, at the outset, as pure propaganda. In both *The Conjure Woman* and *The Colonel's Dream* Chesnutt uses the conventions of plantation literature in a unique manner which gives the southern version of the Arcadian dream a new and disturbing dimension.

The Conjure Woman, according to Chesnutt himself, was "a collection of short stories in Negro dialect, put in the mouth of an old gardener, and related by him in each instance to the same audience, which consisted of the Northern lady and gentleman who employed him." Chesnutt's own evaluation of the stories was that they were "naïve and simple," yet when comparing them to Joel Chandler Harris' Uncle Remus tales, Chesnutt was quick to point out that his stories were not "folk tales" at all, but were "the fruit of my own imagination."[10] Harris, while providing a storyteller for the tales of Brer Rabbit, prided himself on preserving the tales themselves as they existed in the oral tradition of the Negroes from whom he heard them. And while Harris added plantation "backdrops" and some narrative sense to Uncle Remus' preliminaries to the tales, the kind of plantation story that Chesnutt's imagination led him to write was in fact far more intricate than most of those of his famous predecessors in the

7. William Dean Howells, "A Psychological Counter-Current in Recent Fiction," *North American Review*, CLXXIII (December, 1901).

8. Helen M. Chesnutt, *Charles W. Chesnutt*, 178.

9. Quoted *ibid.*, 178.

10. Charles W. Chesnutt, "Post-Bellum—Pre-Harlem," in Elmer Adler (ed.), *Breaking into Print* (New York, 1937), 49, 50.

genre. As he noted, the treatment of the Negro in most of such literature was not realistic; he cited Thomas Nelson Page in particular as a writer who depicted only "the sentimental and devoted Negro, who prefers kicks to half-pence."[11] In the same vein he wrote almost desperately to George W. Cable:

I notice that all of the many Negroes (excepting your own) whose virtues have been given to the world in the magazine press recently, have been blacks, full-blooded, and their chief virtues have been their dog-like fidelity to their old master, for whom they have been willing to sacrifice almost life itself. . . . But I can't write about those people, or rather I won't write about them.[12]

Chesnutt in fact did write one story, "The Passing of Grandison,"[13] about a slave whose "dog-like fidelity" seems so strong that he will not procure his freedom even when his master's son does everything in his power to get the slave to go free. (The master's son is trying to please his sentimental sweetheart, but lacks the strength of will actually to free his slave, so instead tries to give his "ebony encumbrance" several easy avenues of escape.) Grandison will have no part of freedom, however, seeming to prefer to remain on the plantation where he is appreciated. He is finally kidnapped by some abolitionists, but even then manages to return home. His loyalty is applauded, since he seems a symbol of unshakable devotion to his master, yet a few short weeks later he disappears again, this time taking with him his wife, mother, and several brothers and sisters. The story is finely told, and offers an ironist's reply to the stereotyped picture of the faithful slave whose image dominates Page's fiction.

When Chesnutt designed the personality of the black man who was to tell tales of conjuring to a white northerner who has recently become his employer, he seems to have had Thomas Nelson Page's faithful black narrators in mind, not as models but as almost direct opposites to the kind of person he wanted for his stories. In Page's *In Ole Virginia* collection of stories there is a series of darkies who try to escape into pleasant memories of their lives as slaves while they tell

11. Helen M. Chesnutt, *Charles W. Chesnutt*, 58.
12. *Ibid.*, 57–58.
13. Charles W. Chesnutt, "The Passing of Grandison," in *The Wife of His Youth* (Ann Arbor, 1968), 168–202.

romantic episodes of plantation life to uninitiated northerners. There are no close relationships between master and slave in *The Conjure Woman*, none of the Page-type Uncle Billys who become the mainstays of helpless belles. Chesnutt's Uncle Julius is a wily, self-serving freedman who has many purposes of varying subtlety in mind as he tells his employer, John, and John's wife his own reminiscences of slavery times.

In a conjure story not included in the published collection but containing the same three "outer" characters, Chesnutt allows John to recognize something about Julius which does not fit the "traditional darky" myth. In "Dave's Neckliss," published in the *Atlantic Monthly* in 1889, John remarks that "[Julius'] way of looking at the past seemed very strange to us; his view of certain sides of life was essentially different from ours. He never indulged in any regrets for the Arcadian joyousness and irresponsibility which was a somewhat popular conception of slavery." The only reason John can fathom for Julius' distinctly unromantic view is that "his had not been the lot of the petted house-servant, but that of the toiling field-hand."[14] John relies on a familiar cliché concerning slave status to explain Julius' lack of enthusiasm for his former life, yet in *The Conjure Woman* Julius will make much more compelling reasons for his "different" view all too clear to the sensitive listener, who will easily grasp the old man's strategy of irony and see his past for what it was.

One story in *The Conjure Woman* illustrates with particular force this ironic capacity of Chesnutt's Uncle Julius. In "Mars Jeems's Nightmare" the idea of putting oneself in another's shoes is used with comic and ironic effect to teach a plantation slaveowner a valuable lesson. Mars Jeems is guilty of the most insensitive kind of cruelty toward the human beings in his charge; he allows no courting or "juneseyin" on his plantation. As Julius explains, Jeems insisted "he wuz n' raisin' niggers, but wuz raisin' cotton."[15] Even Jeems's fiancée is repulsed by his meanness and breaks off the engagement, which only makes Jeems more unpleasant.

When Mars Jeems separates a plantation hand named Solomon from his "junesy" and sends her away, Solomon is riled enough to ask the

14. Charles W. Chesnutt, "Dave's Neckliss," *Atlantic Monthly*, LXIV (October, 1889), 501.
15. Charles W. Chesnutt, *The Conjure Woman* (Ann Arbor, 1968), 72.

local conjuring woman to put a "goopher" or curse on Jeems that will make him change his ways. Aunt Peggy arranges for Jeems to be transformed into a Negro who, when he is found wandering the roads, is given to Jeems's brutal overseer to be tamed. After many "lashins' en cussins' en cuffins'" the "noo nigger" is sent away again. According to Julius' explanation, this particular "black" man couldn't seem to get it through his head "dat he wuz a slabe en had ter wuk en min' de w'ite folks" (CW, 84). Just before he is sold "down de ribber" to New Orleans, the goopher is removed from Mars Jeems and he returns to his plantation a much chastened man who immediately fires his overseer and begins, finally, to treat his slaves like human beings.

Julius' employer thinks he knows why the old Negro has told this particular story. He has just fired Julius' good-for-nothing grandson, and Julius is hoping to get John to take a more lenient view toward the boy. Still, this rather obvious ruse does not disguise the story's real significance for a sensitive reader. Jeems learns to be kind to his slaves, but not before he has degraded them to the condition of livestock and not until he has been forced to experience such degradation himself. Still, Julius himself offers a moral for his story which casts him back into the role of grateful, obsequious darky: the tale "goes ter show," he says, that white folks who are so hard on "po' ign'ant niggers" are liable to have bad dreams. John answers Julius' sly commentary sarcastically: "I am glad, too, that you told us the moral of the story; it might have escaped us otherwise" (CW, 100–101). The real moral, of course, *has* escaped John. His wife shows more sympathy to the tale and its teller by rehiring the lazy grandson, but it is the reader alone who is meant to understand fully that Julius, through his story, has indicted the plantation system and exploded the myth of benevolent master-slave relationships.

"Mars Jeems's Nightmare" employs another important feature of Chesnutt's ironic "dream" strategy. The Negro as pastoral rustic is shown to have a deeper understanding of what constitutes life and a far closer relationship to nature and reality than the civilized white man is capable of achieving. In the conjure stories, the white plantation owners frequently refuse to allow their slaves to mate or to raise children. Thus when natural, moral order is considered, the Negro slaves of Chesnutt's collection can be seen to have one important kind of superiority over their white masters. In the broadest sense, it is the

superiority that the pastoral shepherd always has over the sophisticated city dweller, involving a higher knowledge of the fundamentals
of existence. But of course when the pastoral shepherd is also a Negro slave, the superiority he gains can have only ironic value; in spite
of his greater imaginative capacity and more sensitive moral facul-
ties, he is without power to exercise control over his own life.

We see in all of the conjure stories that the blacks are able to identify with the natural world, while the whites are usually excluded from
it, either because they are too civilized or because for them nature,
like their slaves, is valued as commodity only. In "The Goophered
Grapevine" the slave, Henry, becomes conjured after eating grapes
from a goophered vine. His life processes follow those of the vine;
when it grows and flourishes in the spring, so does Henry, and when
the vine withers in the winter, so does he. His master is a man about
whom Henry says, it would have to be "a monst'us cloudy night when
a dollar git by him in de dahkness" (CW, 24). So Mars Dugal sells
Henry each spring when the slave is in his prime and buys him back
again each autumn "w'en de sap went down."

Mars Dugal's system works well until his greed destroys both his
grapes and Henry. He allows a Yankee to give a special fertilizing
treatment to his vines in hopes of increasing their productivity, but
the treatment only serves to kill the vines and Henry along with them.
In Julius' tales very seldom do the charms that are concocted finally
result in happy endings for the characters who use them. In most of
the stories, the conjuring becomes necessary because white slave-
owners have violated some natural, human right and the slave has no
other course of redress. Mars Jeems drives Solomon to seek the conjure woman by refusing to allow him to court his girlfriend; in other
stories, conjuring is requested to help deal with such situations as a
mother separated from her baby and two young lovers forced apart
by the demands and whims of their master.

Unfortunately for the slaves, the effects of the spells they get from
the conjure woman are usually too short-lived or they work a little
too well, as in the case of Henry and the grapevine. In "Po' Sandy,"
a young girl with conjuring powers turns her husband into a tree in
order to keep him close to her on the plantation; her solution back-
fires when the tree is chopped down while she is away. Thus one finds
in most of the stories that the forces of nature, like the Negroes

themselves, are not as strong as the force of civilization, which uses both nature and the Negro with respect only for their material value.

"Mars Jeems's Nightmare" and "Sis' Becky's Pickaninny" are two stories in *The Conjure Woman* in which the conjuring spells are allowed to work as planned to provide happy endings; however, even in these stories we have the sense that it is not magic but human nature which is finally responsible for the good results. In Jeems's case, it is learning firsthand how it feels to be a slave that causes his reformation. In Becky's story, it is a mother's love for her child that ultimately causes events to turn in her favor. Becky is a slave whose sole joy is her little boy. As is the case in Harriet Beecher Stowe's *Uncle Tom's Cabin*, she has a kindly master, whose fault is not that he is consciously cruel to his slaves but that when there is a question of economics involved, he is too weak to prevent his slaves from being treated like mere property. The result, as both Chesnutt and Stowe took pains to point out, is the tragedy of broken homes. Becky is to be traded to a horse dealer for a fine horse, and even though her master is willing to include her child for free in the bargain, the horse dealer will not have the baby. "I doan raise niggers; I raise hosses," he says, adding that "niggers is made ter wuk, en dey ain' got no time fer no sich foolis'ness ez babies" (CW, 142).

Both Becky and her child suffer during their separation; finally, Aun' Nancy, in whose charge the baby has been left, seeks the conjure woman's help. The old woman turns little Mose into a mockingbird, and in this form he is sent to visit his mother. His periodic trips as songbird cheer him and Becky for a while, but Aun' Nancy would like a permanent cure. The conjure woman's solution is based on a sly knowledge of human nature more than on her conjuring prowess. She commands a hornet to sting the knees of the fine race horse. Once done, Becky's owner is infuriated, as he believes he has been tricked into swapping a good slave for a lame horse. Meanwhile, Becky has grown so despondent that she is no longer able to work, so her new master and her former one are quickly able to agree to reverse their trade. The horse goes home, and so does Becky, where she and little Mose live happily ever after. When Mose grows up, he is paid to sing at functions throughout the county, and finally has enough money to buy his own and his mother's freedom.

It is not so much a magic spell in "Sis' Becky's Pickaninny" as it is the natural bond of mother and child love which effectuates the final outcome. And this is a fact which Julius and the employer's wife understand, but which John himself never grasps. To Julius he says, "That is a very ingenious tale," and he laughs at his wife's assertion that the story "bears the stamp of truth." As he points out the fantastic nature of the doings of the mockingbird and hornet, she replies, "Those are mere ornamental details and not at all essential. The story is true to nature, and might have happened half a hundred times, and no doubt did happen, in those horrid days before the war" (CW, 159). To display the truth of the reality under the guise of the dream is Chesnutt's goal in each conjure story.

In *The Conjure Woman*, Chesnutt utilized two quite different elements of the plantation tradition to achieve a victory for his ironic point of view. First, we see him exposing the artificiality of the white South's supposedly idyllic Arcadia. The plantation world is not the haven from greed and materialism that the popular myth of Chesnutt's day had established, and Chesnutt proved this by taking the standard features of the myth and twisting them into a very different shape. So, while Uncle Julius may seem to be the traditional darky defender who upholds the assumptions and values of his white masters, what he really does is to destroy the foundations of those assumptions by taking a hard, unromantic look at the way things really were on the black man's side of the fence.

Secondly, although Chesnutt denied the validity of associating the values of a truly Arcadian society with plantation culture, he did locate some pastoral values within the black man's special portion of the plantation. The black slave was spiritually close to nature and developed an imaginative alliance with its mysterious powers. Page and Joel Chandler Harris used the myth of the Old South as a kind of pastoral rebuke to the materialistic, technological orientation of their northern readers. Chesnutt, on the other hand, used the black man's ironic faith in the magic charm of nature to make the point that the white man's Old South was itself artificial and materialistic.

To move from Chesnutt's first collection to his last published novel is to move from a black former slave's ironic vision of the antebellum South to a white colonel's romantic dream of a South of the future which would unite the finest qualities of the "old" and "new" region. It is to move stylistically from the realm of subtlety to that of "avowed purpose"; whereas *The Conjure Woman* aimed to "mine" the enemy's position without his knowledge of the process, *The Colonel's Dream* faced the opposition squarely and defined the battle lines. Both works apply with mocking twists some aspect of pastoral tone and mood in order ultimately to criticize traditional conceptions of the Old South as Arcady.

The colonel's dream is to preserve the best of the Old South by grafting its ideals onto the enlightened progressivism available to the New South. In this connection he resembles rather pointedly the Atlanta orator Henry Grady, whose speech "The New South," delivered in New York City in 1886, opened a new era in the Reconstruction South. Grady hoped to bring progress to his region without sacrificing anything that it had stood for in the old days. Thus in almost the same breath he talked of both the "hero in gray with a heart of gold" and "a diversified industry that meets the complex needs of this complex age."

Like Henry Grady, Colonel French does not see why the best of both worlds cannot be preserved and maintained in the region of his birth. After a long and prosperous business career in New York, he seems to feel, as do the heroes of Thomas Nelson Page's Reconstruction novels, that there is something lacking in the system of values and lifestyles of the urban North. But unlike Page's heroes, Colonel French does not return to the South to repudiate completely the ideals of the North. His aim instead is to apply the practical knowledge he has learned there to the South's desperate economic situation and thereby redeem its most admirable traditions. At no point is he motivated by the urge to escape modern complexities which seems so often the aim of Page's white Reconstruction-era heroes.

There is at the beginning of *The Colonel's Dream* a rather standard pastoral indictment of the excesses of capitalism; Colonel French's business firm is being bought out by a larger, more ruthless competitor, and the strain of bargaining and dealing leads to French's physical collapse. Consequently, the journey he takes to his southern birthplace, the small town of Clarendon, is given symbolic suggestions of a pilgrimage. The South is seen in the early description of his homecoming as a place for renewal and restoration: "The travellers had left New York in the midst of a snow-storm, but here the scent of lilac and of jonquil, the song of birds, the breath of spring, were all about them."[16] Yet scarcely a paragraph later Chesnutt turns the tables on the idea of the South as moral rejuvenator; French senses that in the home of his youth "ripeness was almost decay . . . quietness was scarcely distinguishable from lethargy" (CD, 15–16).

Colonel French mixes realism and romanticism rather incongruously in his observations on the South. There are many features of the Old South ideal which he sees the need to save, including the gentility of his southern friends, their simplicity and graciousness, their "breeding" and closeness to the soil, their reverence for tradition. These are the qualities he plans to rescue by providing the financial security necessary for their preservation.

Chesnutt's last novel thus becomes the story of the colonel's great plan, from his first enthusiasm to his ultimate disillusionment. In the process of dramatizing the colonel's dream, Chesnutt adds details which seemed important both to his reforming zeal and to his sense of the kind of melodrama the public wanted from fiction. He attacks the convict-lease system, the policy of buying prison labor, through the creation of the character of Bill Fetters, a stereotyped image of the new southerner motivated by greed and ambition. Fetters owns not only most of the convicts, who are black, but also most of the mortgages and loan notes of the white citizens. Much of Chesnutt's plot deals with Colonel French's undeclared war against Fetters, who is a rather poorly portrayed villain with no redeeming features. Chesnutt adds other embellishments: a lost treasure, two star-crossed young lovers (she wants to go north and be rich; he wants to save his decaying plantation from ruin), the lynching of a young black man driven to violence by the terrible injustices perpetrated by race prejudice. Still, the novel's attraction remains in seeing Chesnutt's formulation of the colonel's dream for the South and in watching the progress and failure of his goal. The melodrama, the stock characters, the trite stage devices do not dim the poignancy of viewing one man's hope for bettering his world as it grows and finally dies.

The quality in *The Colonel's Dream* which strikes deepest is its fatalism. Chesnutt's irony in this novel is less incisive and less dramatic than the irony of *The Conjure Woman*; nonetheless, his stance gives us an insight into Colonel French's dream which will not allow us to

16. Charles W. Chesnutt, *The Colonel's Dream* (Upper Saddle River, N.J., 1968), 15.

share in his enthusiasm and which makes us aware very early that his disappointment is inevitable. The dream is doomed from the start, and largely because the colonel bases it on too simple a faith in values which are more a staple of his memories of the Old South than they are a feature of the Clarendon to which he returns. Chesnutt's novel in a way depicts the education of an idealist who thinks he has an objective enough vision of reality to make his dream workable, but who underestimates the negativism of the people he wants to help and overestimates the positive power of the values he finds preserved in one isolated area of Clarendon.

It is not coincidental that the colonel's love for the Old South and his sense of mission concerning its future are first kindled on a visit to a cemetery. Here he finds, living in a past well-symbolized by the marble slabs and time-worn monuments to the dead, the two people who will be most responsible for motivating his zeal to bring new life to Clarendon—his former slave, Peter, and an old romantic interest, Laura Treadwell.

Old Peter and Miss Laura bring back to Colonel French the associations of charm, permanence, and simplicity which belonged to his youth in the South before the war. Peter awakens in him a dormant sense of "family pride" and class loyalty. The old servant's rebuke to his former owner frames his master's future goal; he tells the colonel, before he knows to whom he is speaking, that he tends the French family graves "jes' lak I s'pose Mars' Henry'd 'a' had it done ef he'd 'a' lived hyuh in de ole home, stidder 'way off yondah in de Norf, whar he so busy makin' money dat he done fergot all 'bout his own folks" (CD, 24).

Laura Treadwell also rebukes him in her gentle southern way. Pointing out the troubles that she, as a representative of the Old South tradition, has faced in the years following the war, she says, "Had you, and men like you, remained with us, we might have hoped for better things" (CD, 50). Colonel French does not see the problems Laura has had in maintaining the antebellum lifestyle in postwar Clarendon, but only the charm her efforts have produced. "This is your daily life," he marvels, sitting on her piazza enjoying the warm spring evening air; "to me it is like a scene from a play, over which one sighs to see the curtain fall—all enchantment, all light, all happiness" (CD, 50). Colonel French does not make the connection that the qualities he admires in Miss Laura's lifestyle have no more reality than a scene from a play. Even while he talks, his former slave is being hauled off to jail for vagrancy, a charge trumped up against him for the purpose of offering him for sale the next day under the terms of the convict-lease system.

The convict sale brings Colonel French back to reality, reminding him that in Clarendon he will find not only "the charming life of the old South" which is being "perfectly preserved" in Miss Laura's household, but also other features less charming to look upon. He makes the observation that "evidently Clarendon needed new light and leading" (CD, 69), yet the plan of action he decides upon demonstrates all too clearly that he cannot use the ideal light of a former time to change the benighted attitudes of this southern town.

Colonel French's engagement to Laura Treadwell is a predictable occurrence in Chesnutt's scheme. What makes it work better than the other sentimental touches of the plot is that Laura is made to stand for all the things French values about the Old South; she is, we are told, "a true child of the Soil." The planned marriage would symbolize French's commitment to the preservation of these features, and yet Laura recognizes that if he is choosing her only because she is "an abstraction—the embodiment of an ideal—a survival from a host of pleasant memories," the union will not work. She, and not he, comes to the realization that he is perhaps "cherishing expectations which might be disappointed" as he works for reform in this southern town, and it is she who foresees that "his disillusion might be as far-reaching and sudden as his enthusiasm" (CD, 189). French has come to Clarendon "to bring fresh ideas, new and larger ideals to lift and broaden and revivify the town" (CD, 189). Laura rightly suspects that he associates his marriage to her with those goals, and her fears of what will happen to her personal future if his abstract aims meet with defeat are what make their romance interesting.

The colonel seems, in spite of his fiancée's fears, to be able to hold on to his dream even in the face of the fiercest opposition. He begins work on a mill which will bring industry and prosperity to the town; he plans improvements for both the white and colored schools and hopes to build a library. All of his endeavors meet with a negative reaction from a lazy and prejudiced white populace, yet even personal tragedy does not dim his resolve. His beloved son and Old Peter die after being struck by a train. Colonel French has them buried side by side, as was his son's wish, in the "white people's" cemetery. Not sensing the controversy that this act will provoke, Colonel French, on the night after the burial service, resumes his plans for bringing new light and life to Clarendon. In spite of his deep personal grief, his dream that night is of a happy future. He envisions "a regenerated South . . . where every man, having enough for his needs, was willing that every other man should have the same" (CD, 280). As the dream is described, it becomes a familiar version of Jeffersonian idealism which couples southern conservatism with prosperity and self-sufficiency, adding the all-important goal of equal opportunity: "But that each man, in his little life in this our little world might be able to make the most of himself, was an ideal which even the colonel's waking hours would not have repudiated" (CD, 281).

Yet Colonel French must be awakened in a double sense, and one of the finest touches of the novel is the way in which Chesnutt contrives to have the colonel's dream end, as it began, with the image of the old cemetery. At the end of his revery on the night after his son's and Old Peter's burial, French sees the time "when he too rested with his father, by the side of his son" (CD, 281). Immediately after this, however, he is wakened by a terrified servant and goes out to find that the angered white citizens of Clarendon have disinterred the remains of Old Peter and deposited the disfigured casket on his front porch.

Colonel French's thoughts of doing something for the South were first stirred by his visit to the cemetery, where his pride in the tradition and charm of the old life was evoked by Old Peter and Miss Laura. When Old Peter is refused burial in the cemetery, Colonel French finally awakens to the fact that the ideals on which he had based his dreams are dead. He had hoped to preserve the best features of the Old South and to redeem the New South by grafting the two together. He finds that race prejudice is stronger than ideals, and stronger, too, than his own resolve. He abandons his schemes with an alacrity which would be scarcely credible if Chesnutt had not foreshadowed his surrender through the early cemetery scenes and Laura Treadwell's misgivings. When Colonel French tells Laura of his decision to leave Clarendon, she refuses to accompany him, explaining, "You remembered me from my youth . . . and it was the image in your memory that you loved" (CD, 284). Her words offer a judgment of his relationship not only with her but with the South as well. His hopes for regenerating the South had been based on an image of its past glory and future possibility but had no foundation in the realities of the present, which he either ignored or tried to circumvent in the genteel manner of his gentlemanly ancestors. The ideal he championed is shown, through his retreat at the end, to be inadequate and unpreservable, given the South of the present with its stubbornly entrenched ignorance and prejudice.

Chesnutt, however, does not condemn the colonel, either for his naïve idealism or for his final defeatism. He even asks the reader, in a long, closing authorial comment, "But was not his, after all, the only way?" He closes the case of the colonel by saying, "And so the colonel faltered, and having put his hand to the plow, turned back" (CD, 293). Chesnutt intimates that the colonel's dream will one day be realized elsewhere by others; visible "to the eye of faith," he says, are changes in the attitudes and conditions of the South. But for Clarendon itself, he sees no hope. This rural community is doomed to decay. Chesnutt shows us Laura Treadwell tending the graves of the French family. Birds nest in vines that have overgrown the walls of the colonel's unfinished cotton mill: "The pigs and the loafers—leaner pigs and lazier loafers—still sleep in the shade" (CD, 294). The state of Clarendon symbolizes no pastoral sort of triumph of nature over civilization. As in *The Conjure Woman*, Chesnutt here indicts the popular image of the Old South as a pleasant dream. It is not a rural paradise but only a cultural and moral backwater. In Clarendon progress is rejected not because the community believes in a timeless set of nonmaterial values, but because it fears change of any sort, particularly change in its social habits regarding racial separation.

At the time *The Colonel's Dream* was published it was regarded only as an "avowed purpose" novel dealing with the South's unjust convict-lease system. Yet this interpretation has obscured its author's more personal and more significant purpose. It is a novel of awakening, intensely pessimistic, in which Chesnutt denounces the optimism of well-meaning white writers who hoped to make the New South over in the Old South's image. The novel shows that no land offers valid images for a dream of Arcady in which "white men go their way, and black men theirs, and these ways grow wider apart, and no one knows the outcome" (CD, 294).

Thomas Nelson Page's Reconstruction-period heroes return to their southern communities to find a pastoral peace which rebukes the North's barbaric materialism. Chesnutt's hero in *The Colonel's Dream* returns to find conditions which show the South itself to be barbaric. The only peace in Clarendon is in the cemetery where the gravestones are a memorial to a simpler, more gracious time, a time whose existence in reality has been submerged in a wish-fulfillment dream of Arcady. In his portrait of Clarendon one of the most important targets of Chesnutt's mockery is his own literary generation's use of pastoral forms of any sort to deal with a Southland unwilling to come to terms with the realities of its moral responsibilities.

Chesnutt offered little quarter in his evaluation of the need for radical change to right the wrongs of the South's method of dealing with problems of race. When his friend George W. Cable wrote an article suggesting that perhaps the white southerner deserved "one more chance" to deal fairly with the Negro, Chesnutt's reply rejected any compromise: "It is easy enough to temporize with the bull when you are on the other side of the fence," he wrote Cable, "but when you are in the pasture with him, as the colored people of the South are, the case is different. . . . Give the Negro a show. . . not five years hence, or a generation hence, but now, while he is alive, and can appreciate it; posthumous fame is a glorious thing, even if it is only posthumous; posthumous liberty is not, in the homely language of the rural Southerner, 'wu'th shucks'—."[17] This earnest letter indicates what was to be Chesnutt's method in both his literature and his life: he was an advocate of protest and progress who would always be less concerned with adjusting to changes wrought in and for the past than with trying to prepare for a future founded on justice and opportunity. To this end he might employ the language as well as the settings of an idealized rural South, but always and only as an ironic counterpoint to his own ideals. For Chesnutt the pastoral mode as a strategy for dealing with the black man's problems in a world controlled by whites was a form to be mocked or undermined from within.

Chesnutt's "antipastoral" strategy, as it has been called, marked him as being very different from the man whose utterances most directly shaped racial attitudes of Americans during his lifetime.[18] Chesnutt

17. Helen M. Chesnutt, *Charles W. Chesnutt*, 53–54.
18. Bone, *Down Home*, 73.

and Booker T. Washington were both born in 1858; both had as their cherished aim the advancement of their race in a country that had freed the slave but never acknowledged the full humanity of the Negro. Yet the founder of Tuskegee Institute employed tactics that vividly evoked positive images of the rural South not, as in Chesnutt's case, in order to expose the injustices of the black man's experiences there but instead to identify what, for Washington, had to constitute, at least for the time being, the black man's "place." Of these two southern strategies, Chesnutt's seems by far the more realistic as well as forward-looking. It is yet one more irony in a history full of them that the imagery of Washington, which firmly grounded black identity and promise in the soil of the South, would have so much more to do with the immediate future of black literature in the twentieth century than would the progressive strategy of Chesnutt, which would earmark his works as well as the last twenty years of his literary career for relative obscurity.

When Chesnutt's daughter wanted to attend Tuskegee Institute, he reacted to her choice with alarm, writing to her, "I see the South with the chastened eye of experience; it may look very different through the rosy spectacles of youth, to one who has never seen it."[19] His idea of "giving the Negro a show" included no option for a return to a South which for him could only be associated with degradation and exploitation. Yet the young black writers who moved to the urban centers of the North in the 1920s would turn their eyes to the South, to their ambiguous image of it as a land of vitality and value, in order to create a literature of enduring merit.

Booker T. Washington, in his Atlanta Exposition address of 1895, would counsel his people that "no race can prosper till it learns that there is as much dignity in tilling a field as in writing a poem." In the fall of 1921 Jean Toomer would spend three months in rural Georgia and, through his association with black tillers of fields and singers of folksongs, would write the poems and prose of *Cane*, the acknowledged masterwork of the Harlem Renaissance. It is a work whose pastoral design allows Toomer to explore some of the implications of the trip away from, as well as the imaginative return to, the deceptive Arcady of the South that Chesnutt had exposed in his fiction.

19. Helen M. Chesnutt, *Charles W. Chesnutt*, 168.

SIX

Jean Toomer's *Cane*:
The Pastoral Return

Rhobert wears a house, like a monstrous diver's helmet, on his head." He is suffocating under the weight of it, and it is "a sad thing to see a banty-bowed, shaky, rickety-legged man straining the raw insides of his throat against smooth air."[1] Like Thoreau's farmer, who has become the tool of his tools, Rhobert is a victim of a system of values. He is no longer a man, but only a housekeeper. "The best works of art," Thoreau says, "are the expression of man's struggle to free himself from this condition."[2] Jean Toomer writes, as Rhobert sinks into the mud still clinging stubbornly to his dead-weight house, "Lets open our throats, brother, and sing 'Deep River' when he goes down" (C, 75).

Jean Toomer's *Cane* can be read as an expression of one man's struggle to free himself from the condition of America's Rhoberts—the robots of an industrial society who have forgotten how to live. Examined in this light, the book can be said to employ a pastoral design, moving from a lyrical delight in a primitive, simple world, to a recognition of the forces that are destroying that world, and on to a consideration of alternatives: is restoration possible? can any sort of pastoral ideal be affirmed in the face of material reality? Toomer's work is organized around the traditional pastoral motif of a journey away from society, toward nature, though he recognizes, as good

1. Jean Toomer, *Cane* (New York, 1969), 73.
2. Henry David Thoreau, *Walden* (Cambridge, Mass., 1893), 61.

105

pastoral must, that the sojourn is temporary, that his Arcadia is being, as Thoreau would say, "whirled past and away." "Though late, O soil, it is not too late yet," he says, "to catch thy plaintive soul, leaving, soon gone" (C, 21). Toomer works in the first section of *Cane* to catch the plaintive soul of the people who inhabit a fast-disappearing pastoral world; these folk are juxtaposed, in Part Two, against the Rhoberts of a modern urban society, and in Part Three one of the Rhoberts makes his return to the land of his ancestors, seeking salvation and identity. It is a clear-cut pastoral pattern, involving the simple ideal, the threat to it from a complex world, and the attempt to achieve a resolution.

But there is more to *Cane* than this. The idea of the pastoral, as used by artists to analyze dichotomies in their society, is that it involves putting the complex into the simple, and this definition of the mode is one which can be applied effectively to *Cane*. For Rhobert is a black man—the world that he attempts to uphold is not just a sterile, industrial world; it is, more significantly, the white man's world. The house that enslaves him is made of the "white and whitewashed wood of Washington. Stale soggy wood of Washington" (C, 71). And the Arcadia that is eulogized by a black poet-narrator in Part One is the South, land not only of red soil, pine, cane field and folk song but also land of lynching and prejudice, primitive violence as well as pastoral peace. The hero who makes his pilgrimage to Georgia in Part Three does so without essential faith or hope. In response to the "pain and beauty" of the South he prays, "Give me an ugly world. . . . Stinking like unwashed niggers" (C, 161).

Thus irony informs every aspect of Toomer's version of pastoral. The struggle to get free from the conditions which were "bastardizing" the educated, city-bred Negro of the twenties took Toomer south in search of his "roots"; seemingly triumphant, he could write, "Georgia opened me . . . for no other section of the country has so stirred me. There one finds soil, soil in the sense the Russians know it,—the soil every art and literature that is to live must be embedded in."[3] Yet locating his roots in the red soil of Georgia provided Toomer not with an escape but only with a new confrontation, for there were disturbing moral ambiguities in this landscape, too, which could not be ignored by a man out of the modern world.

3. Jean Toomer, in Alain Locke, *The New Negro* (New York, 1925), 51.

Cane therefore becomes a work expressive of both the joy of discovery and the frustrations of loss; it contains partial answers and partial negations, recorded in smooth, lyrical poetry and harsh, disjointed prose. Toomer's ironic conclusion leaves only the ambiguities clear: the potential savior flees, his cowardly antithesis ascends at dawn carrying a bucket of dead coals. Thus the closing action and imagery suggest both triumph and defeat. It is *Cane's* pastoral design which provides continuity and a certain measure of stability for the complex and often contradictory urges reflected in the work as Toomer confronts the world that he, as both black man and modern man, must negotiate.

Toomer's trip to Georgia in 1921 was only one of a series of journeys oriented from his need to "find" himself and also to escape the problems of his personal life. He had grown up in the home of his maternal grandfather, Pinckney B. S. Pinchback, an early black activist who had served as acting governor of Louisiana during Reconstruction. Because of the disappearance of his father when he was very young, because of his light skin, and also because of his grandfather's position and domineering personality, Toomer found it difficult to establish a single identity or to place himself within the black bourgeois world of Washington, D.C. Evidently he also resented pressures from his grandfather to be productive; after completing high school he enrolled in an agriculture curriculum at the University of Wisconsin, perhaps in reaction against the attitudes fostered in the Pinchback household. Agricultural studies proved not to his liking, and there followed a physical training course in Chicago, a history course at the City College of New York, an attempt to join the armed forces as World War I began, and much more: "He sold Fords in Chicago, taught physical education in Milwaukee, and did a ten day stint as a ship-fitter in a New Jersey shipyard."[4] In 1920 Toomer went back to his grandfather's world in Washington, but not to acknowledge failure. He spent months in reading modern authors and in writing, preparing himself to be an artist.

Little wonder that Toomer wrote of the chaotic years before *Cane*, "Personally my life has been tortuous and dispersed."[5] The accep-

---

4. S. P. Fullenwider, "Jean Toomer: Lost Generation or Negro Renaissance," in Frank Durham (ed.), *Studies in Cane* (Columbus, Ohio, 1971), 68.

5. Jean Toomer, letter to *The Liberator*, quoted in Arna Bontemps, "Introduction" to Jean Toomer, *Cane*, viii.

tance of a job as temporary superintendent of a small Negro industrial school in Georgia provided, for a time, relief and restoration. Toomer wrote that seeing the Negro, "not as a pseudo-urbanized and vulgarized, a semi-Americanized product, but the Negro peasant, strong with the tang of fields and the soil," had the effect on him of giving "birth to a whole new life."[6]

The image of birth, which Toomer used so often to describe what he thought his experience in Georgia had done for him, is one of the most important and also ironic symbols in *Cane*. It is ironic too, as a definition of Toomer's feelings about his discovery of relation with the southern Negro. He proclaimed that a "deep part" of his nature "sprang suddenly to life" as he responded to the "Negro peasants." Recognizing that his "roots" were in the southern black man's world was what made him an artist, according to a letter he wrote to Claude McKay not long after his venture had borne fruit in several poems and stories. His need for "artistic expression" had pulled him "deeper and deeper into the Negro group," and it had "stimulated and fertilized whatever creative talent I may contain within me."[7] Toomer, seemingly, had found himself and a way to express himself through his association with blacks who were managing to retain their native vitality and kinship with nature in an isolated pocket of land still unspoiled by modern civilization.

The first section of *Cane* records, on one level, Toomer's excitement and newfound sense of belonging. Yet it records, too, his separateness and also his awareness that the vitality and kinship with nature to which he was witness were fast disappearing. In another letter of this period he wrote that "the Negro is in solution, in the process of solution. As an entity, the race is losing its body." The question, the implications of which Toomer at the time did not seem fully to recognize, was this: if the "song-lit race of slaves" with whom he associated his own artistic being was passing into oblivion, what of his own future as an artist? He wrote that "if anything comes up now, pure Negro, it will be a swan song."[8] So, while his own birth as an artist

6. Jean Toomer, "Outline of Autobiography" (MS in Toomer Collection, Fisk University Library, Nashville, Tenn.), 57.

7. Jean Toomer, letter to *The Liberator*, quoted in "Introduction" to *Cane*, viii–ix.

8. Jean Toomer to Waldo Frank, undated, in Toomer Collection, Fisk University Library, Box 14, Folder 1, No. 59.

is celebrated in *Cane*, the book also acknowledges the passing of his primary source of inspiration. The critics wanted more works like *Cane* from Toomer, more works in which he would continue, in Waldo Frank's words, "to turn the essences and materials of this Southland into the essences and materials of literature."[9] But the essence of his Southland, for Toomer, was the fact that it was passing away. "In those pieces that come nearest to the old Negro," he said in his own analysis of *Cane*, "the dominant emotion is a sadness derived from a sense of fading."[10] In *Cane* he was able to take the pastoral ideal represented by the southern Negro, and while admitting its impossibility of realization in any actual terms, to restore it metaphorically in art. But there could be no second *Cane* for Toomer, and his life after the writing of it shows a series of new but usually abortive "births" as he sought for other ways to define and expose himself.

It is hard to avoid the temptation to use the knowledge of what happened to Toomer after *Cane* in analyzing the book's motivations and themes. Yet *Cane* needs to be examined on its own terms, and not, as is so frequently done, for hints it might give us of the reasons for Toomer's supposed disappearance from the literary scene and his open denial, from 1930 on, that he could be called only a Negro. It is enough, perhaps, to say that *Cane* represented an awakening in Toomer's life, and that from there he went on to other things, other concerns. In the novel his concern was specifically for the black man in the modern world; it is a concern which he defined in pastoral terms and which caused him to mold his book into a unique version of southern pastoral as viewed with the black man's double vision of deep belonging and forced alienation.

The Negro artist, as Alain Locke once wrote, had an advantage over the white artist in that through his art he could fashion "a return to nature, not by way of the forced and worn formula of Romanticism, but through the closeness of an imagination that has never broken kinship with nature."[11] Toomer, like the poet-observer of the first section of *Cane*, seems to have discovered and mastered this advan-

9. Waldo Frank, "Foreword" to *Cane* (New York, 1923), in Durham (ed.), *Studies in Cane*, 18.

10. Toomer to Frank, undated, in Toomer Collection, Fisk University Library, Box 14, Folder l, No. 59.

11. Locke, *The New Negro*, 52.

tage through sympathy as he describes the landscape and in particular the black women of Georgia. Of an old Negro woman's face, he says, "Her channeled muscles are cluster grapes of sorrow/purple in the evening sun/nearly ripe for worms." Observing a girl singing, he notes, "She does not sing; her body is a song. She is the forest, dancing." He explains, and sounds proud: "When one is on the soil of one's ancestors, most anything can come to one." This man seems to be one who has returned freely to something that his imagination never really left; to the land and soil he says, "Thy son, in time, I have returned to thee."

Cane contains in its first part the open exuberance of Toomer's discovery of himself as artist; too, it boasts of his kinship with the land that he found so rich in inspirational value. In this section are stories of six women, one white, the rest black, done in prose that often soars into poetry. There are also poems, most celebrating the primitive vitality of the southern Negro. In all it is the presence of the soil which dominates. Toomer asserts in each piece that the Georgia Negroes who live so close to the soil receive therefrom, as Frank Durham notes, "a rare untrammeled elan alien to the white man with his materialism, his unnatural Christian ethic, and his increasing urge to move into towns and cities." [12] The black southern women, all sexually disturbing, are defined in terms that bind them closely to the fertile land they live on. Carma has a "mangrove-gloomed, yellow flower face"; Louisa's skin is "the color of oak leaves on young trees in fall; the countryside flows into Fern's eyes, "flowed into them with the soft listless cadence of Georgia's South."

There is, as J. Saunders Redding notes, "a subjective tide of love" in all of these descriptions. [13] Yet it is significant that no one ever possesses the women who are so lovingly portrayed here. The men who seek them feel their mystery and promise but cannot grasp their essence by the taking of their bodies, which are given almost indifferently. The imagery of Part One gives a sense of fresh and primitive joy, but the end result of the stories themselves is, as Toomer pointed out, "a sense of fading," and there is a desperate futility about the situations he relates. Karintha, in the first sketch, is a "growing thing ripened too soon." In her story we have the first of many births that

12. Durham, "Jean Toomer's Vision of the Southern Negro," in *Studies in Cane*, 104.
13. J. Saunders Redding, *To Make a Poet Black* (Chapel Hill, 1939), 104.

end immediately, violently in death: "A child fell out of her womb onto a bed of pine-needles in the forest . . . weeks after Karintha returned home the smoke was so heavy you tasted it in water" (C, 4). Karintha, herself, is sweet, full, potent like the land, but like the land, too, indifferent.

Thus there is imagery of life and birth in most of the poems and sketches of the first section, but most often it is overpowered by imagery of death. The poem "November Cotton Flower" is an example; full of "beauty so sudden for that time of year," the bloom appears in late autumn during a drought (C, 7). Too, the setting of the stories and poems in Part One is dusk. From Karintha, who carries beauty "perfect as dusk when the sun goes down" to the black sawmill workers who with "vestiges of pomp" leave the factories as the sun sets (C, 22), the people of the land are associated with the idea of fading—"The Negro is in solution," as Toomer said.

Toomer's position in Part One is, then, certainly ironic. Redding talks of his moods as "hot, colorful, primitive . . . but more akin to the naïve hysteria of the spirituals than to the sophisticated savagery of jazz and the blues."[14] Yet Toomer wrote in a letter soon after his return from Georgia, sometime during the period in which he was preparing the material for *Cane*, that "the Negro of the folk-song has all but passed away: the Negro of the emotional church is fading."[15] Part One thus exhibits two opposite moods. On the one hand, Toomer approaches a kind of hysterical rapture when he attempts to display the vitality of the "song-lit" race of blacks and the Southland they inhabit. But there is also, as David Littlejohn notes, an objectivity born of distance: "In 'Song of the Son,'" says Littlejohn, Toomer "tries to identify himself with the Georgia soil, but the very effort makes clear his distant view; the view of a sophisticated surrealist among an alien peasantry, a peasantry he transforms into something duskily primeval."[16]

The poet who records the black man's energetic recasting of the white man's Christianity in the poem entitled "Conversion" must also

14. *Ibid.*

15. Toomer to Frank, undated, Toomer Collection, Fisk University Library, Box 14, Folder 1, No. 59.

16. David Littlejohn, "Before *Native Son:* The Renaissance and After," in Durham (ed.), *Studies in Cane,* 101.

record the inroads that white man's civilization has made into the black's more primitive, more poetic world. Thus no one associates with the white Becky, who has given birth to two black children. Esther, near-white-skinned daughter of a black merchant, cannot offer herself to black prophet Barlo, because of the taboos of her near-white world. She dreams of the child they might conceive: "Black, singed, woolly, tobacco-juice baby—ugly as sin" (C, 41). In "Blood-Burning Moon" Louisa gives herself freely, with a childlike innocence, to both a black man and a white man. Uninhibited, primitive, she represents the liberated soul of the South. Yet given the terms of the actual world she inhabits, her situation is impossible. The black lover kills the white one and is burned alive by the white lover's friends. Toomer describes the lynching party as it moves toward Louisa's home: "The moving body of their silence preceded them over the crest of the hill into factory town. It flattened the Negroes beneath it" (C, 65). This is a description, too, of the effect of the white man and his culture on the southern Negro. Too strong to be resisted, the white man's world, Toomer believed, would soon either destroy or absorb the more vigorous but also more vulnerable black man's world.

The pastoral world Toomer creates, then, is one on the verge of collapse. Its primitive inhabitants exhibit "vestiges of pomp"; their lives are, like the story of Carma, "the crudest melodrama," full of violence, sensuousness, raw emotions never repressed. But as Toomer makes his attempt to join them, he becomes aware of another quality— indifference—which seems a product of pervasive fatalism.

In the first section's best sketch, "Fern," this indifference is sensitively dramatized. The narrator, like all the men who have ever seen Fern, wants to do something for her, "some fine, unnamed thing." She captivates all men—the possessive, aggressive aspect of them—with eyes that "sought nothing—that is, nothing that was obvious and tangible and that one could see, and they gave the impression that nothing was to be denied" (C, 24). Fern, cream-colored, part-Jewish, part-black, seems to absorb and reflect the land around her. She is full of life-giving potential but also full of unrelieved longing. Her reaction to her world is an attitude of listless acceptance that hides an intense suffering. She is thus an unforgettable image of the southern Negro's plight and his response to it. He accepts the "fading" of his race in the same way that the land accepts the exploitation of the civilizing forces that have gained control over it. And his fatalism is a trademark of pastoral literature, since true pastoral must show the ideal world to be temporary, even incomplete.

Thus Toomer's return to Georgia, as memorialized in the first section of *Cane*, must take into account the "temporariness" of the world recovered or become only an escape fantasy or an exercise in exoticism. This does not mean that the love and longing expressed for the Georgia soil are invalidated, or that the poet's experiences there in the end gain him nothing. The return to nature is essential. Any true pastoral design recognizes and celebrates the restorative powers of nature, as does Toomer in the first part of *Cane*. The work with such a design then must move on, however, to an acknowledgment of the powers of civilized society which counteract the raw vitality of the simpler world, and Toomer provides for this through his ironic vision in the first section. Still, as his black brethren head up Dixie Pike toward the cities, the poet of Part One reminds them that the road they travel had its starting point in a rich past that needs to be remembered: "Dixie Pike," he says, "has grown from a goat path in Africa" (C, 18).

Part One of *Cane* shows the black southerner in his twilight hour, his strength and beauty still discernible against the complementary background of Georgia pine forest and cane field, but his future jeopardized by the encroachment of the white man's values and oppressive designs. In Part Two the background changes, becoming now the streets and "white-walled" buildings of northern cities. Here the black man stands out against his surroundings instead of merging as with his source; here "nigger life," like a wedge, thrusts "unconscious rhythms, black reddish blood into the white and whitewashed wood of Washington" (C, 71). In Leo Marx's terms, here we have the counterforce essential to literary pastoral, the real world that qualifies and forces an ironic slant on the poet's vision of Arcadia.[17] Toomer's particular version of pastoral is, here again, doubly ironic as he views not just the rural thesis being called into question by the urban antithesis, but also the black man's increasingly weak resistance to the temptation to give in to the white man's world—a world which disdains him and is disgusted by his most admirable qualities.

17. Marx, *The Machine in the Garden*, 70.

The central images of Part One carry over into the second section with significant alterations, all of which suggest sterility and corruption. Footpaths are now busy streets; the soft glow of the sun is replaced by theater footlights; tall pines "rustling like guitars" become trees planted in boxes, "whinnying like young colts to be free." The changed regard for the element of sexuality marks the most dramatic difference between the two sections. "That the sexes were made to mate is the practice of the South," Toomer's narrator observes in Part One. In Part Two, a black man feebly rationalizes his inability to make love to a girl he desires and who desires him: "Her suspicion would be stronger than her passion. It wouldn't work" (C, 94).

The black women in Part Two are afraid of their sexuality, and men are afraid to approach them. Civilization stifles them; the pressure to conform makes them impotent. Symbolic of the frigidity that the city's social taboos produce is the woman in "Calling Jesus" who locks herself in her house at night, shutting out her soul which is "a little thrust-tailed dog that follows her, whimpering." Toomer equates soul and sex in the image of the dog, who symbolizes the essence of the southern Negro and what he has lost in the city. Only when the dog's mistress forgets in sleep "the streets and alleys, and the large house where she goes to bed of nights" is she receptive to the "soul" of her southern Negro heritage. As she dreams, "her eyes carry to where builders find no need for vestibules, for swinging on iron hinges, storm doors" (C, 103).

In "Calling Jesus," the woman's house is her prison, as in "Rhobert" the house that Rhobert carries on his head is a symbol of his resignation to an alien, stultifying philosophy: "God built the house. . . . It is good to die obeying Him who can do these things" (C, 74). The property instinct belongs to the white man's world, and the black man who gives in to it is, like Rhobert, on his way down. Houses represent confinement, limitation, and inhibition in Part Two. In "Box Seat" a Negro savior-figure comes to his "withered people" in the city to "call them from their houses and teach them to dream" (C, 104). Dan Moore appears as a sort of transplanted Barlo, a fertility symbol from the South who has come to "stir the root-life" of a people so afraid of what he is that they go indoors when they hear him coming.

The imagery of "Box Seat" is primarily sexual; the conflict, pastoral. The prim, cool, city-girl Muriel is pitted against Dan, whose "fingers and arms are fires to melt and bars to wrench and force and pry." Dan sees himself breaking into "virginal houses"; he hears the roots of "underground races" when he puts his ear to a wall. The story's tension reaches a peak at a theater house where Muriel has gone to escape Dan. The theater represents all that is artificial, unnatural, escapist in these people's lives. Dan brings rude, raw nature to bear on this world through his sensual interpretations of what he sees. Sitting next to a "portly Negress," Dan recognizes in her a "soil-soaked fragrance" and he has a vision that "through the cement floor her strong roots sink down . . . and spread under the river and disappear in blood-lines that waver south" (C, 119).

Dan is sensitive to the still unconquered animalism of his people, who in spite of "zoo-restrictions and keeper-taboos" have passionate natures that might save them from the certain sterility they face in the white world they are trying to adopt. Yet Dan saves no one, and seems to lose his own soul after witnessing the mockery of life on the stage that is being accepted as real by the audience. Two dwarfs have a slug-fest as a part of the show; Dan challenges an irate theatergoer to a real fight outside, but as the crowd follows the two to an alley, Dan disappears. Having seen his philosophy rejected, he grows incoherent and impotent, "cool as a green stem that has just shed his flower." The natural man, it seems, cannot survive in this environment.

In both Parts One and Two, Toomer uses his female characters as passive reflectors of their environment. In Part One the fate of all of his women, with the notable exception of Esther, demonstrates the passion, violence, and spontaneity of the rural South, while the women of Part Two are "whitewashed" like the cities they inhabit. The sketches of the first section, as Darwin Turner points out, deal with women who are either "isolated or destroyed because they have ignored society's restrictions on sexual behavior."[18] If failure to live by society's standards results in such disasters, is not the self-denial practiced by the characters of the second section preferable; are not their fears of sex well grounded? The answer lies in Muriel's desperate attempts to conform, in Dorris' futile effort to break out of the mold society has cast for her, in Bona's hypocrisy and Avey's resignation. The overt

18. Darwin Turner, *In a Minor Chord* (Carbondale, Ill., 1971), 27.

violence of the sketches of Part One is replaced in the city stories by repression; physical damage, like physical fulfillment, is thus avoided, but we witness instead the deterioration or distortion of potentially vigorous, valuable personalities. In Part One the women, who are close to the earth, are shown experiencing all of life, its tragedies included. In Part Two they experience only frustration.

The male characters of Part Two take a more active role. The point of view changes in this section so that we have no longer one calm, reflective vision of life, as was provided by the narrator of Part One, but many fragmented pictures seen through the consciousness of several of the male protagonists. John (the stage manager's brother in "Theater"), Paul, and the nameless narrator of "Avey" are three men who have been made impotent by their overly intellectual approach to sexual encounters as well as by the conventions and taboos of their society.

Darwin Turner approaches this shift in viewpoint by suggesting that in Part Two Toomer was reproducing "his satiric, self-pitying, or idealized image of himself." Turner finds the shift unfortunate, saying that "whereas Toomer could sing of women, he could not write effectively about Jean Toomer."[19] Yet the new tone caused by Toomer's more personally subjective view in Part Two is functional in pastoral terms. Perhaps Toomer "joined the dance," as Turner calls it, in order to acknowledge the force of pressures always being applied by the real world, modern society. Part One is a dream; it suggests the subconscious mind creating fantasies of violence and fulfillment. This, as Leo Marx notes, is a valid object of the pastoral design as it re-creates a purely natural world: "What is ascribed to 'nature' in the design may plausibly be understood as the vitality of unconscious or preconscious experiences."[20] The vision of Part One seems to offer restoration through release: the narrator of that section accepts the primitive side of his nature as a valid, vital part of his personality. Yet the other side must be given its due. The return to conscious reality is necessary as a balance.

In Part Two we see the conscious mind of the black man at work in Toomer's characterizations of men who are paralyzed by thought. They think instead of acting, and their actions are thus self-con-

19. *Ibid.*, 27, 28.
20. Marx, *The Machine in the Garden*, 70.

scious, artificial as in a play. The theater itself is thus a telling image
for Toomer. Watching a group of black chorus girls as they relax and
talk naturally, the stage manager's brother thinks, "Soon the director
will herd you, my full-lipped, distant beauties, and tame you, and blunt
your sharp thrusts in loosely suggestive movements, appropriate to
Broadway. (O dance!) Soon the audience will paint your dusk faces
white, and call you beautiful" (C, 93). This man recognizes the artificiality of his world and its designs on the freedom and true beauty
of the Negro woman. Yet he himself is trapped by the same world:
"John's body is separate from the thoughts that pack his mind," says
Toomer, and the chorus girl who dances out her longing for him, when
looking for approval in his face, finds only "a dead thing in the shadow
which is his dream" (C, 92, 99). Dorris runs to her dressing room
where "her eyes, over a floor of tears, stare at the whitewashed ceil-
ing" (C, 100).

Everything in the second section is "whitewashed," people as well
as ceilings, buildings, and cities. The color white symbolizes nega-
tion. Most of the characters in Part Two, like Esther of the first section, are debilitated by their white blood. In Esther's case, the longer
she represses her longing for the coal-black Barlo, the whiter her skin
seems to become and the weaker she seems to be: "Her face pales until
it is the color of the gray dust that dances with the dead cotton leaves"
(C, 33). "Perhaps for some reason, white skins are not supposed to
live at night" (C, 141), thinks Paul in Part Two. Paul, himself white
enough to "pass" at the school he attends in Chicago, is unable to
acknowledge fully his Negro heritage. He knows that the whites
around him see in his blackness "not attractiveness . . . but difference," and this awareness pains him, in spite of his effort to be superior. In the end he feels a need to explain in platonic terms his passion for a girl when he is seen leaving a dance hall with her; he comes
back to discuss his motives with a black doorman who has understood his desire all too well. When he returns to the spot where he
left the girl, he finds she has disappeared, unable, as he himself is, to
bear the consequences that a sexual relationship might bring.

Paul dreams in his sketch of a southern Negro woman giving birth
to a song: "She weans it, and sends it, curiously weaving, among lush
melodies of cane and corn" (C, 138). The message of the song is lost
to him, however, as he opts for the city, its artificial lights and music

and concepts. Here is another aborted birth which leads the way into Part Three, in which a black man from a northern city dreams and denies, like Paul, the song that is the South—simple, unspoiled, regenerative.

In the third and final section of *Cane* Toomer dramatizes the coming to Georgia of a man who is very different and yet closely related to the narrator of Part One. The narrator of Part One responds to the South; Ralph Kabnis in Part Three can only recoil from it. Coming between them and causing the difference is the mechanical world of Part Two. Thus Ralph Kabnis travels to Georgia as a man who has long since "broken kinship" with nature, with the soul of his ancestors. He longs for the same gift of unflinching responsiveness to the land that is exhibited in Part One. He thinks, "If I, the dream (not what is weak and afraid in me) could become the face of the South. How my lips would sing for it, my songs being the lips of its soul" (C, 158).

Part Three draws together the opposing strains of the first two sections into a dramatic enactment of the concerns of the book as a whole. *Cane* was not written as a novel, with the novel's sort of unity. Jean Wagner, in fact, goes so far as to say that "the only literary genre to which one can assign the work is poetry, for ultimately the entirely personal meaning of Toomer's pilgrimage, and the poetic symbolism which gives it expression, are the elements that maintain the unity of this interlocking succession of poems, tales, sketches, and impressions that lead on to the book's final drama."[21] Part Three, the dramatic piece "Kabnis," does not aid the attempt to classify *Cane* generically, but it is crucial, nonetheless, in completing the book's symbolic design. Through this drama we see that the book definitely has a unified structure, which is pastoral, and a major theme, which might be called resurrection. Each section has its savior figure, with Lewis in Part Three achieving an amalgamation of Barlo and Dan Moore. Each section also follows a symbolic pattern of darkness going into light, and the third section ends with a significant sunrise. In each section, too, there is a preoccupation with birth, and with pastoral images like the November cotton flower or the trees in boxes which hold in tension the warring forces of life and death. The third section

21. Jean Wagner, *Black Poets of the United States* (Urbana, Ill., 1973), 266.

dramatizes two symbolic births, each having a different message concerning the possibility of rebirth for the black man in the modern world. Hope and despair alternate in the emotional atmosphere of the third section, which in terms of the pastoral works at a synthesis involving the rural paradise, the loss of this due to the pervasive, corrupting influence of urban civilization, and the recognition of the need to regain the values if not the actuality of the simpler time.

For the black man, the return in imagination to the rural South involves not just a desire to regain the peace of the simpler world, but also a recognition and acceptance of his black heritage, rooted in soil, savagery, and slavery. Ralph Kabnis is described as being "suspended a few feet above the soil whose touch would resurrect him" (C, 191). As in Part One, there is here the pastoral suggestion that the soil, the land, possesses a regenerative force. However, in the last section the struggle to become "rooted" is complicated by the fact that the characters involved here have been exposed to the debilitating pressures of the white man's artificial, mechanical civilization.

There is Hanby, a black school superintendent who copies the white man's habits, groveling before them and tyrannizing other blacks. There is Halsey, a potentially vigorous man who has given up trying to get ahead; he finds escape in manual labor and evenings of meaningless debauchery. None of the blacks in this section are free to express or fulfill themselves according to their nature, because "the whole white South weighs down" upon them, and "the pressure is terrific." Kabnis represents the most extreme case of "uprootedness" in this group. The others are confused about their racial heritage, but they do not deny it. Kabnis, returning to the South from an urban world totally dominated by white restrictions, carries with him that world's deep sense of alienation and fear of belonging.

Ralph Kabnis is portrayed as "a promise of soil-soaked beauty; uprooted, thinning out" (C, 191). He cannot accept the capacity for joy and suffering that characterizes the people of his race who live in the more primitive, violent South. The folk songs, revival hymns, and church shouts that form a constant background music in this section alternately irritate and frighten him: "We don't have that sort of thing up North," he says. His continuous sneering is a measure of his self-contempt and his envy of those around him who can live at peace with the land. Their natural responsiveness and resignation infuriate him, while "he totters as a man would who for the first time uses artificial limbs. As a completely artificial man would" (C, 163). He has come to Georgia seemingly to find himself, but only feels more "cut off" in the South because he is so close to the answers that he is unable or unwilling to understand. "Things are so immediate in Georgia" (C, 164), he complains.

In direct contrast to Kabnis is Lewis, a northern Negro who "lets the pain and beauty of the South meet him there." Like Kabnis he has come to Georgia "on a contract" with himself, but unlike Kabnis he resembles the narrator of the first section, who is fully receptive to the land and the people around him. Yet the people he encounters, including Kabnis, mistrust him: both "suspicion and open liking" greet him when he seeks out the men of the town. Most of them turn away.

Lewis is a savior figure, like King Barlo without Barlo's primitivistic rhetoric and like Dan Moore without his violent manner. Both Barlo and Dan Moore blend African-pagan and Christian symbolism; both exhort their people to "look unto the heavens." Their religion is thus a religion of escape, and neither can sustain his faith in the face of the corruption of the real world. In comparison Lewis' religion seems rather one of confrontation. He asks those he meets to forget the "sin-bogies" that artificial conventions have forced them to obey, and he speaks directly to the conditions that are destroying his people. To Kabnis, for instance, he says: "Can't hold them, can you? Master; slave. Soil; and the overarching heavens. Dusk; dawn. They fight and bastardize you" (C, 218). Here Lewis defines the basic problem of the black man who lives in a white man's mechanical world: he has a need to belong to the land of his ancestors, to define himself in terms of his racial inheritance, but also a need to transcend the indignities of the past that the Southland still suggests.

Lewis would seem to offer an answer, a way through. He has Kabnis' poetic vision coupled with a strengthening sense of mission that Kabnis lacks. He is able to see the significance of Father John, who for Kabnis represents only the ignominies and bigotry that the black man is made to bear and, moreover, is a living sign of the African slave ancestry that Kabnis has tried to deny. To Lewis, on the other hand, Father John is potentially a "mute John the Baptist of a new religion" as well as "a tongue-tied shadow of an old" (C, 211). Lewis recognizes that the past is part of the future, and it is this knowledge which frees him from Kabnis' rootless soul searching.

Yet Lewis, like Dan Moore, ends up fleeing a scene that suggests things too painful for him to bear. Looking at Father John, Lewis manages to "merge with his source" and to accept both the pain and beauty of the South. But later in the night, when he watches Halsey and Kabnis carry on meaningless affairs with two prostitutes, the loneliness of his deeper understanding of the black man's needs becomes too chilling, and he rushes out: "Their pain is too intense. He cannot stand it" (C, 226).

What it is that Lewis understands about the South and what plan he has to offer for its salvation are matters never clearly defined. His responsiveness and directness, "purpose guided by an adequate intelligence" as Toomer calls it, seem to indicate a productive way to meet and transcend the dilemma of the southern black man facing "solution." Yet he runs away from the challenge represented by Kabnis' bitter rejection of his racial identity. Like the other Negroes of the southern town, he too seems to become "burdened with an impotent pain" (C, 205). His meeting with Carrie Kate, Halsey's younger sister, is the only positive scene involving him in the role of savior, and even here he is denied complete power.

Carrie Kate seems to be an extension of the women figures who dominate Part One. Like them she is the product of a pastoral environment—simple, innocent, naturally responsive. When Lewis draws her attention, she impulsively gives herself to him, recognizing in his eyes a dream of something superior to her familiar surroundings: "The sun-burst from her eyes floods up and haloes him. Christ-eyes, his eyes look to her. Fearlessly she loves into them" (C, 205). Yet there is something else in Carrie Kate that is foreign to her environment, and it prohibits her from yielding to Lewis. As she is about to make a commitment to him, she recalls the conventions of her society, a society that is trying to stifle its own most creative urges. "The sin-bogies of respectable southern colored folks clamor at her: 'Look out! Be a *good* girl. A *good* girl. Look out!'" (C, 205).

Frank Durham points out that in the meeting of Lewis and Carrie Kate, Toomer "possibly offers a solution to the Negro's subjection by the white." Carrie represents the Negro's spirit, "his life force drawn from the soil and the sun and the primal past." Lewis is the modern black man, educated and involved in the present. The possibility of the union of the two, combining the best of North and South, past and present as influences on the black race, symbolizes perhaps a hope for the Negro's future. Yet as Durham points out, it is only a possibility, cast in doubt by Carrie Kate's fear of social recriminations, which represents a "hint that the solution will be delayed until the Negro can cast aside the restrictive, bourgeois moral-religious taboos of the white code."[22]

Carrie Kate is often considered by readers of *Cane* to represent hope, for Kabnis' diseased will as well as for the race as a whole. Patricia Chase interprets her as being "all of [Toomer's] women in one self-actualizing woman," and sees in her a figure of light, "advancing toward the future carrying the relevant past, i.e., Father John, with her."[23] The symbolic potential of her role is complicated and advanced by the last scene in "Kabnis," during which she functions as food bringer, healer, mother, Madonna, and midwife. This concluding act brings all the major symbols and themes together, and while the drama ends ambiguously with no clear statement of possibilities, the final focus is on symbols of hope rather than those of despair.

Early in the drama, Kabnis was told the story of a pregnant black woman killed in the street of a southern town by whites. As she dies her child is born living, but a white man takes it, "jab[s] his knife in it and [sticks] it t'a tree" (C, 179). The child represents the soul of the southern Negro. Kabnis, deeply impressed by the story, later makes the wish that some "lynchin white man" would take his soul and "stick his knife through it an pin it to a tree" (C, 225). His death wish, like the murder of the newborn black baby, seems to indicate only hopelessness.

In the final scene, there is another birth; in symbolic terms, it is the rebirth of Kabnis himself. Left alone in Halsey's basement after a night of joyless debauchery, Kabnis curses Father John, representative of his own debased past. Then Carrie Kate appears, "lovely in her fresh energy of the morning, in the calm untested confidence and nascent maternity which rise from the purpose of her present mission" (C, 233). Father John speaks of the sin of the "white folks"; Kabnis is contemptuous. Yet all this time the dark basement is slowly being lightened by the first rays of a "new-sun." Carrie's palms draw the fever out of Kabnis and she helps him to take off a robe that he had worn

---

22. Durham, "Jean Toomer's Vision of the Southern Negro," 113.
23. Patricia Chase, "The Women in *Cane*," *C L A Journal*, XIV (March, 1971), 272–73.

during the night to mock himself and his race. The basement, dark and clammy, is like a womb, and Kabnis, now disrobed, goes up the stairs to sunlight.

Is Kabnis a new man? The drama does not give a conclusive answer. What he meets as he takes up his life again at the end may be the same violence that ended the life of the black baby. Probably he will simply continue to fade, in "impotent pain." There are no clear signs from his own actions that he has found the necessary compassion or perception to survive, other than the fact that he "trudges upstairs to the workshop." Carrie Kate remains behind, praying for Jesus to come, and this too is an ambiguous act, since the book throughout has demonstrated that Christian faith offers no help but only recommends passivity to the Negro.

Yet in terms of *Cane's* symbolic design, the sunrise described in the last paragraph is highly significant. It is the book's only dramatic description of a true dawn: "The sun arises. Gold-glowing child, it steps into the sky and sends a birth-song slanting down gray dust streets and sleepy windows of the southern town." *Cane* begins with sunset scenes, with a description of a woman who is "perfect as dusk when the sun goes down," with a song that speaks of the sun "setting on a song-lit race." There is, then, from the very beginning, a realization that the life represented in the southern scenes is a dying thing which might be captured in art but not preserved as an escape from or a cure for modern ills. The sunrise at the end of *Cane*, then, is a symbol of hope, but not hope based on the kind of pastoral existence that is given lyrical treatment throughout the book. Rather, because of the sunrise we are able to visualize a sort of reconnection or rerooting process through which a modern black man might find renewal through an acceptance of the land and the past that have molded his racial identity. We see Kabnis first in the dead of night, waiting for daylight. At the end he is bathed in sunlight, after an evening which presents to the reader a dramatic possibility of catharsis.

Cane's conclusion points to possibilities through the inclusion of symbols of rebirth and sunrise. The resolution provided is aesthetic, then, not actual, which is as it must be in a pastoral design. Toomer's own conception of the direction of his collection shows that he was seeking no dramatic climax at the end of "Kabnis," which was written before the sketches of the second section were added to give

Toomer enough material for a publishable manuscript. From a letter that Toomer wrote to Waldo Frank in December of 1922 comes a description of the movement of the different segments of *Cane* in terms of curves and arcs that are never completed (as the graphics at the beginning of Part Two and "Kabnis" also indicate). Toomer wrote:

From three angles, *Cane*'s design is a circle. Aesthetically, from simple forms to complex ones, and back to simple forms. Regionally, from the South up to the North, and back into the South again. Or, from the North down into the South, and then a return North. From the point of view of the spiritual entity behind the work, the curve really starts with Bona and Paul (awakening), plunges into Kabnis, emerges in Karintha, etc., swings upward into Theater and Box Seat, and ends (pauses) in Harvest Song.[24]

So, for Toomer, *Cane* in effect has no ending when viewed in terms of its spiritual course. There is not an end but a "pause," and this a little more than halfway through the book, before it takes a downward plunge into the gnawing world of disconnection that is chronicled in "Kabnis." The reaper of "Harvest Song" looks both ways; he has "been in the fields all day" and seeks "the stack'd fields of the other harvesters." His evocation of harvest time takes us back to the poem "Georgia Dusk" in Part One, "where plowed lands fulfill / Their early promise of a bumper crop." Yet in "Harvest Song" is no fulfillment but only the thirst that Kabnis will feel:

> I am a reaper. (Eoho!) All my oats are cradled.
> But I am too fatigued to bind them. And I
> Hunger. I crack a grain. It has no taste to it.
> My throat is dry. . . .

"Harvest Song" also contains a call to the brother harvesters, a sort of plea for recognition, response, connection.

> O my brothers, I beat my palms, still soft, against the
>   stubble of my harvesting. (You beat your soft
>   palms, too.) My pain is sweet. Sweeter than
>   the oats or wheat or corn. It will not bring me
>   knowledge of my hunger.

24. Jean Toomer to Waldo Frank, December 12, 1922, in Toomer Collection, Fisk University, Box 3, Folder 6, No. 800.

As Charles T. Davis notes, "There is no sign that the cry is responded to . . . and without response there is not satisfaction for hunger, not even the knowledge of what hunger is."[25]

The last section of *Cane* begins with Kabnis' pain and hunger. It ends with Carrie's bringing food to Father John and Halsey's call: "The axle an th beam's ali ready waitin f y. Come on." The black man's idealized, primitive past is figuratively joined to his brutally immediate present in "Kabnis." Here a sophisticated man from a northern city and a white world returns to the rural South and the black people who form his folk culture. Through the experience of Kabnis in Georgia, Toomer displays two options for the black man whose distress Kabnis typifies: he can be "suspended from his roots" like Kabnis or he can "merge with his source" like Kabnis' double, Lewis. Neither man, neither choice is offered as a solution or ultimate course of action, but only as a suggestion for direction. Neither can save the race or the individual from the debilitating influence of modern life. Yet through his inclusion of these dual possibilities, Toomer examines his own and his race's inheritance—the pain and beauty of the South—and restores to it an artistic vitality through the pastoral design of *Cane*.

Much of the power of *Cane* comes from its "doubleness," its looking both ways, its acknowledgment that the routes of connection with the past are open now only to the energizing focus of the artistic mind. In this respect *Cane* pinpoints problems of concern and design that relate to other matters besides the Harlem Renaissance. In writing of the pastoral tendencies of the black literature of this period, Robert Bone asserts that "at the center of the Harlem Renaissance, in short, was a generation in process of becoming *deprovincialized*," yet one which also felt "compelled to deal with rural life and to assume a more or less affirmative stance toward rural values." In noting that at this same juncture many white writers were also flocking to the cities, and particularly to Chicago, as "young provincials in search of big-city sophistication," Bone remarks that "for these white authors, the theme

25. Charles T. Davis, "Jean Toomer and the South: Region and Race as Elements Within a Literary Imagination," *Studies in the Literary Imagination*, VII (Fall, 1974), 30.

of personal liberation was not at odds with any traumatizing historical event. For them, it was all expansion and no recoil. Their provincial origins, far from serving as a touchstone, were largely regarded as a curse."[26] While this might be a useful distinction to make in relating the work of white writers of the Chicago Liberation whom Bone mentions, such figures as Sherwood Anderson, Edgar Lee Masters, and Sinclair Lewis, still we might note considerable ambivalence in their attitudes toward the "provincial" world left behind. And for another group of white writers of the same era whom Bone does not assess, the issue of rural origins as "touchstone" or "curse" is even more complex and has an important bearing on the work of the writers of the Harlem Renaissance.

The ambiguity of *Cane* in its expression of the essences of the rural South is matched in mood and implication by the work of a group of white southerners who, like Toomer and other young blacks of the early 1920s, faced a sense of cultural dislocation as they opted for life in a modern, industrial, urbanized America. And while the name they chose for the magazine which displayed their poems, the *Fugitive*, might seem to mark them as being as eager to "revolt" from southern villages as their Chicago contemporaries were from midwestern ones, the most important members of the group also came a little later to be known by a label that suggests not flight from, but return to, rural beginnings—the "Agrarians."

To recognize how similar some of the Fugitive-Agrarian approaches are to Toomer's, one has only to compare the character Kabnis, "suspended from his roots," to the narrative personality who appears in Allen Tate's "Ode to the Confederate Dead." Tate's narrator, a modern southerner standing by the gate of a Confederate soldiers' cemetery, illustrates, as Tate himself has written, the "cut-off-ness" of modern man from the world, particularly the world of his own personal past, and this is certainly the condition with which Toomer informs Kabnis' every reaction to the Southland he visits. Indeed, both "Kabnis" and "Ode to the Confederate Dead" are concerned with the difficulties the artist as modern faces when confronting an "immoderate past" which is both too close in its physical and familial associations and too remote in its operations on the intellect

26. Bone, *Down Home*, 112, 124.

and spirit: as Kabnis prays, "Dear Jesus, do not chain me to myself and set these hills and valleys, heaving with folk-songs, so close to me that I cannot reach them" (C, 163).

The narrator of Toomer's "Harvest Song" is another of *Cane*'s figures whose situation resembles that explored in much of the Fugitives' poetry. In this poem, which Toomer felt was a proper place to "pause" if not to end in one's reading of the book, the singer looks both back to the earlier celebration of rural richness and forward to the spiritual starvation of Kabnis. As in other poems of *Cane*, Toomer here links the function of the harvester with the role of the artist; the dilemma of this reaper who has cradled his oats but is "too fatigued to bind them" is the dilemma that Toomer recognized as his own at the time he was completing *Cane*—how to resolve productively his sense of the richness of the black man's heritage in the South with his knowledge that the black man's fate was now inextricably linked to a modern world that was sterile and inhumane. The harvester seems disillusioned about the power of art to bring about the necessary resolution; at any rate, he seeks new support and defines a potential new role as he calls the other harvesters, his "brothers" in toil, to his "field." The functions of prayer and prophecy are identified by his "closing" poem, and these are functions which Toomer would take up in more openly religious endeavors for himself very soon after *Cane* was published.

In his poem "The Antique Harvesters," which like Toomer's "Harvest Song" uses the imagery of reaper and harvest to explore the poet's vocation, John Crowe Ransom would, like Toomer, define a religious function for the writer of the modern world with a similar avowal that the pain of faith was "sweeter" than any actual harvest. How to reap the harvest of the South, as image of a land that has preserved elemental, traditional human values, is a question that *Cane* defines in terms of the black man's sometimes violently contradictory experience there. It is a question for which the Fugitive-Agrarians would propose a variety of answers in the period of a dramatic southern renascence in literature which, like its Harlem counterpart, would begin with a search through a simpler past for identity and direction.

SEVEN

Agrarian Quarrel, Agrarian Question:
What Shall This Land Produce?

In the poem "Antique Harvesters," which John Crowe Ransom wrote in 1925, a number of opposing directions and images are balanced through the language and situation. The title itself presents something of a contradiction that is complicated by Ransom's choice of adjectives. The harvesters of the poem are old men of the South, far past their own moment of fruition; still the poet characterizes their age not with the word *old*, or *aged*, or even *ancient*, but with the word *antique*, which suggests the richness of relics, of something preserved, as well as the value of aging beautifully through time. The antique harvesters speak primarily of matters of time as they talk of harvest in their declining land; of young men who prefer the songs of passionate birds to the "croak of raven's funeral wing"; of the yellow tinge of "moon" time as well as "noon" time; of the "sons of the fathers" charged with service to "Our Lady" the spirit of the land, who herself has not "stooped" though her "servitors" have lost their vigor. And yet, while the imagery and the direction of the poem seem to be headed toward a portrayal of decline, even decay, in an old region whose yield is "meager," the opposite is actually affirmed. Here is a place that is vital not in spite of but because of its very "antiqueness."

The Proud Lady, certainly symbolic of an Old South in a modern world, is a lady for all seasons: "And by an autumn tone / As by a gray, as by a green, you will have known / Your famous Lady's image." The harvesters themselves endure because their service is to the land: "Trust

not but the old endure, and shall be older / Than the scornful be-
holder." Though the leaves have turned "tawny," they "still hold," and
starting with this description of the durability of nature in time, the
poem asserts a position of faith that is never seriously assaulted. Four
questions are asked during the course of the poem, but they are all
purely rhetorical, shaped specifically to set up their answers, answers
that proclaim the value of the South's historical experience and the
triumph of a pastoral ideal. The poem's oppositions are formally balanced by a tone which adheres to a pastoral mood; it is both elemental and ornamental, as these lines from the first stanza demonstrate:

> And it is harvest; what shall this land produce?
> A meager hill of kernels, a runnel of juice;
> Declension looks from our land, it is old.

The effects of change are ordered under the laws of nature. Here is
not restless, forward progress, but the reassertion of permanence
through natural process. If asked to forsake the Proud Lady, the
"dainty youths" of this land know how to answer: "the sons of the
fathers shall keep her worthy of / What these have done in love." The
instruction of the antique harvesters to the youths on this matter admits no equivocation, as the verb form of the line emphasizes: "Angry as wasp-music *be* your cry then" (my italics).

One might be more than a little surprised to find this kind of unqualified affirmation for a pastoral lifestyle in a southern poem of 1925,
a year when the Old South and its ways were, or soon would be,
through the Scopes trial in Dayton, Tennessee, and other events as
well, attacked both from within the region and without. It does not
lessen the surprise to note that the author of the poem belonged to
the "Fugitive" group, who had proclaimed that as artists they fled
"from nothing faster than the high-caste Brahmins of the Old South."[1]
The antique harvesters seem rather singularly unperturbed by the
"scornful beholders" and those who whisper that they might "more
prosper in other lands." Their faith in their task as servitors in a distinctly unmodern vocation is allowed to proclaim itself without any
interior challenges. This is indeed an unusual quality to find in a
Ransom poem, as Louis Rubin notes when he says of "Antique Har-

---

1. *The Fugitive*, I (April, 1922), 1.

vesters" that it is "quite unlike most of Ransom's poetry in that it lacks the customary qualifying of the speaker's position." In this poem, Rubin says, "the poet, having come upon his identity, proceeds to proclaim its meaning."[2]

With the poem's virtually unqualified assertion of identity in mind, we might at this point consider the speaker of the poem (and in this case the poet as well) in light of a theory proposed by Allen Tate in his essay "A Southern Mode of the Imagination." In the essay Tate discusses the forces behind and some of the implications of "the shift from the rhetorical mode to the dialectical mode" which was "redis-covered" (having been first discovered in terms of southern literature by Mark Twain) by twentieth-century writers of the South.[3] The de-scription of "the old Southern *rhetor*, the speaker who was eloquent before the audience but silent in himself," seems relevant to the speaker in "Antique Harvesters," who states his case with a carefully de-signed colloquial eloquence, answering his own questions with a self-assurance that does not admit to a "quarrel with himself," to use Tate's terms. If the speaker has questioned his own position, he gives no evidence of it in the poem. The harvesters have assembled to gather a harvest for their lady and to instruct their posterity in the rites of their profession; they are not there to argue with "scornful behold-ers," whom they acknowledge only to dismiss.

The harvesters are masters of the rhetorical mode which, Tate says, "presupposes somebody at the other end silently listening." In this case "sons of the fathers" listen silently to a recitation of the timeless value of their tradition spoken by their elders who, like the hunters of the scene, are themselves "keepers of a rite." Thus the pastoral and the rhetorical merge as method and concern in "Antique Harvesters"; along with the formal art of persuasion, the harvester-speakers prac-tice the art of balancing and resolving opposing standards in a way that affirms the simpler, the more natural, the more traditional. Rob-ert Bone's definition of pastoral is helpful here:

2. Louis D. Rubin, Jr., *The Wary Fugitives: Four Poets and the South* (Baton Rouge, 1978), 284, 180–81.
3. Allen Tate, "A Southern Mode of the Imagination," in *Collected Essays* (Denver, 1959), 567.

Like paradox, it is essentially a means of reconciling opposites. . . . The harsh dichotomies of poor and powerful, provincial and metropolitan, simple and complex, innocent and sophisticated, natural and artificial, ideal and actual, timeless and historical, active and contemplative, are momentarily dissolved. The result is a gain in balance and proportion, and a greater complexity of moral vision.[4]

In "Antique Harvesters" the rhetorical mode is employed in a poetic ceremony celebrating this pastoral process of reconciling opposites to gain a particularly complex moral vision. Because the rhetorical mode is applied consistently, the sense of interior threat and tension, the specters of doubt and divided consciousness that seem so often to impel a writer toward a pastoral strategy, have been excised from the poem's mood. The oppositions evoked by the title between harvest or "fruition" and age or "declension" are resolved or, to use Robert Bone's term, "dissolved," with the promotion of the religious image of the Proud Lady who has "aged" but does not "stoop" and with the assertion that the harvesters themselves are "nothing" in the frail duration of time; the "bronze treasure" of ritual and reverence that they "garner for the Lady" constitutes the only valuable object.

The matter of the relation of the rhetorical mode to overall pastoral design in this poem at this particular moment in the history of southern literature is of special significance. Tate theorizes that the important creative major literature that came to constitute the works of a southern renascence was the result of a shift during the 1920s from a rhetorical to a dialectical mode, a shift which demanded the injection of the "perception of the ironic 'other possible case.'"[5] In art that employs the dialectical mode, says Tate, "the action is generated inside the character: there is interior dialogue, a conflict within the self." In one sense "Antique Harvesters" constitutes the assertion of faith that needs to precede the conflict within the self that has engaged the attention of so many modern writers of the South, the conflict which concerns the individual's changing, struggling relation to the traditional rural society of the past as represented by some vision of life in the South.

4. Bone, *Down Home*, 133.
5. Tate, "A Southern Mode of the Imagination," 567–68.

Thomas Nelson Page constructed out of rhetoric a "pleasant dream" of the Old South which, says Tate, had more to be said for it than Henry Grady's New South "nightmare"; yet neither rhetorically posed dream "could lead to the conception of the complete society." Not until the South, reentering the world after the First World War, "looked round and saw for the first time since about 1830 that the Yankees were not to blame for everything" could the "Southern dramatic dialectic of our time begin."[6] It is not surprising that a black writer, Jean Toomer, would offer the first dramatic example for modern southern literature of how an essentially pastoral vision of the South might lend itself to dialectics. Within the rural sensibility that informs the southern scenes of *Cane*, Toomer incorporates his own and his race's often violent vacillation between acceptance and alienation. The poetry of the Fugitive group, as well, usually operates through a dialectically based perception of the "ironic 'other possible case,'" which is why Ransom's "Antique Harvesters" is significant to study as an exception or at least a variation from an important trend.

"Antique Harvesters," as Rubin demonstrates, is a poem which "signifies Ransom's arrival at a point in his career at which he had pretty much decided where he stood in the cosmos."[7] It is, then, a poem which elaborates the consequences of decision instead of the dynamics of making that decision; in Rubin's words, "It is as if the modern poet has discovered a strategy whereby it becomes possible to recapture the fervor, faith, and moral ordering of the old-time religious outlook, through a renewed concern with the South and its tradition." The discovery of this strategy was to have important ramifications beyond the poem itself, for in "Antique Harvesters," as Rubin notes, "we have the prescription for *I'll Take My Stand*."[8]

I'll Take My Stand was a book which defined, primarily in rhetorical terms, several mythic visions of southern tradition which, taken together, form a pastoral ideal of what life should be, but is not, in the modern world. Whereas a poem like "Antique Harvesters" firmly establishes the characteristics of such an ideal, the essays of *I'll Take My Stand*, with the same purpose in mind, are somewhat less useful in providing solid images of the good life than they are in identify-

6. *Ibid.*, 566, 568.
7. Rubin, *The Wary Fugitives*, 284.
8. *Ibid.*, 41, 42.

ing and assailing the threats to that life contained in the policies of industrialism and progress being endorsed on the American scene at large. What stands out in the essays is not so much the sense of ceremony or the contentment that comes with strong belief but instead a reaction of dismay and rebellion against the dehumanizing tendencies of modern life. It is a feeling that would certainly seem better served by the forceful persuasion of a rhetorical stance than by the questioning spirit of a dialectical one.

In the work of the writers who have come to be known as the "Fugitive-Agrarians" we can witness not so much a shift as an alternation between rhetoric and dialectic within one southern group who, as Tate explained it, were learning that they could not blame only the Yankees for the condition of their region and their own ambivalence toward it. *I'll Take My Stand* represented in a way a rallying point or a "statement of principles," which indeed its introduction was titled. In other works—poetry, novels, essays on aesthetics and religion and history—they would give magnificent expression to what Tate cites as the "Southern legend . . . of defeat and heroic frustration," but in 1930, the need, as they saw it, was to persuade their own generation of southerners and Americans "to look very critically at the advantages of becoming a 'new South' which will be only an undistinguished replica of the usual industrial community."[9] A quarrel was beginning in *I'll Take My Stand* which, though directed there largely against enemies seen as being for the moment outsiders to the southern garden, would in its ultimate assessments bring many questions to bear on the garden itself. In time the engagement in agrarianism as a pastoral rebuke to America's progressivist, industrial tendencies would lead to works by southern writers, among them Tate himself, William Faulkner, and Eudora Welty, which would shape what Tate called "the Southern dramatic dialectic of our time" into an enduring "universal myth of the human condition."[10]

I

The story of the Fugitives' turn to agrarianism during the 1920s is one not unlike that of Toomer's turn, or return in art, to the Negro

9. "Statement of Principles," Twelve Southerners, *I'll Take My Stand: The South and the Agrarian Tradition* (New York, 1930), xx–xxi.
10. Tate, "A Southern Mode of the Imagination," 568.

"peasant" South during the early years of the same decade. It is a story heavy with pastoral implications covering the rejection of the modes of modern, industrialized America and the discovery of value and identity in a past which, if far from perfect in actuality, still embodied in its relation to the present a force by which one could measure the diminishment of humane standards in modern times. Ransom and the other poets who began publishing their magazine in Nashville after World War I belonged to the changed world. The situation that pertained has been explained by Ransom's fellow Fugitive Robert Penn Warren in a *Paris Review* interview:

> After 1918 the modern industrial world, with its good and bad, hit the South; all sorts of ferments began. As for individual writers, almost all of them of that period had some important experience outside the South, then returned there—some strange mixture of continuity and discontinuity in their experience—a jagged quality.

Yet Warren also stated, in the same interview, "It never crossed my mind when I began writing fiction that I could write about anything except life in the South. . . . Nothing else ever nagged you enough to stir the imagination."[11] And as the 1920s wore on, the imaginations of several of the Fugitive poets, particularly Ransom, Warren, Tate, and Donald Davidson, were increasingly nagged and stirred in the direction of seeing the South as an embattled ideal composed of memories and attitudes of a way of life very different from the present one, a way of life in a simpler, rural world that all of them had been brought up to respect.

We might say, using Warren's terms, that in the last years of the tumultuous twenties these members of the Fugitive group were seeking to stress the traditional values of their early experiences in the South by the means of some strategy that could serve as a corrective for the "jagged quality" that life had taken on. The writers who turned to agrarianism had grown away from their region, and in reestablishing their connection to a rural, regional identity, they seem to have hoped to recover, first and foremost, the sense of continuity that life in the real world, both southern and American, lacked. They looked,

11. Malcolm Cowley (ed.), "Robert Penn Warren" in *Writers at Work: The "Paris Review" Interviews* (New York, 1959), 193.

as John Crowe Ransom explains, back to "a certain terrain, a certain history, a certain inherited way of living" that might serve as a formal "reproach" that a nation enamored of the fruits of industrialism might be made to "reckon with" (ITMS, 1). In the ultimate design that its twelve essays developed, the book *I'll Take My Stand* represents a programmatic use of the South as pastoral image to provide the terrain, the history, the inherited way of living by which the modern industrial world might successfully be reproached.

In a July, 1929, letter to Allen Tate, who was studying in France on a Guggenheim fellowship, Davidson outlined a plan for a symposium on the South and its relation to the rest of the country that he and Ransom had tentatively discussed. The "project" would take the form of "a collection of views on the South. . . . It would deal with phases of the situation such as the Southern tradition, politics, religion, art, etc., but always with a strong bias toward the self-determinative principle. It would be written by native Southerners of our mind—a small, coherent, highly selected group, and would be intended to come upon the scene with as much vigor as is possible—would even, maybe, call for *action* as well as ideas." [12] Tate replied enthusiastically and eventually supplied a list of suggestions for contributors and subjects as well as a sense of urgency; [13] the project went forward rapidly and the twelve essays, with an anonymous "Statement of Principles" (actually written by Ransom and approved by the others) placed at the beginning as an introduction, were published late in 1930 as *I'll Take My Stand: The South and the Agrarian Tradition*.

In addition to Ransom, Davidson, Tate, and Warren, there were, as contributors, "kindred spirits who," in Davidson's words, "shared our deep concern about the future of the South, in the field of affairs no less than in arts, ideas, and literature." [14] Andrew Nelson Lytle, Frank Lawrence Owsley, John Donald Wade, Lyle H. Lanier, Herman Clarence Nixon, and Henry Blue Kline were all either students

12. Donald Davidson to Allen Tate, July 29, 1929, in *The Literary Correspondence of Donald Davidson and Allen Tate,* ed. John Tyree Fain and Thomas Daniel Young (Athens, Ga., 1974), 227.

13. Allen Tate to Donald Davidson, August 10, 1929, *Literary Correspondence,* ed. Fain and Young, 232.

14. Donald Davidson, *Southern Writers in the Modern World* (Athens, Ga., 1957), 52.

or professors at Vanderbilt University; Stark Young was a Mississippian, a distinguished man of letters and well known in the area of drama and criticism of the theater, and John Gould Fletcher from Arkansas was primarily a poet, a friend of the Fugitives, particularly Tate and Warren. As their collection of essays was put together, there was a last-minute argument over the title. Tate and Warren objected to "I'll Take My Stand" on the grounds that it would stir up prejudices and make an "emotional appeal." "It makes my ears burn," wrote Tate.[15] But Ransom and Davidson prevailed; for them the excerpt from the song "Dixie," when coupled with the theme of "the agrarian tradition," combined the necessary sense of the local with the universal ideals involved. Ransom and Davidson wrote to the dissenters that for them the title meant "a statement of convictions by Southerners; take them or leave them; specifically we unite Southernism with agrarianism, on grounds both historical and philosophical."[16]

II

"Take it or leave it" is a rhetorical demand which aptly indicates the "angry as wasp music" mood of the southerners who published *I'll Take My Stand* as the first step in what was intended to be, but never actually became, a broad agrarian offensive. Ransom's lead-off essay, "Reconstructed but Unregenerate," seems in a way to have picked up the thread launched in "Antique Harvesters," to have worked out by a systematic rhetoric the challenge to "live and die in Dixie" that the poem defines through its eloquent sense of ceremony. As Ransom describes in his essay's first paragraph the "unreconstructed Southerner, who persists in his regard for a certain terrain, a certain history, and a certain inherited way of living," he seems to have had in mind the same figure that he developed as a speaker in "Antique Harvesters." The important difference is that in the essay this "backward looking" southerner was introduced from the outside according to how he would appear to those moderns whose lifestyle he contradicted just by his presence: he was "an anachronism," a "harmless reproach," regarded "like some quaint local character of eccentric

15. Allen Tate to the Contributors to the Southern Symposium, July 24, 1930, *Literary Correspondence*, ed. Fain and Young, 406.
16. Donald Davidson and John Ransom to Allen Tate, Robert Penn Warren, and Andrew Lytle, September 5, 1930, *Literary Correspondence*, ed. Fain and Young, 407.

but fixed principles who is thoroughly and almost pridefully accepted by the village as a rare exhibit of the antique kind." It is as
though Ransom was, at the start of his essay, exploring the implications of the discovery he chronicled in his poem, examining the consequences of making a commitment by faith to a traditional religious
ordering of life according to rural and southern patterns.

His first task, Ransom said, was to describe the backward-looking
southerner, this "rare exhibit of the antique kind," in "the position he
seems now to occupy actually before the public." The "other possible
case," to use Tate's term for what exists in the dialectical mode, did
not have its view represented in like manner in "Antique Harvesters," except insofar as the harvesters indicate that there are certain
"degenerate specters" who say that "easily will your hands / More
prosper in other lands." In "Reconstructed but Unregenerate" the
skeptical public's view was posited, but only because Ransom wanted
to go on record as acknowledging that the southerner's "antique
conservatism does not exert a great influence against the American
progressivist doctrine" (ITMS, 3). The lesson of the antique harvesters had been directed to their sons, to those who were nurtured in the
value of a backward-looking heritage. The audience to whom Ransom's essay was directed was obviously quite different, and Ransom's
willingness to admit that his southerner's devotion was "to a lost cause"
allowed him to take some of the enemy's ammunition at the outset.

Ransom began "Reconstructed but Unregenerate" with the image
of the kind of "keeper of a rite" whose presence symbolizes the religious value of the rural, southern tradition in "Antique Harvesters,"
yet in the essay this was just the starting point for an exploration of
the basic principles underlying his agrarian preferences. The principles were advanced by a method which, as in the poem, worked
through a number of pastoral oppositions. Ransom set up clusters of
associations around certain concepts that would not ordinarily spark
either positive or negative responses, yet as he developed them through
carefully balanced emotional suggestions they stimulate judgments
of two opposing philosophies of life. And while it might look like a
dialectical system of give and take was being established, this was
hardly the case. What Ransom did in this keynote essay of *I'll Take
My Stand* was to establish without question the philosophical grounds
upon which a mechanized, commercialized urban society must be

rejected in favor of the southern-styled rural community experience. Using the rhetorical mode, Ransom set out to engage our loyalty for a metaphor of a way of life whose practitioners must celebrate the status accorded by their fellows of being "rare exhibits of the antique kind."

Ransom established his premises through a series of concisely framed definitions which carry an overtone of logic without damaging the element of poetical association that attracts the reader to his descriptions on a far less rational level. Of particular significance as an example of his adroitness is his definition of the farmer, which uses, Ransom admitted, "some terms which are hardly in his [the farmer's] vernacular":

> He identifies himself with a spot of ground, and this ground carries a good deal of meaning; it defines itself for him as nature. He would till it not too hurriedly and not too mechanically to observe in it the contingency and the infinitude of nature, and so his life acquires its philosophical and even its cosmic consciousness. (ITMS, 20)

This is not poetry, certainly, but it comes very close to the poetical sense of the fifth stanza of "Antique Harvesters":

> Resume, harvesters. The treasure is full bronze
> Which you will garner for the Lady, and the moon
> Could tinge it no yellower than does this noon;
> But grey will quench it shortly—the field, men, stones.
> Pluck fast, dreamers; prove as you amble slowly
> Not less than men, not wholly.

In the essay not less than in the poem, it is the metaphor, not the literal image, that matters more; the poem's harvester and the essay's farmer stand for a philosophical orientation that is imaged by but in no way restricted by their vocation: a feeling for the "infinitude of nature"; the identification of meaning with concrete experience, "a spot of ground"; an insistence on leisure, tilling "not too hurriedly," plucking fast but ambling slowly, as the basis for knowing life well and fully.

At one point Ransom proposed a pair of definitions that again indicate by their associations the nature of the life he was endorsing. The definitions were similarly constructed yet their parallelism only serves to make their differences in meaning all the more apparent. "It is the character of the seasoned provincial life that it is realistic, or successfully adapted to its natural environment, and that as a consequence it is stable, or hereditable" (ITMS, 5). Ransom balanced the definition of provincial life with its opposite: "But it is the character of our urbanized, anti-provincial, progressive, and mobile American life that it is in a condition of eternal flux." The clusters of associations that surround each definition develop into a definitive judgment when examined together. Provincial life is characterized by such terms as "seasoned," "realistic," "successfully adapted," "natural," "stable," and "hereditable." The evaluative word "successfully," injected quietly enough into the construction, has an intriguing effect. We are led to associate our concept of what is realistic with what is here pronounced natural, stable, and hereditable. In the next definition, which has a parallel construction, the words *American, mobile*, and *progressive*, when lumped together with *urbanized, anti-provincial*, and *flux*, carry definitely negative associations that were calculated to cause a rejection. The sentences which follow these two equations provide a kind of "clincher": "Affections, and long memories, attach to the ancient bowers of life in the provinces; but they will not attach to what is changing. Americans, however, are peculiar in being somewhat averse to these affections for natural objects, and to these memories" (ITMS, 5–6). Without ever having to expose himself by frontal assault, Ransom could assert through the mere shape of this rhetoric that (1) the provincial life was realistic and natural, that (2) what is stable and hereditable is successful, that (3) the antiprovincial life (which just by its prefix is charged with negativism) was in a state of flux connoting a confusion that projected into the very condition of being urbanized, progressive, and mobile. Ransom's rhetorical strategy ended by making it seem, purely by association, that what was "American" or "progressive" was also unsuccessful, unnatural, "peculiar," and damaging to one's affections and memories.

Throughout his essay Ransom associated nature, and through it the condition of being natural, with the agrarian experience. His contention was that progress, the gospel of the urbanized, industrial society, was at war with nature, was therefore *un*natural, and therefore doomed eventually to fail. The clusters of associations surrounding the two opposing attitudes toward nature that we see developed in the following passage leave a clear impression of which course has the power to endure:

Nature wears out man before man can wear out nature; only a city man, a laboratory man, a man cloistered from the normal contacts with the soil, will deny that. It seems wiser to be moderate in our expectations of nature, and respectful; and out of so simple a thing as respect for the physical earth and its teeming life comes a primary joy, which is an inexhaustible source of arts and religions and philosophies. (ITMS, 9)

Ransom's definition of progress portrayed it as a policy by which man, as he gained ascendancy over nature, destroyed himself: it was "a concept of man's increasing command . . . over the forces of nature; a concept which enhances too readily our conceit, and brutalizes our life" (ITMS, 10). The definition which Ransom shaped for industrialism was even sterner in its implications, using a logical outer "vehicle" in combination with a very emotional inner "tenor": "Industrialism is a program under which men, using the latest scientific paraphernalia, sacrifice comfort, leisure, and the enjoyment of life to win Pyrrhic victories from nature at points of no strategic importance" (ITMS, 15).

At the same time that Ransom was working through a series of definitions which contrasted the southern, agrarian way with the American, progressive way, he was also tracing the South's historical relation to the Union in terms of an ideological struggle between a region "committed to a form of leisure" and a nation committed to "a principle of boundless aggression against Nature" (ITMS, 14, 17). The South was associated at every period of its history with two elements that seem hardly compatible, much less contingent—farming and passivity. However, as Ransom saw it, the Old South "pioneered her way to a sufficiently comfortable and rural sort of establishment, considered that an establishment was something stable, and proceeded to enjoy the fruits thereof" (ITMS, 12). The defeated South "did not repair the damage to her old establishment" but instead tried "to live the good life on shabby equipment." In the twentieth century, one might see "great numbers of these broken-down Southerners . . . in patched blue-jeans, sitting on ancestral fences, shotguns across their legs and hound-dogs at their feet, surveying their un-kempt acres while they comment shrewdly on the ways of God." This was, as Ransom himself admitted, a "grotesque" and rather "piti-able" image, but even so not one without its redeeming graces. We are not so far from the antique harvesters as we might think, for Ransom felt that the defect of these "broken-down" southerners was only that their "aestheticism" was based "on insufficient labor." There was, at least potentially, "something heroic, and there may prove to be yet something very valuable to the Union, in their attachment to a certain theory of life." Like the antique harvesters the southerners portrayed here "have kept up a faith which was on the point of per-ishing from this continent" (ITMS, 16).

There was an important rhetorical purpose for Ransom's fusion of the rural with the passive or "leisurely" elements that he noted on the southern scene. As he defined it, progress, the gospel of the modern industrial state, was the policy of boundless aggression against na-ture; the gospel of "the farmer who is not a mere laborer" (*i.e.*, the agrarian) had to be defined through associations which opposed this aggression in order to offset it through the particular rhetorical style that Ransom had chosen for the essay. Leisure became almost the essential ingredient of Ransom's agrarian construct, as aggression and frantic mobility were the essentials of the industrial progressive so-ciety to which it was opposed. Ransom shaped for his ideal the im-age of a lifestyle which by its very definition could not be aggressive, and in doing so he paved the way for the consideration of solutions which themselves would have to rest in the contemplative or aes-thetic realm rather than in spheres of definite, or militant, action. Thus the crisis before the South in the twentieth century was presented through a form of pastoral threat, in these terms: Americans at large intended to become "infinitely progressive," an intention which "cannot permit of an established order of human existence, and of that leisure which conditions the life of intelligence and the arts" (ITMS, 21).

Ransom's strategy of balancing and dramatizing, through the shape of his language, the elements of clash between the American and the agrarian way was useful at the end of his essay as he opposed, again through parallels and equations, the crucial question involved in his cause. As with the questions in "Antique Harvesters," the question here is rhetorical, the answer existing in the very manner and language in which it was framed:

> The question at issue is whether the South will permit herself to be so industrialized as to lose entirely her historic identity, and to remove the last substantial barrier that has stood in the way of American progressivism; or will accept industrialism, but with a very bad grace, and will manage to maintain a good deal of her traditional philosophy. (ITMS, 22)

The South's way had, in Ransom's historical interpretation at least, always been one of acceptance, and in this passage one is met with the contingency that the South *must* accept industrialism. Only after this positive half of the statement has been digested does the all-important negative qualification, that the South must accept industrialism "with a very bad grace," enter the picture. The statement makes it clear that what matters is not the defeat or rejection of industrialism itself but the preservation and maintenance of the South's "traditional philosophy." What triumphs throughout the essay is not any literal agrarian program or even any particular image of the good life, as we have in "Antique Harvesters"; what triumphs is the value of the humane principle itself, the philosophical, actively religious ordering of existence around a stable, natural, leisurely, hereditable, and in other words, for Ransom, a southern tradition. The premise that Ransom established more firmly than anything else was the absolute necessity of taking matters of mind and heart seriously; his definitions of progress and industrialism indicated that these modes would not serve the human situation because the only matters they could seriously consider were those of the material and the mechanical. And Ransom conceived for this premise a successful rhetorical language that worked not so much through eloquence or passion as through a delicate balance of the emotional nuances with which he surrounded the opposed systems that were involved in his argument.

III

Other essays in *I'll Take My Stand* employed a great variety of rhetorical strategies as they made their agrarian and humanistic assertions. In relation to Ransom's essay, Andrew Nelson Lytle's "The Hind Tit" was more piquant and picturesque, if more flamboyant, as it portrayed an ideal southern yeomanry at work and play; Donald Davidson's "A Mirror for Artists" stressed in more elemental terms the nature of the aesthetic life, achieving a broader emotional range and perhaps a more dramatic accounting of what happens to the artist in a society controlled by an industrial norm; Allen Tate's "Remarks on the Southern Religion" launched a far more incisive investigation into the religious grounding necessary to sustain one's faith in a richly concrete, yet spiritual experience of life. Tate brought an inherently skeptical spirit to bear on the issue of how fully or how well the Old South might adequately be made to symbolize a valid religious ideal with which to confront and rebuke the ways of a modern technological society. Stark Young's "Not in Memoriam, But in Defense" made a fitting conclusion to the book with the tone of courtly indignation and carefully controlled aristocratic earnestness which it brought to the discussion of southern manners and customs.

Ransom's unique achievement in his *I'll Take My Stand* essay was, as with so much of his poetry, the eminently appropriate matching of style to mood and thought. The essay was written to define a conflict, and its language and structural mode were designed to capture the tension of that conflict; words explode against one another, and Ransom's ideal prevailed in part because of the resiliency of the language associated with it. In terms of rhetorical effect, the only other essay of *I'll Take My Stand* that is as engaging in its management of style is John Donald Wade's "The Life and Death of Cousin Lucius," which readily impresses any reader with its control of tone. "Cousin Lucius" was a part-fictional biography of an actual agrarian relative of Wade's who found his ideals challenged from within and without by the lust of modern men for the material products of a technological system. What he became was a full-bodied extension of Ransom's conception of the "antique harvester," a laborer by faith in a garden of the mind who enshrined more than anything else a simple, humanely ordered approach to dealings with his fellow man. The tone that Wade employed was what carried an essay whose theme might easily have tended toward the maudlin or the melodramatic. The account was told in a third-person perspective, but the mind and feelings of Lucius were directly rendered without elaboration; the style is notable for the same qualities we come to associate with Lucius— a directness and simplicity, a gentleness that was never querulous or fawning, a dignity that was never remote or patronizing. The possession of these qualities made Cousin Lucius one of agrarianism's most memorable champions, even though he was never shown taking the offensive against the forces that threatened everything he valued.

Like Ransom's "unregenerate Southerner," Cousin Lucius knew himself to be an anachronism, "an old fogy" as he heard himself called. Yet hearing it, Lucius responded as a man of Ransom's passive, or accepting, South must: "He did not know whether to go out and defend himself, or to hold his peace, and later, when appropriate, to clarify his position as best he could for a race that had become so marvelously aggressive" (ITMS, 291). When even his own children deserted the farm and headed for the prosperous lights of the city, Lucius' response became a metaphor for the activity of mind that engaged many southern writers during these years:

He went about fortifying himself by his knowledge of history and ancient fable, telling himself that man had immemorially drawn his best strength from the earth that mothered him. . . . "But what have history and ancient fable," the fiend whispered, "to do with the present?" Cousin Lucius admitted that they apparently had little to do with it, but he believed they *must* have something to do with it if it were not to go amuck past all remedy. (ITMS, 282)

Cousin Lucius, in his own life, found a way to make history and fable have "something to do" with the present. The example of his father, his college training in the classics, and his own "instinct for the mastery of the land" made it impossible for him to follow his friends and neighbors as they abandoned their farms and villages, heading for the industrial fruits of the cities. He became, within his community, a teacher, a farmer, and a banker and thus succeeded as an agrarian—but Wade showed just as conclusively that his South was failing as a region capable of sustaining the agrarian vision. It is rather remarkable that Wade's was the only essay in *I'll Take My Stand* to dramatize agrarian principles in terms of the life history of an actual agrarian, yet it was also the essay which most dramatically acknowledged the hostility that the agrarian thesis was to meet with even in the South which fostered the rural tradition. Cousin Lucius was positive in his conviction that the industrial program was not suitable for the rural South, that it was "not suitable even for an industrial community if it was made up of human beings as he knew them." But he finally saw that the farmer seemed to have only three options—in the South as elsewhere: "He could run alongside [the industrialists' motorcar], or hang on behind the car, or sit beside the road and let the car go on whither it would" (ITMS, 294). Though he himself was a strong-minded enough individual to opt for the third alternative, Lucius did so with the result that he became an "old fogy" even within his own community.

As a farmer-philosopher mourning the fact that his friends and neighbors were moving to the city, Lucius would be at best a spokesman only for a policy of fatalistic acceptance. But Lucius did more than mourn, and so for the agrarian cause and for the modern southern writer he could symbolize a more positive function than that of being caretaker of a neglected garden. Lucius asserted that only certain universal human values are durable and therefore hereditable as he denied his neighbor's new faith that "happiness was to go faster and faster on less and less." Lucius "would not concede that we are no better than flaring rockets, and he would never get it into his old-fashioned head that anything less than a complete integrity will serve as a right basis for anything that is intended to mount high and to keep high" (ITMS, 292).

What the *I'll Take My Stand* essays as a whole condemned was not the technological system of American society per se, but the general weakening of faith in human dignity and worth that seemed to accompany a whole society's increasing attachment to purely material proofs of value. A man who lived close to the land and who kept his knowledge of his past in active perspective could know himself for what he was and would be equipped to assess properly both limitations and strengths. Cut off from an understanding of nature or an awareness of the past—as modern man in an urban, technological environment was seen to be—a human being could only ask questions for which there were no answers.

IV

Allen Tate's *I'll Take My Stand* essay, "Remarks on the Southern Religion," is concerned with this matter of modern man and his unanswerable questions, as are his most famous poem, "Ode to the Confederate Dead," and his mysterious novel, *The Fathers*. Both the poem and the novel were written during the period of Tate's deepest involvement in the agrarian movement, and both are important instances of Tate's point in "A Southern Mode of the Imagination" concerning the shift "from melodramatic rhetoric to the dialectic of tragedy." Both the poem and the novel, moreover, illustrate the point that Tate borrowed from Yeats to close that essay: "Out of the quarrel with others we make rhetoric; out of the quarrel with ourselves poetry."

During the late 1920s and the 1930s Allen Tate was one of the most firmly committed of the Agrarians, yet it is interesting that his *I'll Take My Stand* essay came closer than the others to laying a large share of the blame for the South's dilemma in the modern world on conditions inherent in the region itself in antebellum times. The problem that Tate identified in the essay was that the old southerners, die-hard agrarians though they were, lived a rational life that "was not powerfully united to the religious experience," the result being that "when the post-bellum temptations of the devil, who is the exploiter of nature, confronted them, they had no defense." Tate suggested the imaginative possibility that "the South would not have been defeated had it possessed a sufficient faith in its own kind of God" (ITMS, 173, 174). The kind of faith that Ransom projected into his poetical figure of the antique harvester was not an actual attribute of the old civilization, at least not as Tate interpreted it.

Thus Tate demonstrated in "Remarks on the Southern Religion" the exact condition which he would later cite as being responsible for the change in southern literature from rhetoric to dialectic; he looked in that essay to the southerner himself as a cause for the modern South's failure to sustain a humane principle. Tate's final remark on southern religion implied a question that itself implied that there might very well be no satisfactory answers: the southerner, Tate had said earlier, must take hold of his tradition "by violence" (ITMS, 174). Yet the essay's last sentence raised serious doubts and fed no simple hopes: "I say that he must do this," said Tate, "but that remains to be seen." The quarrel within the self was surely intimated in this very much less than optimistic conclusion.

The quarrel within the self had actually been going on in Tate and the Fugitive-Agrarians, as well as in other southern writers such as Jean Toomer, Thomas Wolfe, and William Faulkner, for a good while before *I'll Take My Stand* was formulated as one kind of resolution to the problems inherent in taking hold of one's tradition and the identity inextricably bound to it. "Ode to the Confederate Dead," first published three years before *I'll Take My Stand*, was Tate's poetic dramatization of the extreme difficulty that the modern southerner would encounter as he made that attempt to take hold of his tradition. In his essay on the poem, "Narcissus as Narcissus," which was written in 1938, Tate said that the poem's structure was "the objective frame for the tension between two themes, 'active faith' which has decayed, and the 'fragmentary cosmos' which surrounds us."[17] The poem used the ordering of a kind of pastoral ode in order to confront man's loss of connection with a grandly heroic, simpler past. Tate wrote of the poem's protagonist, a modern descendant of chivalrous southern forbears, that "in contemplating the heroic theme, the man at the gate never quite commits himself to the illusion of its availability to him." With the loss of the "illusion" that one's past, one's heritage, is available to him, through art if not through more literal access, comes the stimulus for dialectic. No longer are the most important questions generated from a well-defined enemy whose arguments one has already dismissed, but now the questions come from within: "What shall we say who have knowledge / Carried to the heart?" and the only answer can be only another question, and then another: "Shall we take the act / To the grave? Shall we, more hopeful, set up the grave / In the house? The ravenous grave?"

Tate's novel *The Fathers*, published in the same year that he wrote his essay "Narcissus as Narcissus," is very much caught up in the same artistic as well as ideological dilemma that the poem presents: how to take hold of one's tradition, how to evaluate it justly when one's own identity is indicted along with every criticism that is made of the tradition itself. In *The Fathers*, to use distinctions which Tate makes in "Narcissus as Narcissus," the "active faith that has decayed" is easily recognizable in Major Buchan, who is the father of Lacy Buchan, narrator of the novel. The "fragmentary cosmos of today" is aptly represented by Lacy's brother-in-law, the "admirable" George Posey, who is another father figure (he almost always calls Lacy "Son," or "my boy"). George Posey and Major Buchan are "the fathers"; they

17. Allen Tate, "Narcissus as Narcissus, in *Collected Essays*, 254.

represent two diametrically opposite possibilities for inheritance, two completely different orientations for Lacy to choose between concerning what life is and how it should be measured. The opposed standards involved in the agrarian reaction to modern industrial existence are embodied in the two men and also in the environments they inhabit by nature. Major Buchan belongs to Pleasant Hill, a country "place" where farming is practiced in a way that makes a relative exclaim, "A Buchan understand business? You are all gentlemen."[18] George Posey's family has long since moved to the urban environment of Georgetown, on the northern side of the river, and George himself crosses the bridge between North and South many times as an arms dealer during the war, during which time his loyalties are somewhat suspect, as the South's in modern times have become for the Agrarians.

George Posey exhibits in every move the trait that Tate talked about in "Narcissus as Narcissus," a "preoccupation with self" reflecting "the remarkable self-consciousness of our age."[19] Lacy Buchan himself exhibits, as a narrator, some of this preoccupation with self. For his narrative this means that ambiguity will reign; the facts themselves will become subordinate to Lacy's self-interested concern for what they reveal about his own state of mind as a boy, when the events he tells were taking place, as well as now, as he is telling the story: "In my feelings of that time there is a new element—my feelings now about that time" (TF, 22). In terms of the novel's overall thematic direction, Lacy's self-consciousness as narrator shows he has inherited much from George Posey, more probably than from his actual father, whose traits are altogether of a different and, one might assume, a better order.

Yet Major Buchan's order is not necessarily better, as it is developed; he has designed himself to be a kind of "keeper of a rite," the upholder of a once "active faith," but that faith has quite dramatically decayed. Faith has degenerated into mere formality. If George Posey is responsible for providing a model of solipsistic behavior for Lacy to follow (as Lacy dreams often of following George over a precipice), then Major Buchan is responsible for projecting an alternative that lacks a deeply felt religious base to make it work. The judgment

18. Allen Tate, *The Fathers* (Rev. ed.; Baton Rouge, 1977).
19. Tate, "Narcissus as Narcissus," 251.

of southern religion that Tate made in *I'll Take My Stand* is the one that he makes of Major Buchan. In the essay Tate said of the old southerner, "He cannot fall back upon his religion, simply because it was never articulated and organized for him" (ITMS, 175). It is the same for Major Buchan when George Posey breaks all the rules of propriety in his dealings with him. In every meeting between the two the major is incapable of asserting his position. Lacy is always on hand at these skirmishes, which are described as tactical maneuvers in very much the same mode that the battle scenes of the Civil War are depicted later: "Papa had run into a panther, and he had fired a charge that had hitherto been good enough for his game; but the game had been rabbits" (TF, 36).

Writing about the novel in a letter to the *Partisan Review*, Tate said that he did not understand a reading by Lionel Trilling which interpreted his story as "an indictment of the Old South; I think it may as easily be seen as a justification of it, quite apart from the style."[20] In *The Fathers*, the Old South cannot be said to be indicted as a culture whose value system was wrong, but it is indicted as one which made its very fine apprehension of life unavailable by retreating into formalities instead of lining up a strong moral reaction when threats from an alien world appeared. Lacy explains:

Our lives were eternally balanced upon a pedestal below which lay an abyss that I could not name. Within that invisible tension my father knew the moves of an intricate game that he expected everybody else to play. That, I think, was because everything he was and felt was in the game itself; he had no life apart from it and he was baffled, as he had been baffled by George Posey, by the threat of some untamed force that did not recognize the rules of his game. (TF, 44)

What the Old South had to offer, what Major Buchan might have offered to Lacy, was a heritage of conduct that was designed to allow people to be fully "human beings living by a humane principle," as Tate put it in *I'll Take My Stand*, and the major's failure is not one of principle but one of will.

The other alternative, George's way, is to live in active horror of what

20. Allen Tate, Letter to the Editors, *Partisan Review*, VI (Winter, 1939), 125.

being human means. George is horrified by death, seeing no formal process in it but only the "ravenous grave" and the cadaver; he is terribly embarrassed to see animals going about their procreative business; he "was a man who received the shock of the world at the end of his nerves" (TF, 185). It would seem that Lacy comes to understand that the modern, traditionless, totally self-conscious life that George embodies could provide no acceptable model. He seems to reject it when, after George has killed Lacy's brother Semmes, Lacy returns to Pleasant Hill and takes great pleasure in the thought that his identity is bound up in a concrete place: "The house, the big sugar tree, the back gallery, papa's affectionate glance were all that I was; under the chestnut tree was all that I would be" (TF, 281). Yet the house is destroyed by Yankee soldiers, Lacy's father commits suicide, and Lacy's life is thus cut off from the past. His future is ambiguously handled; he narrates the story as an old man who has had a "competent" life as a bachelor-doctor living in George Posey's house in Georgetown. Yet he sees his life as a series of questions, and while he is concerned enough to ask them, he has no answers. He knows what has happened and usually how, but never why. Creating a frame for his story at the start, he asks a number of questions that grow out of one another as do the questions in "Ode to the Confederate Dead":

Is it not something to tell, when a score of people whom I knew and loved, people beyond whose lives I could imagine no other life, either out of violence in themselves or the times, or out of some misery or shame, scattered into the new life of the modern age where they cannot even find themselves? Why cannot life change without tangling the lives of innocent persons? Why do innocent persons cease their innocence and become violent and evil in themselves that such great changes may take place?

His only reply is to say, "These questions must go unanswered. I have a story to tell but I cannot explain the story" (TF, 5).

Yet at one very dramatic moment in the novel Lacy receives an explanation and an answer to the questions with which the story began, an answer that bears on all the other expressions of agrarian concern that we have considered. It relates back to John Donald Wade's Cousin Lucius, who when challenged by his children's defection to

the city, went about "fortifying himself by his knowledge of history
and ancient fable," as though these held the secret key to the present's
chaotic state of affairs. It relates as well to the image in "Antique
Harvesters" of the old men who bolster their vision by remarking on
the hunters, "archetypes of chivalry," who ride by their fields. In *The
Fathers*, Lacy, who admits that he was "never . . . able to say to myself that George Posey was not right about everything, even to the
point of rectitude" (TF, 132), is given a mode of perception that allows a clear judgment of George's way of life. It comes to him through
a vision of a conversation with his dead grandfather, who begins by
noting, "My son, in my day we were never alone, as your brother-in-
law is alone" (TF, 268). Here is another father figure for Lacy, projected at a critical time by his own need to have a hereditable dream.
His grandfather speaks through history and fable, making an analogy between George Posey and the mythical Jason, who could not
"master certain rituals." "It was Jason's misfortune," Lacy conceives
of his grandfather telling him, "to care only for the Golden Fleece and
the like impossible things, while at the same time getting himself involved with the humanity of others, which it was not his intention
but rather his very nature to betray." The judgment that one can make
of George is the judgment that Grandfather Buchan makes of Jason:
"He was a noble fellow in whom the patriarchal and familial loyalties
had become meaningless but his human nature necessarily limited him,
and he made an heroic effort to combine his love of the extraordinary and the inhuman with the ancient domestic virtues." Grandfather Buchan ends his analogy of Jason with a question that is, importantly, answered. "If the Fleece had been all-sufficing, would he
have taken Medea with him back to Greece? My son, I do not think
so" (TF, 269).

That the golden fleece is, quite absolutely, not all sufficing is the answer that the Agrarians advanced rhetorically in their essays in *I'll Take
My Stand* as they sought to reproach a world that had gone, to use
Lacy's evaluation of George, into "communion with the abyss" (TF,
185). It is an answer which is wrought, in *The Fathers*, through a
portrayal of father figures who come to symbolize opposed interior
longings that compose a dialectical quarrel with the self. There emerges

through Tate's handling of the "invisible tension" of Lacy Buchan's life a powerful statement on human nature that indicates the full possibilities of a "Southern dramatic dialectic" applied to the potentially pastoral question of how to inherit the past. And in the same tradition as Tate, William Faulkner, bringing a "dialectic of tragedy" to bear on the question, would convert regional legend into the southern literary renascence's fullest and most complex expression of the "necessary limitations of human nature." Tate once wrote that the "South reentered the world—but gave a backward glance as it stepped over the border."[21] The literary accomplishments of the Fugitive-Agrarians as well as Faulkner have endowed their backward glance with a vitality that has caused their visions to endure as expressions of the questioning spirit of man.

21. Allen Tate, "The New Provincialism," *Collected Essays*, 292

EIGHT

Faulkner's Sons of the Fathers:
How to Inherit the Past

In Allen Tate's *The Fathers*, the characters are taken from a home and heritage that had seemed immune to time and "scattered into the new life of the modern age where they cannot even find themselves" (TF, 5). The young protagonist who feels most keenly this disruption alternates between the examples of two father figures as he seeks to find himself. His actual father, like the past of which he is a part, has become too formal and too remote to touch him deeply: attractive in his idealism and innocence, still Major Buchan "could not allow anybody to be personal." Major Buchan cannot fathom or survive the present, and so Lacy follows George Posey into the modern age, not so much by conscious choice as in puzzled response to circumstance. George Posey is a man who typifies the present moment cut off from time. The South with its codes, its "elaborate rigamarole—his own forfeited heritage," can only tease him "like a nightmare in which the dreamer dreams a dream within a dream within another dream of something that he cannot name" (TF, 180). Lacy Buchan is too much an heir of his tradition not to be repelled by George's excessive, insensitive vitality, yet losing George as a model for dealing with the present throws him into a crisis of anguish that is temporarily resolved when he yields to the influence of the past, as it is projected not by his ineffectual father but by the vibrant image of his grandfather who appears in a kind of dream. What Lacy inherits from this dream of the past is the knowledge that there is a proper mode of

153

vision that does not lose its relevance by its association with times that are gone. Grandfather Buchan can teach Lacy through an old fable, he can explain the motivations of George Posey by explaining Jason and the golden fleece, so that what he explains most clearly is that a man's identity is not isolated in the present but is defined by its connections through time to all who have lived before. Grandfather Buchan asserts through the relevance of his vision the necessity of history as well as the unity and permanence of man's life in time.

In another story by another Fugitive-Agrarian, Robert Penn Warren's "Blackberry Winter," another young man turns between two father figures at the critical moment when he is on the verge of discovering the true nature of time. The world of his actual father was a quiet, changeless place where time, he thought, "is not a movement, a flowing, a wind then, but . . . rather, a kind of climate in which things are," a thing like a tree "which is alive and solid."[1] It was a world of childhood whose passing is symbolized in the story by the cold spell of weather in June and by a flooded river that people go down to the bridge to watch, since "it made something different from the run of days." And with the flood, into a boy's life which has been protected by a caring father and a stable home, comes a tramp, walking up the path "like a man who has come a long way and has a long way to go." The boy can discern "no place for him to have come from." Like George Posey of *The Fathers*, the tramp is a man without the identity that comes from place and people. He belongs to the sheer forward movement of time which, like a flood, pushes everything away from its established order. The boy's mother sets the tramp to work repairing the damage done by the flood, a job for which he is palpably unsuited, and when the father returns, the tramp is sent away. No great alteration has taken place in the boy's actual existence, yet the experience here recorded is the initiation into essential knowledge of life as change and disruption. The boy's father cannot permanently keep the tramp of time from the door, and it will be this out-of-place, "unmemorable" representative of the alien future whom the boy means when he says, at the end of the story, "That was what he said, for me not to follow him. But I did follow him, all the years."

1. Robert Penn Warren, "Blackberry Winter," in *The Circus in the Attic and Other Stories* (New York, 1947), 63–64.

In both of these works the image of the father is used to suggest the traditional mode of connection between the present and the past—through family, heredity, inheritance. Yet in both cases the father is somehow inaccessible or ineffectual; he has lost his relevance to the changing world that beckons insistently to the son. In "Blackberry Winter" time forces the inevitable break with the past; watching the tramp, the boy is forced into an awareness of his own very tenuous hold on his life in a certain place. He hears, as he sees the tramp coming from the river, a sound that "seems to measure out something, to put an end to something, to begin something, and you cannot wait for it to happen and are afraid it will not happen, and then when it has happened, you are waiting again, almost afraid." In *The Fathers* the situation is a cognate of the cultural condition of the South itself in the early twentieth century. The Civil War setting of the novel is symbolic of what for Tate was an even greater crisis for the South—the loss of its heritage in a modern nightmare society bent on barring all access to the past. In the novel Lacy Buchan comes to an understanding of the present through an imaginative projection of himself back into his inheritance, the past of his fathers, and thus he bridges the gap between two worlds.

In "Antique Harvesters" John Crowe Ransom had rebuked a modern age cut off from the past through a statement of faith in the durability of a southern garden dedicated to "Our Lady," a religious image suggesting man's traditional place in nature: "the sons of the fathers shall keep her worthy of / What these have done in love." In his essay in *I'll Take My Stand*, Tate had asked, "How may the Southerner take hold of his tradition?" In a modern world that had turned the past into "an elaborate rigamarole, a forfeited heritage," the only answer that Tate could endorse was, "By violence." *The Fathers* answers the question in a way that translates violence momentarily into an act of artistic vision. The work of William Faulkner dramatizes the same problem, often using a similar symbolic construction of inaccessible fathers and disinherited sons in a world where active faith in a traditional society has decayed, and often directing his characters to a similar answer—a violent, potentially self-destructive attempt to seize an inheritable dream of the past and make it relevant to the "fragmentary cosmos" that is life in the modern world.

I

Near his thirtieth birthday Faulkner found himself at work on two manuscripts simultaneously, both of them significantly different from his first two published novels, *Soldiers' Pay* and *Mosquitoes*. The two projects he began some time in 1926 seemed to indicate a new direction, though the themes were very different. One manuscript, tentatively titled "Father Abraham," dealt with the patriarch of the Snopes clan; the other chronicled the history of the Sartoris clan, whose first illustrious member resembled, in outline at least, Faulkner's own great-grandfather. By early 1927, as Joseph Blotner relates in his biography, Faulkner set aside the work on "Father Abraham" in favor of the other manuscript, tentatively titled "Flags in the Dust." And two years later, in a set of notes which may have been intended as a kind of introduction to this work but which was never published, Faulkner gave some clues as to why the Sartoris project had more relevance than the other at that time in his life. It had occurred to him, Blotner says, that he was losing his sense of "the simple bread-and-salt of the world"; the life of his youth, the traditions and values that had been easy to accept, were fading:

All that I really desired was a touchstone simply; a simple word or gesture, but having been these two years previously under the curse of words, having known twice before the agony of ink, nothing served but that I try by main strength to recreate between the covers of a book the world as I was already preparing to lose and regret, feeling, with the morbidity of the young, that I was not only on the verge of decrepitude, but that growing old was to be an experience peculiar to myself alone out of all the teeming world, and desiring, if not the capture of that world and the feeling of it as you'd preserve a kernel or a leaf to indicate the lost forest, at least to keep the evocative skeleton of the dessicated.[sic] leaf.[2]

Throughout this passage the infinitives that Faulkner uses to express his concern are especially revealing: *to recreate, to lose, to regret; to indicate the lost forest; to keep the evocative skeleton*. The purpose that Faulkner defined for his fiction is couched in the language of pas-

    2. Quoted in Joseph Blotner, *Faulkner: A Biography* (2 Vols.; New York, 1974), I, 531–32.

toral writing generally. The mode as it has operated from Virgil's time forward begins with an awareness of the imminent loss of an Arcadian condition; this emotional foreboding, usually combined with a sense of childhood passing, is followed by a determination to re-create the lost world by some form of imaginative escape from or indictment of the new condition; the artistic impulse culminates in the important perception that what can be captured in art is not the "living kernel" of the lost world but only the "evocative skeleton" of it as a "touchstone" with the past. Faulkner found a personal as well as an artistic challenge out of a pastoral urge to control the effects of time.

Flags in the Dust evidently satisfied Faulkner as a "touchstone." It was a mammoth work in which he shaped an "evocative skeleton" of the entire Yoknapatawpha country, and he felt that with it he would make his mark as a writer. Yet Horace Liveright, who had published his first two novels, rejected it immediately, partly because it ranged so widely over what was to become Faulkner's "postage stamp of native soil." Finally, after substantial cutting engineered by Faulkner's friend Ben Wasson, the novel was published by Harcourt, Brace in January, 1929, with a new title, Sartoris. Flags in the Dust was not to be published until 1973; neither work, as Cleanth Brooks says, "occupies a place among his great novels."[3] Flags in the Dust is undoubtedly the more important of the two in providing a key to the saga that developed out of it. Sartoris, however, centers more closely on the Sartoris clan itself, fathers and sons, and their dream of inheriting the grandeur of the past through actions that imitate the feats of the first great forebear. For this reason we focus on it as the clearer dramatization of Faulkner's mood of "loss and regret" about the world he wanted to re-create as he was beginning to work on his first Yoknapatawpha book.

Sartoris and several of the novels which followed it begin with a dream of the past which in the minds of the characters is associated with an inaccessible heritage or a threatened inheritance. The dream tends to establish itself in some fixed symbol of purity and simplicity that becomes distorted as romantic associations are built up around it. Four different versions of such dreams in Faulkner's fiction shed

3. Cleanth Brooks, Toward Yoknapatawpha and Beyond (New Haven, Conn., 1978), 391.

light on his attitude toward the southerner's particular relationship to his past. Each version involves one of the four leading baronial families of the Yoknapatawpha territory: the Sartorises, the Sutpens, the Compsons, and the McCaslins. In each some fixed element of an ancestral, family-related past acquires the status of symbol or myth and ends by controlling the responses a character is able to make to his world, both present and past.

In *Sartoris* it is the figure of Colonel John Sartoris who dominates the scene from the opening pages, not as man but as myth, as two old, deaf men sit in the banker's office shouting stories of the colonel's exploits into the empty air. In *Absalom, Absalom!* the vision of Sutpen's Hundred is conjured out of the "hot weary dead September afternoon" and with it the portrait of a man who sacrificed his sons to gain what he wanted. In *The Sound and the Fury* the controlling image, the focus of four different points of view, is that of a little girl's muddy drawers as she climbs into a pear tree to look in a window where her grandmother's funeral service is taking place. It is an image of childhood sullied, of virginity lost, of purity inevitably stained and corrupted, and for Quentin Compson, a symbol of an order, a whole way of life, betrayed. And in "The Bear," actually in *Go Down, Moses* as a whole, the image of the wilderness itself, constantly receding, haunts and motivates and yet almost always eludes the men who seek it.

The four novels use the father-son relationship to varying degrees to symbolize a loss of order; old Bayard and his nephews are dominated by his father's heroic exploits; Sutpen, in adopting the South's system of values, must deny his own and his sons' humanity in order to uphold a dead tradition; Quentin Compson has a model for despair in a father who, in his own disenchantment with the present, teaches him that the sweep of time negates the value of any action; Ike McCaslin has the courage to free himself from his grandfather's corrupted inheritance and to assert his claim to Sam Fathers' more natural one; yet he, like Faulkner's other sons, will have difficulty in finding a way to live actively in a present that does not conform to his dream of the past. In each work, these major characters involve themselves in a more or less futile attempt to make some symbolic memory into a kind of literal program for achieving recognition or significance. The loss or rejection of a father figure is a starting point;

from there the ritualistic search goes out for something in the South's past that is endowed with a natural sort of permanence.

II

As Faulkner explained it, his purpose in beginning the novel that became *Sartoris* was "to recreate between the covers of a book the world . . . I was already preparing to lose and regret." The book he was to write, then, represented an attempt to hold on somehow, imaginatively, to some valuable quality of a world past or quickly passing out of actuality and into memory. With this in mind, we can be struck with Faulkner's use in *Sartoris* of Keats's poem on the theme of myth making, "Ode on a Grecian Urn." The novel ends with Faulkner's rearrangement of the first two lines of the poem; "Thou still unravished bride of quietness, / Thou foster-child of silence and slow time" becomes, in Faulkner's description of evening, the following: "beyond the window evening was a windless lilac dream, foster dam of quietude and peace."

There are other references to the "Ode" as well. Horace Benbow refers more than once to his sister Narcissa as the "still unravished bride," and rhapsodizes over a vase he has made, "richly and chastely serene," in the same manner. Other sections of Keats's description of the "Cold Pastoral" bear direct relevance to the Sartorises and to a central urge for most of the characters in the novel. The question of the poem, "What leaf-fringed legend haunts about thy shape / Of deities or mortals, or of both?" is a crucial question in *Sartoris*; the novel shows the heirs of Colonel Sartoris ever haunted by the glamor and the doom he represents, as a figure who, "freed as he was of time and flesh . . . was a far more palpable presence" than the living who discussed his deeds.

The longing expressed in Keats's poem for permanence, for a way to achieve some peace above "all breathing human passion," is a key to the motivation of many of the characters of *Sartoris*. Both works involve a search for meaning; both tend to see in some former time "the dales of Arcady"; both note how, with the losing of their actual force to the "sensual ear," men become gods, passion becomes bliss, traditions become myths as memory attempts to fill the universal need for romance and simplified significance. Keats's poem tries to satisfy the longing through the equation of beauty and truth. The Sartoris clan seeks to use the figures of famous and doomed fathers to provide their valuations of themselves and their world. This method provides a basis for action for the modern Sartorises but does not offer any concurrent meaning to make those actions worthwhile.

Sartoris begins in almost mock-seance fashion, as old Will Falls visits Colonel John Sartoris' son, now an old man himself, in order to relive with him the moments of greatness of the first baronial Sartoris. It is a symbolic feature of their conversation that both are deaf; in a rather comic turn of Keats's meaning, they are quite literally piping to the spirit "ditties of no tone." In Old Bayard's office, Colonel Sartoris lives without the need of words to conjure him up, "far more palpable than the two old men cemented by a common deafness to a dead period." Faulkner here judges these men, not without sympathy or humor, as being incapable of living in the present and, moreover, as preferring their "citadel of silence" since it keeps them from having to face the reality of either present or past.

Old Bayard looks at the teeth marks left in his father's pipe, a memento Will Falls has brought, and thinks of his father as resembling "creatures of that prehistoric day that were too grandly conceived and executed either to exist very long or to vanish utterly when dead from an earth shaped and furnished for punier things." The comprehension is here in Old Bayard of something in his ancestry doomed to extinction even as it was conceived, and yet with a fatalism that is self-serving, Old Bayard accepts, as the rest of his family does, this definition of his own identity.

Sartoris becomes a series of studies in myth making and its consequences. Keats asks, "What men or gods are these?" In *Sartoris*, by turning men into gods, and then by according the legends the status of myth by associating timeless as well as personal valuations with them, the characters find value for themselves. The major importance in the novel of this process involves young Bayard. As the last Sartoris, born into a world far different from the world of his Civil War era ancestors, young Bayard finds that his quest for meaning takes on the shape of nightmare, not myth. For him, certainties about the old cherished values are gone, and yet he finds himself still trapped by an obligation to uphold them. In his case the obligation is made even more bitter a challenge because his twin brother seems to have had the ability to accept its importance unquestioningly. Johnny was able to duplicate the Civil War Bayard's suicidal charge into a Union camp by engaging a German aviator in a futile battle from his own inferior airplane. Young Bayard is paralyzed by guilt that he himself has survived while his reckless brother has continued a "tradition" somehow expected of all Sartorises. At the same time, he is sensitive enough to question the value of his brother's act, which has deprived him of the only person he has ever loved.

Young Bayard's family feeds his guilt while at the same time they too are aware that the myth they have created has gained nothing by Johnny's sacrifice to it and will gain nothing by Bayard's. Their ambiguous attitude toward his high-powered automobile is one way that they show their own confusion about the value of the Sartoris tradition. Old Bayard and Jenny constantly nag him about driving too fast; yet it is significant that Old Bayard takes to riding with his grandson, and everyone knows that his reason is not to keep the boy from killing himself but to participate in the recklessness, the suicidal quality, of what he is doing.

The key to the tension of this early Yoknapatawpha novel lies in young Bayard's paradoxical attitude toward the past, both his own remembered past and his family's legendary past that has been made into a myth to be perpetuated at any cost. Johnny, he knows, was, like the first Bayard, a fool. Yet in trying to find some meaningful definition of his own existence, young Bayard is often driven into making Johnny a hero. Faulkner describes his talk of Johnny's death as "not of combat, but rather of a life peopled by young men like fallen angels, and of a meteoric violence like that of fallen angels, beyond heaven or hell and partaking of both: doomed immortality and immortal doom."[4]

The point is made through all the attitudes about World War I, including Horace Benbow's refusal to remember it at all, that this war lacks any unifying conception to give it value. As comic vignette, or nightmare, it provides no clear proving ground for making men into gods or altering the course of human events. The experience of it seems to Bayard to resemble being "caught timelessly in a maze of solitary conflicting preoccupations, like bumping tops" (s, 320). The recent past is not yet legend, much less myth, which only time and the re-

4. William Faulkner, *Sartoris* (New York, 1929), 126.

tellings of generations can accord. Yet young Bayard cannot accept this, since his family has made the question of personal identity one of ability to perpetuate a myth that itself started as one meaningless action by one reckless Sartoris.

The myth by which the Sartorises define themselves, excuse themselves, and finally destroy themselves is a myth falsified by excessive romanticism. The best that can be said for the courage and glamor associated with the Sartoris tradition is that it provides a fine-sounding justification for suicide. Faulkner's final rumination concerning the fate of the Sartoris men indicates the irony of this family's myth-making game: "The dusk was peopled with ghosts of glamorous and old disastrous things. And if they were just glamorous enough, there was sure to be a Sartoris in them, and then they were sure to be disastrous." One quality of myth is its durability and the significance it gives to life and positive action. Yet of the Sartoris name Faulkner says, "There is death in the sound of it"; perhaps Sartoris is just a game, "a game outmoded and played with pawns shaped too late and to an old dead pattern, and of which the Player Himself is a little wearied" (s, 380).

There seems almost a note of regret in this final assessment of Faulkner's, as if, caught up in the Sartorises' romantic attachment to fine-sounding doom, he admires the way this game has been played and wished these pawns had been shaped in such a way that their lifestyle might provide a more significant pattern for action in the modern chaos of the 1920s. The novel's most serious flaw, perhaps, is Faulkner's failure to judge the "game" decisively himself. On the one hand, the world of the first Sartorises is not brought into sharp or compelling focus. The shaping of Colonel Sartoris' code is never powerfully enough promoted to be useful in accounting for the force it has in motivating the lives of his descendants. Likewise no other standard of value operates successfully to provide any comparison of the code the Sartorises choose to live by. Later works would correct this flaw as Faulkner learned to increase dramatic tension between ideals by including more than one perception on a particular past and its meaning.

For the Sartoris legend itself Faulkner provided a kind of corrective through the story "An Odor of Verbena" in *The Unvanquished* volume. Here Bayard, the Old Bayard of *Sartoris*, breaks the chain of suicidal violence in order to promote the idea that human values cannot be isolated into one particular code of behavior, certainly not one that denies the value of human life itself. Drusilla Hawk Sartoris becomes the spokesman for the Sartoris myth, "the Greek amphora priestess of a succinct and formal violence."[5] The novel *Sartoris* has no such compelling figure to provide sufficient evidence that the Sartoris standard is or ever was worth the price it exacts of those who follow it.

The Sartoris goddess of "formal violence" makes her case dramatically relevant through her own pure commitment to it. She says to Bayard in her effort to incite him, "If [a dream] stays alive long enough, somebody is going to be hurt. But if it's a good enough dream, it's worth it. There are not many dreams in the world, but there are lots of human lives" (s, 257). Bayard objects not so much to her faith in his father's dream as to the devaluation of human life that she is willing to make for the sake of that dream. For this reason he does not continue the cycle of violence in the manner expected of a Sartoris. When he goes to meet his father's murderer without a gun, Bayard steps out of legend and into the kind of reality from which true myths might spring.

III

In a letter to Malcolm Cowley, Faulkner attempted to explain the lack of a "literate middle class" and hence the lack of literature in the Old South. He used Thomas Sutpen to make his point. "In the pastoral cityless land they [the small farmers] lived remote and at economic war with both slave and slaveholder. When they emerged, gradually, son by infrequent son, like old Sutpen, it was not to establish themselves as a middle class but to make themselves barons too."[6] Something dreamlike and compelling about the Old South tended up to and even through the Civil War to attach her sons, of all races and classes, to the pursuit of a goal which only the slaveholder stood to profit from. Thus *Absalom, Absalom!*'s hero, emerging from West Virginia as a ten-year-old boy, had "never even heard of, never imagined, a place, a land divided neatly up and actually owned by men who

5. William Faulkner, "An Odor of Verbena," in *The Unvanquished* (New York, 1934), 252.

6. Quoted in Malcolm Cowley, *The Faulkner-Cowley File* (New York, 1966), 79.

did nothing but ride over it on fine horses or sit in fine clothes on the galleries of big houses while other people worked for them."[7]

Yet four years later Sutpen has committed himself to achieving and perpetuating that very design. He makes himself a "baron," a defender of the status quo more rigid in his adherence to the system than Colonel Sartoris himself. *Absalom, Absalom!* begins, as did *Sartoris*, with figures of the twentieth century dwelling in memory and imagination on the events that created the colonels of the Old and Civil War South and their mythic world. Yet *Absalom, Absalom!* succeeds where *Sartoris* failed in bringing the world of the barons to life and in showing how, if not always (in terms logical or well ordered) why, their shadows are cast so long and demandingly over the present.

In *Absalom, Absalom!* four narrators brood over the fate and fortunes of the Sutpen family. They are not like the Sartoris narrators—Will Falls, Miss Jenny, the Old and the young Bayard—who have the direct tie of blood to make the mystery of the past innately compelling. Perhaps this is to Faulkner's advantage, because in a way it forces him to develop Sutpen more directly as an "imaginative construct"[8] and to show more convincingly the motivations for the narrators' obsession with the past. Only one of *Absalom, Absalom!*'s narrators, Miss Rosa, has any directly personal cause to "exhume" Thomas Sutpen forty years after his death. Yet Harvard-bound Quentin Compson, his father, and later his college roommate all take up the tale as well. Mr. Compson explains the fascination that the past as Sutpen illustrates it has for them all:

We see dimly people, the people in whose living blood and seed we ourselves lay dormant and waiting, in this shadowy attenuation of time possessing now heroic proportions, performing their acts of simple passion and simple violence, impervious to time and inextricable. (AA, 101)

Each of the narrators might be said to see in Sutpen a kind of father figure for themselves, someone, as Mr. Compson says, "in whose living blood and seed we ourselves lay dormant and waiting." Sutpen has a way of supplying a lack or filling a void that exists in each nar-

7. William Faulkner, *Absalom, Absalom!* (New York, 1936), 221.
8. Cleanth Brooks, *William Faulkner: The Yoknapatawpha Country* (New Haven, Conn., 1963), 312.

rator and by attachment to him their own identities achieve some definitive shape. Thus Sutpen satisfies Rosa's need for a villain for her gothic imagination as well as her pathetic craving for attention, even if it be in the form of insult; he acts as a proof for Mr. Compson's theory that life in modern times has, by comparison to earlier eras, lost its potential for yielding heroic challenges; he is for Quentin what his own father is not—an active, purposeful man who is willing, at any cost, to make life conform to his ideal. And lastly, Sutpen's goal of establishing an inheritable dream out of the shape that he gives to his own life functions for Shreve, as in a way for the reader, as a concrete embodiment of the inscrutable force in the South itself, an embodiment through which he can attempt to understand the southerner's "kind of vacuum filled with wraithlike and indomitable anger and pride and glory at and in happenings that occurred and ceased fifty years ago" (AA, 361).

Sutpen and Sutpen's dream become inseparable as his story is reconstructed. He is his dream, and because of this anything that does not conform to the strict lines of the dream pattern cannot be acknowledged or accounted for. Thus wife, sons, daughters, and slaves all function just as fixtures for a house might; if they do not fit properly or produce desired effects, they must be cast aside for substitutes. It is terrifyingly simple. "I had a design. To accomplish it I should require money, a house, a plantation, slaves, a family—incidentally of course, a wife. I set out to acquire these, asking no favor of any man" (AA, 263).

The full horror of Sutpen's design rests in the series of awful ironies that surround it. The design itself is clear and pure. Sutpen would become not just the image of, or the imitation of, the Tidewater slaveholder who ordered his slave to insult Sutpen as a boy, but he would become that man's reincarnation, the inheritor of his kingdom, possessing duplicates of his possessions, upholding his standards, creating in turn his own sons to perpetuate all that the man in the big house, and through him the Old South, stood for so clearly and simply.

So, the first irony is that the design to which Sutpen commits himself is not his own design at all; it is the design of the representative of a culture that Sutpen despises, the program of a man who has treated Sutpen in a way that, for all his innocence, Sutpen knows no human being should be treated. And to complete this design fully, Sutpen will have to treat others as he has been treated, with the same inhumanity which motivated his own search for a way to put himself out of reach of that kind of treatment forever. He will have to dispossess *both* of his sons of their humanity, just as he has been dispossessed.

The second irony involved in Sutpen's borrowed design is that he cannot and will not ever be able to achieve it. The reason, as Quentin's grandfather diagnoses it, is his innocence. (There is great irony as well, of course, in this "innocence," since it allows Sutpen to become totally corrupt while it keeps him from being able to recognize what corruption is.) "Sutpen's trouble was innocence" (AA, 221), not innocence as purity but innocence as lack of knowledge, in his case not only of evil but also of good.

The first result of this ironic innocence is that it keeps Sutpen from understanding that while he can imitate the mannerisms of men who have been born into the landed gentry, he cannot duplicate them. He was hopelessly, helplessly "underbred," yet he believed that by practice he could achieve what only time could allow men like General Compson and Judge Benbow to do unconsciously. "He may have believed that your grandfather or Judge Benbow might have done it a little more effortlessly than he, but he could not have believed that anyone could have beat him in knowing when to do it and how" (AA, 46). But time was in this, as in all things, against him. Just as in later life he would find that money could not buy him a sufficient future in which to produce another son and heir, so at the beginning of his program he should have known that neither money nor practice could gain him entrance into that world of respectability that southern opinion accorded only to those who had inherited their status through generations.

Miss Rosa echoes the town's indomitable bias when she points out that "he was no younger son set out from some old quiet country like Virginia or Carolina with the surplus negroes to take up new land" (AA, 17). He is no son and has no father, no past that automatically belongs to him through blood. And this sort of past he cannot buy. Her description of the way in which he built his plantation— "tore violently a plantation" and married and had children—"without gentleness begot" (AA, 9) shows that in substance he violated the public aspect of the dream he was trying to copy in order to establish its form. "He wasn't even a gentleman. He wasn't even a gentleman" (AA, 14), Miss Rosa says.

Thomas Sutpen, then, is defeated before he begins in his quest to design a lifestyle for himself, and he ironically ensures the defeat with every action he takes to avoid being defeated. Before the Civil War comes to destroy the design for the Old South generally, Sutpen has accomplished in material terms all that he has set out to do: he has plantation, mansion, gardens, genteel wife, son, and slaves. Yet he has also created, through the actions by which he established Sutpen's Hundred, the interior means of its destruction. His dream depends absolutely on its being inheritable; it must be capable of being handed on, so that the past that Sutpen wants to embody through his own actions might endure as legend. The success of such a design depends, therefore, upon his sons, whose humanity Sutpen needs but has been from the start willing to deny. The tragic irony here is not just Sutpen's but the South's, whose history demonstrated its willingness to sacrifice the human to the ideal in its system. When Sutpen's white son kills his own older brother, Sutpen's first-born heir through a part-Negro wife, he secures his father's estate, keeping the design of it pure in the sense that the South itself defines purity. Yet Henry is not able to live with the betrayal of human values involved, and so he renounces his patrimony and destroys his father's dream of bequeathing an identity that conforms to his ideal. Sutpen's pathetic attempts after Henry's abandonment to create another son to carry out his program show the full horror of his fixation, the tragedy and the absurdity of that "innocence" that never allows him to see that the design itself was fatally flawed before he ever adopted it and that all he could accomplish by making it his life's goal would be his own destruction and that of his posterity.

What Lacy Buchan's grandfather says of the mythical Jason in Allen Tate's *The Fathers* applies with startling relevance to Sutpen and is a cogent statement of the nature of the tragedy that pervades Faulkner's story, even through its title: "He was a noble fellow in whom the patriarchal and familial loyalties had become meaningless but his human nature necessarily limited him, and he made a heroic effort to combine his love of the extraordinary and the inhuman with the ancient domestic virtues" (TF, 269). The story of Jason teaches that the fleece is "not all-sufficing," that the "humanity of others" cannot with impunity be betrayed. If Thomas Sutpen never learns this lesson, still it is what his own children's response to him affirms, and it is what compels the four narrators of his story, especially Quentin Compson, to take up his tale and project their own lives into it.

IV

In *Absalom, Absalom!* Quentin Compson listens with both horror and fascination to Rosa Coldfield's tale of the fall of the house of Sutpen. He is simultaneously obsessed and repulsed by the story, outraged at having to listen while eager to know more. Faulkner acknowledged that the Quentin of *Absalom, Absalom!* bore essentially the same identity as the Quentin of *The Sound and the Fury*. In one of the University of Virginia conferences Faulkner remarked, "Quentin was still trying to get God to tell him why, in *Absalom, Absalom!* as he was in *The Sound and the Fury*."[9]

There are a number of crucial instances in which what happens to the Sutpens seems to parallel what Quentin can see, in *The Sound and the Fury*, happening to the Compsons. The Compson house seems doomed to fall as did the Sutpen house, with the sins of the fathers being visited upon sons who have no choice but to be martyrs to circumstances they did not themselves plan. Yet the differences between the Sutpens and the Compsons, particularly between Henry Sutpen and Quentin himself in their relation to their fathers and families, would be equally important to Quentin.

Both Henry and Quentin are, in a sense, paralyzed by the past. Both feel compelled to commit desperate actions in order to uphold some arbitrary concept of honor which they associate with the family name. Yet Quentin, looking at Henry, might easily feel envy for him since the circumstances surrounding Henry's act would have an aura of purposeful, tragic grandeur. In Henry's case, the stakes were high, with absolute values of love, kinship, and honor to be weighed, and the final act of murder might also be interpreted as an act of love, and so both horrible and yet somehow ennobling. Henry could become through his act the doomed, fated symbol of an order corrupted by his father but purified anew by his sacrifice. Through his renuncia-

9. Frederick L. Gwynn and Joseph Blotner (eds.), *Faulkner in the University* (New York, 1959), 275.

tion of his patrimony, he could repudiate his father's false dream. These possibilities attract Quentin because they indicate the significance his own options lack. For Quentin would find in his world no place, no compelling demand, no audience even to care, for any action he might conceivably commit in order to etch forever some memorable image in the minds of men.

The last scene on which Quentin's deranged mind dwells before he commits suicide is the one in which he tells his father first of the imagined incest with Caddy and then of his intention to kill himself. Quentin's father denies the meaning and value of both acts. He tells his son that "you cannot bear to think that someday it will no longer hurt you like this."[10] It is an apt remark that pinpoints Quentin's diseased idea that if only he can suffer horribly enough, as did Henry Sutpen, he might redeem the wreck that has been made of his world, his house, his name. Yet Mr. Compson cannot deal with the causes of Quentin's agonized obsession with acts of horror since they lie in a past that he himself is cut off from, and so he ends by denying the significance that Quentin might attach to all action. Speaking in his terribly objective way about suicide generally, he tells Quentin, "No man ever does that under the first fury of despair or remorse or bereavement he does it only when he has realized that even the despair or remorse or bereavement is not particularly important to the dark diceman" (SF, 196).

Quentin might well wonder, as his suicide shows that he does wonder, what the use of any action might be in this modern chaos. The values he associates with life are constantly being undercut—by a mother incapable of giving love, by a sister incapable of preserving his standard of purity, and most tragically of all, by a father so disillusioned that he will tell Quentin, "People cannot do anything very dreadful they cannot do anything very dreadful at all they cannot even remember tomorrow what seemed dreadful today" (SF, 99). Mr. Compson in this statement denies the premise upon which Thomas Sutpen built his whole design; Sutpen's plan was predicated upon the assumption that people could remember, as he himself remembered, the climactic moments of the past which had made them what they were. For Mr. Compson, as for young Bayard Sartoris, there can only

10. William Faulkner, *The Sound and the Fury* (New York, 1946), 196.

be too much time, for they are separated from the only thing that has meaning to them, their dream of grandeur in the past, by each stroke of time that diminishes their families' identities in legend. Yet Sutpen will always have too little time, and in the figure of Wash Jones, time will turn on Sutpen and destroy a dream not yet fulfilled.

Thomas Sutpen and his story might very well be attractive to Quentin, then, chiefly because Sutpen's life so profoundly opposes Mr. Compson's definition of the value of action in the modern world. As Quentin solidifies his resolve to kill himself, he remembers his father's saying "that Christ was not crucified: he was worn away by a minute clicking of little wheels" (SF, 96). Quentin can become another hero by a death which will demonstrate a refusal to sit passively by and see all meaning worn away by the "minute clicking" of time's wheels.

Young Bayard Sartoris, Thomas Sutpen, and Quentin Compson are all trapped or driven into accepting as their life goal a dream which belongs to an inaccessible past. They commit themselves to the goal of completing such dreams with an impenetrable resolve that denies not just to them, but to those who have human claims on them, the possibilities of love and full life. It is not until we read Faulkner's "The Bear," set within the larger framework of *Go Down, Moses*, that we encounter the design of a dream which attempts to include, to account for, even to be responsible for, human nature at the same time that it strives to establish a more permanent ordering of values. Ike McCaslin has Quentin's sensitivity to modern blight without Quentin's incapacitating bitterness against the present. Yet he too is haunted by his forefathers, his personal past, in a way that tends to qualify his success in formulating a design that will hold for the future.

V

Faulkner's "The Bear" is often looked upon as his most primitivistic statement concerning man's place in the modern world. There seem to be two prevailing arguments concerning Ike McCaslin's usefulness in providing a standard for response to such issues as modern materialism, the rape of the wilderness, the guilt of the South for promoting slavery and racial bigotry. In one view Ike becomes a Christlike figure who atones by renunciation for the South's sins against man and nature, past and present. In the other he becomes an escapist, in most radical form almost a Judas, who betrays not just his birthright but his obligation to work out solutions for the region he professes to love. In an important interpretation R. W. B. Lewis makes a case for Ike as a figure representing, through "an act of atonement," the potential of redemption. Yet even Lewis goes on to admit the puzzling complication that Ike "seems never fully to share the demoralizing and magnificent adventure of being fully human."[11]

Two articles which explore the uses of Keats's "Ode on a Grecian Urn" in "The Bear" evaluate Ike more negatively. Joan S. Korenman cites convincing evidence that Faulkner, like Keats, experienced marked ambivalence when considering "the notion of stopping time." Miss Korenman's assessment of Faulkner's attitude toward Ike is that "as a representative of old times and old values, Ike has the author's admiration. However, when he renounces his patrimony and proclaims, 'Sam Fathers set me free,' Ike is claiming freedom from his responsibilities and from time. This is a claim with which Faulkner may sympathize, but, unlike Ike, he recognizes that it is a claim that cannot be realized."[12] Blanche Gelfant takes a stern approach to Ike's desire "to be the human embodiment of virtue by transforming himself into the Hunter-ideal through the initiation ceremony in the woods."[13] This "sterile gesture" is "the very essence of a Romantic desire for escape from the human condition." Both articles point out the crucial confrontation of "The Bear": man's age-old battle against time and change, his perpetual search for a permanence beyond but somehow inclusive of the "human condition."

Within "The Bear" itself there is criticism of Ike's denial of his patrimony and the denial of humanity that this act seems to entail. The most eloquent critic is General Compson, who on other occasions had shown great respect for Ike's relationship with the wilderness: "Because I don't believe you just quit," Compson tells Ike. "It looks like you just quit but I have watched you in the woods too much and I don't believe you just quit even if it does look damn like it."[14] There is implied criticism of Ike as well in the story of his black cousin, Lucas

11. R. W. B. Lewis, "William Faulkner: The Hero in the New World," in *Faulkner: A Collection of Critical Essays* (Englewood Cliffs, N.J., 1966), 217.

12. Joan S. Korenman, "Faulkner's Grecian Urn," *Southern Literary Journal,* VII (Fall, 1974), 20.

13. Blanche H. Gelfant, "Faulkner and Keats: The Ideality of Art in 'The Bear,'" *Southern Literary Journal,* II (Fall, 1969), 64.

14. William Faulkner, *Go Down, Moses* (New York, 1942), 309.

Quintus Carothers McCaslin Beauchamp, who, unlike Ike, claims his inheritance from "old Carothers" as his sister and brother refused to do. Lucas does not seem to feel that his acceptance of his ancestor's stained inheritance in any way binds him or compromises him. He calls himself Lucas instead of Lucius, "simply taking the name and changing it, making it no longer the white man's but his own, by himself composed, himself selfprogenitive and nominate, by himself ancestored" (GDM, 281). Lucas' vitality, his active life as it is chronicled in the earlier *Go Down, Moses* story "The Fire and the Hearth," seems to contrast pointedly with Ike's passivity.

Faulkner himself, whatever his feelings as he wrote Section Four of "The Bear," later was to say that Ike does not go as far as he could to correct the injustices of the world around him. In telling a sort of parable during one of his university conferences, Faulkner classified people dealing with their problems into three "stages," as he called them. The first, he said, responds to life by saying "This is rotten, I'll have no part of it, I will take death first." Faulkner cited Ike McCaslin as a case in point not of the first stage but of the second, a man who says, "This is rotten, I don't like it, I can't do anything about it, but at least I will not participate in it myself, I will go off into a cave or climb a pillar to sit on." The third stage was represented in Faulkner's thinking by the type who might say, "This stinks and I'm going to do something about it."[15]

We recognize Quentin Compson as a representative of the first stage. The third might claim, in a negative way, Thomas Sutpen, a man of action with a fixed design, and in a positive way, Lucas Beauchamp, one of the few Faulkner characters whose life moves fairly persistently in purposeful directions. And Ike McCaslin, though able to face problems more directly than Quentin Compson, still tends to disappoint us, as he disappointed General Compson, because he seems capable only of the second stage, of withdrawal and not action. The greatest stumbling block to our understanding of what Ike is doing in Section Four of "The Bear" is the one General Compson defines: seeing Ike in the woods, where he exhibits the finest sort of perception and determination, we expect more of him than we get in the

15. Gwynn and Blotner (eds.), *Faulkner in the University*, 246.

commissary—his simple act of "quitting," as Sam Fathers had quit after Old Ben was killed. It seems indeed, as Blanche Gelfant says, that "when Ike gives up his heritage, he gives up his means to act."[16]

Most analyses of Ike tend to evaluate him, as Gelfant's does, in terms of his act of "repudiating" and "relinquishing" his patrimony, and most look for the reasoning behind this action in the ledger books that Ike broods over. These books record the incest, the miscegenation, the greed, the total disregard for humanity exhibited in the life of Ike's grandfather, Carothers McCaslin. The usual view is that Ike renounces his inheritance from his grandfather in order to atone for and/or to escape from the effects of the first McCaslin's corruption. It is important to note that it is not Ike who first uses the words *repudiate* or *relinquish* to describe what he is doing. "I can't repudiate it," he tries to explain, since "it was never mine to repudiate," essentially because, as he insists, his grandfather "bought nothing" when he bought the land from Sam Fathers' Indian father. The earth cannot be bought or sold or relinquished, reasons Ike, because it has been given to men only "to hold . . . mutual and intact in the communal anonymity of brotherhood" (GDM, 256–57).

If Ike is not repudiating his grandfather's—and white civilization's—concept of ownership and the dehumanizing greed that accompanies it by relinquishing his title to the land, what is he doing? The answer that *he* gives, again and again, is that he is setting himself free. His explanation is caught up in his theory of the South's bondage, a theory that has at its center the idea that the white race is the enslaved one, because the black race "had it [freedom] already from the old free fathers a longer time free than us because we have never been free" (GDM, 295). What Ike means might best be illustrated by the first story in *Go Down, Moses*, a story that is filtered through Ike's consciousness and deals, as in fact all the stories of the collection do, with kinds and degrees of freedom and bondage. In "Was" it is Tomey's Turl, the slave, who is free to run away, to court his girlfriend on another plantation, to manipulate events and his white owners for his own ends (as Lucas will manipulate Roth Edmonds in "The Fire and the Hearth"). It is Ike's father and uncle, Buck and Buddy McCaslin, who are not

16. Gelfant, "Faulkner and Keats," 65.

free, who do not want to but are forced by the southern code to chase their slave, to don neckties, to miss their breakfast in order to preserve the form of an order that they do not believe in.

It is with his own black kinsmen's special kind of freedom in mind that Ike tells McCaslin Edmonds, on his twenty-first birthday in 1888, that "we [the white McCaslins, the white South in general] have never been free." Two years earlier Ike had had a lesson in freedom that has a bearing on the issues involved. When Ike went in search of his cousin in order to give her part of the McCaslin legacy, he found her living in a terrible squalor that is an ironic symbol of her liberty: a "muddy waste fenceless and even pathless and without even a walled shed for stock to stand beneath." Yet she and her husband did not accept Ike's assessment of their condition; when Ike asked Fonsiba if she was all right, she answered only, "I'm free" (GDM, 280). At the time of his visit, Ike thought that Fonsiba's and her husband's notion of freedom was "the boundless folly and the baseless hope," yet two years later he seems to have inherited their hope, for after first telling McCaslin Edmonds that "we have never been free," he goes on to announce "I am free" and finally, "Sam Fathers set me free" (GDM, 299, 300). As a sort of natural father figure, Sam had shown Ike how to function in the wilderness without compass or watch, he had taught him the code of the hunter, and most importantly, he had illustrated through his own life the possibility of connection with a past that was more vital than the historical or legendary past of actual ancestors whose legacy was possession tainted by guilt and bondage. Through Sam Fathers Ike had become aware of patterns of life belonging to a world in which no race question ever entered into the making of the identity of a man.

It is such a world that Ike had sought entrance to through his apprenticeship to the wilderness and to Sam Fathers as steward of that wilderness. In "The Old People," the story that precedes "The Bear" in *Go Down, Moses*, Ike's feelings are described as he listened to Sam talk about "the old days":

Gradually to the boy those old times would cease to be old times and would become a part of the boy's present, not only as if they had happened yesterday but as if they were still happening . . . until at last it would seem to the boy that he himself had not come into existence yet. (GDM, 171)

In the wilderness with Sam, then, Ike felt the effects of a freedom from both time and racial identity. He saw the gigantic apparition of a buck to whom Sam said, "Oleh, Chief . . . Grandfather" (GDM, 184), and he was eager to claim this dream as his heritage. The gigantic buck of "The Old People" foreshadowed the gigantic bear, Old Ben, and buck and bear and Sam Fathers himself would come to stand in Ike's mind for a freedom from binding concepts that demand subservience.

So, what Ike wants when he reaches manhood is freedom, freedom that he defines specifically in terms of the wilderness, the bear, and the old Indian in whom the blood of three races mingled. Certainly, then, his is a primitivistic kind of freedom and a hopeless freedom as well since the symbols of it—wilderness, bear, and Indian—have vanished, have achieved only the freedom of release in death. Ike longs to participate in a kind of timeless, guiltless Eden that he associates with the wilderness. Joan Korenman goes so far as to say that "like Quentin Compson, [Ike] wants his world to remain the simple untainted existence of his childhood. He refuses to accept change as part of the human condition, insisting instead on the static peace embodied by the timeless woods and Keats's Grecian urn."[17] I think we can agree with her first statement: Ike would like his world to remain simple and untainted. However, this in itself does not make him any more like Quentin Compson than like any other human being; the urge to return to or remain in the state of grace of childhood is a fairly common one.

The question that must be asked concerning Ike's longings is whether or not he recognizes that they cannot be fulfilled in the actual world and whether or not he is able to accept the fact that they may form the basis for ideals but not for acts. To answer with Korenman's argument, that Ike "refuses to accept change as part of the human condition," is to deny some dramatic evidence included by Faulkner that demonstrates Ike's acute consciousness that his wilderness is very much in time. Faulkner, in fact, arranges a series of experiences which teach Ike that he cannot remove himself from time or evil or the realities of life by entering the ever-diminishing confines of his pastoral kingdom. The evidence in "The Bear" that we can

17. Korenman, "Faulkner's Grecian Urn," 19.

assemble to support this view consists of three acts: first, Ike's participation in the killing of Old Ben; second, his salute to the gigantic snake, which is the last "gesture" that he makes in "The Bear"; third, his marriage and his desire for a son, which end in his acknowledgment that "no man is ever free" (GDM, 281).

When Ike, as a boy, hunts the bear, confronts it with a gun in his hands after four years of searching, and still refuses to shoot, his kinsman McCaslin tries to explain his passivity to him by reading Keats's "Ode on a Grecian Urn." McCaslin emphasizes one line: "'She cannot fade, though thou hast not thy bliss,' McCaslin said: 'Forever wilt thou love, and she be fair'" (GDM, 297). We can assume that McCaslin wants Ike to understand that his reluctance to kill the bear is part of a universal urge for permanence, for something impervious to change and death. Keats's urn has this permanence; portrayed on its surface are trees that will never be bare and two lovers who, if they have no consummation of their love, still have the consolation of a sense of love and beauty that can last "forever."

Yet the urn is art, and Keats calls the scene "Cold Pastoral"; it is "all breathing passion far above"—it is not life. And while Ike and the other hunters of the bear are engaged in an archetypal act, a ritual celebrating the permanence that life attests in its ceremonies, they are also human, mortal, and by their very choice of sport, agents of change. That Ike understands this double nature of the hunt would seem to be indicated by the fact that he does not hate the mongrel dog who is found and trained for the sole purpose of trapping Old Ben. Even before Lion is discovered, just after Ike with his tiny fyce has had the chance to shoot Old Ben, Ike speaks to Sam of the inevitable day when someone will do it: "That's why it must be one of us. So it won't be until the last day. When even he don't want it to last any longer" (GDM, 212). Faulkner says that Ike "should have hated and feared Lion" (GDM, 226). If he was only interested in freezing time, surely he would not have encouraged Sam's training of the animal who was strong and ferocious and worthy enough to destroy the very symbol for Ike of timelessness and indestructibility. Yet Ike did not hate or fear Lion, Faulkner says, because "it seemed to him that there was a fatality in it. It seemed to him that something, he didn't know what, was beginning; had already begun. It was like the last act on a set stage. It was the beginning of the end of something, he didn't know what except that he would not grieve" (GDM, 227).

After Old Ben has been killed, Sam Fathers "quits." This, at least, is the doctor's diagnosis: "Old people do that sometimes." Sam and Lion are buried side by side in the deep wilderness, and when Ike visits the graves two years after the killing of Old Ben he thinks that here "was no abode of the dead because there was no death, not Lion and not Sam: not held fast in earth but free in earth and not in earth but of earth" (GDM, 328–29). Ike seems to see death not as an end but, paradoxically, as a fixing of the principle of change, as an "immutable progression." He sees Sam's death, then, not as a "quitting" but as the attainment of a freedom that will give to him (as Keats's urn gave back) "the long challenge and the long chase, no heart to be driven and outraged, no flesh to be mauled and bled" (GDM, 329). Yet Ike himself does not choose to gain freedom through death. He is young and Sam was old; he is inescapably a member of a race and a culture that Sam could largely ignore. Sam's literal freedom is not available to Ike except as an ideal, and it would seem that he recognizes this when he sees in the woods on his visit to the grave site a gigantic snake.

This final scene of "The Bear" was surely intended to parallel the scene in "The Old People" in which Ike sees the gigantic buck whom Sam salutes with the words, "Oleh, Chief . . . Grandfather." As Ike sees the snake he "freezes" in order to avoid being bitten, yet after the snake passes "he put the other foot down at last and didn't know it, standing with one hand raised as Sam had stood that afternoon when Sam led him into the wilderness and showed him and he ceased to be a child, speaking the old tongue which Sam had spoken that day without premeditation either: 'Chief,' he said: 'Grandfather'" (GDM, 330). It is highly significant that while Sam saluted a buck as his symbolic progenitor, Ike salutes a snake, which he recognizes as "the old one, the ancient and accursed about the earth, fatal and solitary and he could smell it now: the thin sick smell of rotting cucumbers and something else which had no name, evocative of all knowledge and an old weariness and of pariah-hood and of death" (GDM, 329).

Ike understands that he belongs to the world of man which is a world of knowledge and not innocence, of death and not timeless freedom. Immediately after the snake vanishes, Ike hears the mechanical clicking of Boon's gun as he frantically tries to put the machine together so that he can kill the squirrels which fill a tree behind him. Boon will not share the squirrels; with the hopeless greed of his race and time he says to Ike, "Get out of here! Don't touch a one of them! They're mine!" (GDM, 331).

Ike does not reject Boon or the civilization that he epitomizes in the last scene in "The Bear." That Ike fully intends to function as a fairly active citizen in the society to which he was born is proved by his marriage and his desire for a son. After he relinquishes his patrimony, Ike moves to a boardinghouse and takes up the carpenter trade. Those who see this last act as another gesture in the series by which Ike seeks to remove himself from the world of men might note Faulkner's qualification; Ike takes up carpentering not "in mere static and hopeful emulation of the Nazarene" because he knows that his own ends, "although simple enough in their apparent motivation, were and would be always incomprehensible to him and his life, invincible enough in its needs, if he could have helped himself, not being the Nazarene, he would not have chosen it" (GDM, 310).

Ike, then, does not see himself as Christ-like. He is neither "static" nor "hopeful" but instead is full of needs that are "invincible," and he is very much aware that he has not been allowed free choice in the direction he finds his life caught up in. In other words, he is fully human and knows it. Ike marries out of need and desire, yet when his wife demands that he either take back his inheritance or lose his conjugal rights with her, he refuses. What Ike's wife does with her proposition is to offer the most difficult challenge he will have to face in order to keep his pledge to himself to be free from the system of inherited possession that his culture has enshrined. The loss of posterity that he is threatened with is a rather logical and inevitable consequence of his argument that no man can project his will upon the future, yet it is a difficult contingency to accept and brings Ike face to face with the possibility that the path he has chosen might, unless care is taken, cause him to sacrifice the vitality of life for some un-human standard of purity.

Thus Ike's marriage brings him to a final position concerning the freedom he has sought all his life; by 1895, Faulkner says, Ike was "husband but no father, unwidowered but without a wife, and found long since that no man is ever free and probably could not bear it if he were" (GDM, 281). He has learned that to be alive and human is to be limited to what the real world offers. So at last the judgment that we can make of him is this: he is able to reach back beyond the sin and guilt of a historical and familial past to find and fathom in a special way a mythic and yet also private past which gives a purposeful ordering to his life. His mode enables him to act not as a force for change but as a force for recognition of the values that Faulkner associates with nature—courage, pride, humility, and a simple but absolute respect for all life.

It is his belief in a special value that is higher than himself but still human that allows Ike a peace that is not an escape but an acceptance of his own humanity. The exact nature of this value is essential to remember when comparing Ike to Faulkner's other past-haunted southern dreamers. Thomas Sutpen's design requires the ruthless establishment of a dynasty for the purpose of attaining a position beyond the reach of time or social pressure; the dreams of young Bayard Sartoris and Quentin Compson pinpoint death as the only instrument for the achievement of significance. It is important, then, that the symbol of Ike's dream is not something fixed, or past, but something fluid and protean. Near the end of his life Ike, having witnessed the diminution of all the things he cherishes most, has this vision that makes the present not unreal to him, but bearable: "He seemed to see the two of them—himself and the wilderness—as coevals . . . the two spans running out together, not toward oblivion, nothingness, but into a dimension free of both time and space . . . where the wild strong immortal game ran forever before the timeless belling immortal hounds, falling and rising phoenix-like to the soundless guns" (GDM, 354).

Ike alone, of those Faulkner characters who dream of inheriting a relevant past, takes the opportunity he is given to re-create the tradition he reveres as a part of an imaginative process that carries through the present. Faulkner himself had desired the capture of a world that he was prepared "to lose and regret" and had recognized that the capturing would involve an act of imagination; what he could preserve in art might be only "a kernel or leaf to indicate the lost forest." Ike has a similar hope and a similar challenge. His last ideal of freedom, of "himself and the wilderness . . . running out together, not toward oblivion, nothingness, but into a dimension free of both time and space," is an ideal of perception, not action, which still celebrates a full life bound by time as the prerequisite to the capture of the long-loved, long-lost forest of Sam Fathers and the bear.

Eudora Welty, Faulkner's Mississippi neighbor, would concentrate on this ideal of perception in her novels' approach to the concern that Faulkner defined as indicating the lost forest. In a short story which uses the same kind of taut imagery opposing the pristine wilderness and the corruption of man that Faulkner applies in "The Bear," Miss Welty in "A Still Moment" directs her artist-hunter, Audubon, toward a perception of an identity that is free of the limitations of whatever ancestry he might claim but not free of the responsibilities entailed upon his humanity: "But if it was his identity that he wished to discover, or if it was what a man had to seize beyond that, the way for him was by endless examination, by a care for every bird that flew in his path and every serpent that shone underfoot."[18]

Audubon's responsibility, as man, hunter, and artist, the one which alone can reveal to him who he is, is to practice a mode of seeing which will bring memory, the "looking inward," into the open light of experience, which is a "looking outward." Audubon must kill the lovely snowy heron in order to know it and to reveal it in his art; as he realizes, "the gaze that looks outward must be trained without rest, to be indomitable" (WN, 90). Miss Welty's development of Audubon's purpose and limitations as an artist indicates that she will carry Faulkner's sense of the relevance of the past for the present, particularly in the creation of fiction, into a different, but contingent, direction. Audubon wants "to record all life that filled this world"; yet even as he relishes the times when "what he would draw, and what he had seen, would become . . . one to him," he realizes that what he has seen and tried to capture, to possess by the destruction of the living thing and the re-creation of it through memory and study, will be "never the essence, only a sum of parts. . . . As he had seen the bird most purely at its moment of death, in some fatal way, in his care for looking outward, he saw his long labor most revealingly at the point where it met its limit" (WN, 92). Audubon, "trained to see well in the dark," becomes the type of seer who is the catalyst for the still moments of perception that achieve great power in Welty's novels, which center on vision and the achievement of perspective as a key to bringing time and place, past and present, into relationships capable of enriching and preserving whatever of experience can live in art.

18. Eudora Welty, "A Still Moment," in *The Wide Net and Other Stories* (New York, 1943), 89–90.

NINE

To See Things in Their Time: The Act of Focusing in Eudora Welty's Fiction

In making a distinction between two forces that are prominent in her fiction, Eudora Welty has written that "place has always nursed, nourished, and instructed man. . . . Man can feel love for place; he is prone to regard time as something of an enemy."[1] The feeling for the difference in the way one responds to place and to time has a quality specifically southern about it. The southerner, who has become the object of so much analysis in recent years, literarily, politically, and sociologically, seems indeed a creature very much at home with the concept of place in his life and not at all comfortable with time.

The South has long been associated, in the popular mind at least, with an ideology that exalts sense of place in order to resist time and progress. Time and progress belong to the world outside, or so the myth goes; on the plantations or in the small, sleepy southern towns that are the popular images of the South, time is held back by the places themselves. Thus Miss Welty describes a group of her own southern characters in their relation to outsiders: "They only hoped to place them, in their hour or their street or the name of their mother's people. Then Morgana could hold them, and at last they were this and they were that."[2]

1. Eudora Welty, "Some Notes on Time in Fiction," *Mississippi Quarterly*, XXVI (Fall, 1972), 483.
2. Eudora Welty, *The Golden Apples* (New York, 1947), 90.

Miss Welty has said of her South as place, "It endows me, and it enables me."[3] Time, on the other hand, seems to act against the urge to preserve, the urge to hold in, and so it is, especially for the southern imagination steeped in a personal and particular sense of place, "something of an enemy." Still the awareness of time is essential to any vision of man's possibilities. Frederick Hoffman warns, in his study of place in southern fiction, that "the most vividly concrete particular can become the worst kind of abstraction if it is allowed to work erosively upon the present. That is why the most successful of place literature is that which presents its details as freshly and intimately renewable."[4]

The danger implicit in resting one's fictional environment on too static a sense of place is avoided in Miss Welty's work, which often, in fact, uses the idea of the need for dynamic concepts of place as a major theme. For Miss Welty a sense of place is where art begins: "The truth is, fiction depends for its life on place."[5] Yet for her place is "mysterious," not fixed, and it is always in its relation to the social, to the human, that place is developed in her stories and novels. Indeed, a place acquires its importance, its mystery only when people find themselves using it to identify and understand themselves. The mystery about place lies "in the fact that place has a more lasting identity . . . than we have, and we unswervingly tend to attach ourselves to identity."[6]

Through Miss Welty's early essay on sense of place in fiction as well as in subsequent writing, a definite design emerges concerning her idea of how place functions, and the design seems to hinge on two qualities—identity and endurance—out of which grows an essential third factor, renewal. Place has "lasting identity"; man, seeking his own identity, "attaches" himself to a place because it offers a concrete mechanism through which he can order and hold onto the beliefs that give meaning to his life.

3. William F. Buckley, "The Southern Imagination: An Interview with Eudora Welty and Walker Percy," *Mississippi Quarterly*, XXVI (Fall, 1972), 493.

4. Frederick J. Hoffman, "Sense of Place," in Louis D. Rubin, Jr., and Robert D. Jacobs (eds.), *South: Modern Southern Literature in Its Cultural Setting* (New York, 1961), 74.

5. Eudora Welty, "Place in Fiction," *South Atlantic Quarterly*, LV (January, 1956), 59.

6. *Ibid.*

In "Some Notes on River Country," Miss Welty explains her concept this way: "Perhaps it is sense of place that gives us the belief that passionate things, in some essence, endure." Yet it is not this endurance of place alone that matters: "Whatever is significant and whatever is tragic in its story live as long as the place does, though they are unseen, and the new life will be built upon these things—regardless of commerce and the way of rivers and roads, and other vagrancies."[7] "New life" must grow out of the "belief in passionate things" that endure "as long as the place does."

Miss Welty's theory of place is hardly static, then, and perhaps it is because she always views place in this social sense that her place images differ somewhat from those of other modern southern writers, most notably her fellow Mississippian William Faulkner. Faulkner gives us the crumbling plantations of Sartoris, Compson, McCaslin, and Sutpen; in "The Bear" there is the wilderness, hallucinatory, breathtaking, but ever receding or "drawing inward," eaten away by man's civilizing greed. In the Snopes novels there is a community, hamlet or town, but men are shown in a primitive, isolated relation to the concept of community. Faulkner shows man frightfully alienated from place; the fear is a disease of many of his characters who are too often painfully aware of their "roots" in the southern place but who can take no nourishment from it and so are forced to cry, as Quentin Compson does, "I don't hate it! I don't hate it!" Miss Welty's most perceptive characters might cherish a certain sense of "separateness" from place, yet they do not become totally uprooted. They must learn to cope with the identities that place endows or even forces upon them.

The dominant place image that emerges through Miss Welty's fiction is the small southern community that acts as an integrating force: we have in Shellmound, Morgana, Banner, Mount Salus, places with a lasting identity that the community uses to define itself, but places also that live themselves because of the living attitudes of the people who dwell in them. The importance of these places, of any places, as vital images for fiction resides for Miss Welty in the way they are *seen*. Place provides knowledge of identity. But eventually "our knowledge depends upon the living relationship between what we see going on and ourselves." "Insight," says Miss Welty, "doesn't happen often

7. Eudora Welty, "Some Notes on River Country," *Harper's Bazaar*, no. 2786 (February, 1944), 156.

at the click of the moment, like a lucky snapshot, but comes in its own time and more slowly and from nowhere but within."[8] It is through what she calls "the act of focusing" that place acquires the sense of identity that men can use to measure themselves and to endure. "The act of focusing itself," she says, "has beauty and meaning; it is the act that, continued in, turns into meditation, into poetry."[9]

Miss Welty's design for the use of place in her fiction might be summarized, then, as this: Place, as the "named, identified, concrete, exact and exacting, and therefore credible, gathering spot of all that has been felt" in a fictional work, can endow characters with a sense of "lasting identity" and, consequently, endurance or "new life." This sense is valid and usable only if it is acquired through "focus" and reflection, when there is a "living relationship" between what one sees and what he understands about himself "entirely from within." Place yields to time; it cannot, therefore, be used to fix identity but exists as a mechanism of insight available to those who can "stand still" to catch the fleeting moment when place reveals its mysteries: "Indeed, as soon as the least of us stands still, that is the moment something extraordinary is seen to be going on in the world."[10]

Welty's four major longer works (*Delta Wedding, The Golden Apples, Losing Battles, The Optimist's Daughter*) dramatize the demands made on characters whose main challenge is to perceive, understand, and transmit the moments when place yields up its "extraordinary" values. For the purpose of discussing the "act of focusing" involved in these works, we can divide her characters into four major groups based on their ability to "stand still" and see themselves in proper relation to their worlds. We might label the types as the objects, the insiders, the outsiders, and the seers or "onlookers" as they have sometimes been called. (In making these classifications, I recognize that each work develops very differently from the others, that the aims and discoveries of the characters are unique to their special situations, and that the general patterns of attitudes grow out of an overall design for achieving perception that Miss Welty applies flexibly and sensitively to the individual case.)

8. Eudora Welty, *One Time, One Place* (New York, 1971), 8.
9. Welty, "Place in Fiction," 63.
10. *Ibid.*

The object character is often at the center of a novel as the one who is watched, almost always seen from the outside by most of the other characters. He both epitomizes his place and stands more or less free from it, and this is the source of his fascination for other characters, most of whom are attracted to him by an urge to define him more firmly in terms of place in order to preserve their own need for stability. George Fairchild is such a character in *Delta Wedding*, so often the center of his family's thoughts, representing for them the security and permanence of their social order but somehow mysterious and in a way threatening because he does not seem to be pinned down in their place, as they themselves are content to be. George marries a town girl, of different caste and class, who has none of their reverence for "roots," and while he himself seems to uphold their system, his unpredictability troubles the family deeply.

In Welty's two most recent novels there appear characters like George who are the center of family or community focus but who by marrying outsiders seem to betray the values which have been invested in them. Jack Renfro in *Losing Battles* and Judge McKelva in *The Optimist's Daughter* are "object" characters who are watched, counted on, and worried over as representatives of order who are not quite to be trusted to stay within the bounds set by family or community. They tend to stray, to exercise an unorderly independence, to be willing to risk uprooting old definitions in order to fulfill some more important need.

In *The Golden Apples* King MacLain is a pure object character, free from his community but somehow at the very heart of it, a wanderer who can never get away from Morgana, who is defined and finally must define himself largely in terms of the behavior that Morgana expects of him. As a center of interest in most of the stories in the collection, he operates as a unifying force for *The Golden Apples*.

The object character can wander freely from his place—George Fairchild moves to Memphis, King MacLain is gone from Morgana for years at a time, Jack Renfro stays away from the reunion long enough to renew his conjugal ties with Gloria after an extended absence at Parchman. Still, this figure functions quite differently from a second type of character, the outsider. The outsider never truly belongs to the place he has come to live. He or she is not a "native," and although such a person may have been born only a few miles down the road from a community or family in question, there is a cultural gulf that cannot be crossed by years of residence or even by marriage. It is interesting to note that while the object characters in all four of the works under discussion are males, the outsider character is usually a woman.

In three cases, the outsiders are wives of object characters. They resent and are in turn resented by the families they enter as brides of favored sons or fathers or uncles. Robbie, as George's wife in *Delta Wedding*, is openly hostile on occasion to the Fairchilds' influence on her husband. Gloria, in *Losing Battles*, has only one all-consuming dream, and that is to settle with Jack away from his demanding clan. Fay, as Judge McKelva's second wife in *The Optimist's Daughter*, has the whole community against her. Robbie and Gloria are allowed some limited acceptance into their husbands' family circles; their roles as intruders are tempered by the love for their husbands that must be shared by all.

Fay, on the other hand, is closer in one sense to two other, more dynamic outsider figures: Miss Eckhart of *The Golden Apples* and Miss Mortimer of *Losing Battles*. The latter two, old maids of great intellectual strength and sensitivity, are much more sympathetically presented than Fay; nevertheless all three have the same sort of effect on the communities they enter. They present a direct threat to the ritualized patterns of life that have been nurtured, protected, and preserved at great cost by the old, closed families of Morgana, Banner, and Mount Salus. Miss Eckhart is a foreigner, inherently strange through her German customs and accent, but Fay and Miss Mortimer too might just as well have come from other countries, instead of different states or counties.

One other outsider figure of somewhat special significance is Judge Oscar Moody, who actually functions in two different capacities in *Losing Battles*. As the judge who sentences Jack to a term at Parchman, he is a classic outsider and a villain as well. But he is grouped with the Beechum-Vaughn-Renfro clan in another respect, his relation to Miss Julia Mortimer. He joins what becomes almost a Greek chorus, or perhaps what more aptly compares to an Irish wake, to sing with the others a paean of somewhat dubious praise to Miss Mortimer after her death. He definitely does not "belong" to the reunion; yet he is absolutely essential, not to impose a foreign perspective but, through his sensitive perceptions, to provide an illuminating response to all the events that are discussed at the celebration. He becomes the closest example of a seer or onlooker figure we are given in *Losing Battles*.

This third type of figure, the seer, is naturally the one who counts most in terms of the act of focusing. From the technical angle this person provides the center of "consciousness" for the reader, making judgments, shaping opinions, adding a dimension of objective distance or subjective depth; from the standpoint of theme, the characters consciously, purposefully involved in the act of focusing are the ones to watch. They alone are not static; the important "plot" of each work usually is much more concerned with their interior growth in awareness than with the exterior events—the weddings, recitals, reunions, funerals—that make up their field of vision.

In terms of measuring the development of Miss Welty's art, the functions and capacities of this third type of character are most revealing. From *Delta Wedding* to *The Optimist's Daughter*, the seer figure has grown more complex, more closely integrated into the kind of dual process of mystery and revelation that it is the author's main purpose to unfold. The seer figures tend to contain within their perspective more concentrated power in each work until, in the story of Laurel McKelva, there are no events, hardly any images, that are not filtered through her watchful, waiting eyes. *The Optimist's Daughter* is, by its title and in every other respect as well, a story about perspective.

Reynolds Price, in one of the first articles to appear concerning *The Optimist's Daughter*, takes note of how the "onlooker" figure, as he calls Laurel McKelva, differs from such characters of earlier works. For him the important change concerns the fact that in Miss Welty's most recent novel, the final look is not one of "puzzlement" as in earlier works; in *The Optimist's Daughter*, by contrast, "the end clarifies. Mystery dissolves before patient watching."[11] This distinction, however, seems not nearly so relevant as one that can be made concerning the increased power of the vision that is attained in *The Optimist's Daughter*, a power that results not so much from Laurel's being less puzzled by what she looks upon than earlier seer figures as it does from Miss Welty's own mastery of the technical and thematic possibilities of such a figure.

In *Delta Wedding* there is no one center of consciousness who op-

11. Reynolds Price, "The Onlooker Smiling: An Early Reading of *The Optimist's Daughter*," *Shenandoah*, XX (Spring, 1969), 62.

erates exclusively or fully as a seer. Usually young Laura McRaven is marked out as the character who is most perceptive and whose impressions of life at Shellmound operate best to clarify or evaluate essential points for the author. Yet in addition to Laura, there is Ellen, the Fairchild mother who is perhaps the most dependable seer and who like young Laura both belongs and is yet a little apart, a Fairchild by marriage and not birth. There are also the viewpoints of Shelley and Dabney, the two oldest Fairchild daughters, whose consciousness that they will not always be only Fairchilds helps them to appraise their family with greater independence.

Taken together all these perspectives form a kaleidoscopic vision of Fairchild life that is constantly being reshaped by many richly varied bits and pieces falling into different patterns. There is a sense of tentativeness that results both from this multiple focus and also from the fact that none of these seers can achieve complete detachment. All of them are a little afraid of the separateness that the act of focusing requires. In their family, togetherness is more than just a virtue; it has been taught as the only reliable mechanism of survival.

The Golden Apples in many ways improves on the mechanisms used to provide focus in *Delta Wedding*. The collection of stories does not form a single plot thread built around one event. Still, in the matter of perspective there is more unity than *Delta Wedding* can impose, largely because the seer figure is given a capacity for greater control over a particular field of vision. Not all of the stories make use of such a figure, but the two most pivotal, "June Recital" and the climactic "The Wanderers," provide dramatic examples of the shaping power of the act of focusing. In "June Recital" we are given the focus of Loch, imaginative, innocent, free-wheeling; and the focus of Cassie, stirred and contained by memory and knowledge—both on the same material. Together the two operate in the manner of a lyric duet, achieving the effect of a piece of music begun at different points, played by hands of different skill, interpreted by differing artistic sensibilities.

Virgie Rainey of "The Wanderers" is the key seer figure in this last story, which brings together the threads of the whole, not to fix them but to arrange them in new ways, building "new life" out of Morgana's old experiences. Virgie Rainey appears as more or less an "object" character in "June Recital," seen entirely from the outside as a figure free to wander, to show her disdain for place but always in an important way imprisoned by Morgana's definition of her, just as King MacLain is. In "The Wanderers" she becomes a seer and shaper herself, forced into a role as onlooker both by her community's demands that she conform and by her need to understand herself.

Losing Battles offers an experiment in focusing that makes it unique among Welty's works. It is a novel without a true center of consciousness who actively *reflects* on the world around him to inform or evaluate or hold events in place. Discussing her technique in *Losing Battles*, Welty has said that she wanted to make the novel proceed "altogether by talk and action, trying to *show* everything and not as an author enter the character's mind and say, 'He was thinking so-and-so.'"[12] Thus the act of focusing, as a mechanism to reveal inner character, becomes a matter of significance almost exclusively in the case of Judge Moody. He is the only character actually called upon in the novel to find knowledge and interpret it as a "judge" out of court as well as in.

There is another method, however, through which Welty reveals the interior worlds of her characters, particularly the two most sensitive, Gloria and the judge. By focusing on the natural world, then blending it with the emotions of her characters through similes, she puts character and place together in dynamic relationship in this novel.

Two examples will suffice to show her sensitive approach in the area of revealing inner character through natural description. One occurs as Gloria sits waiting by the roadside for Jack to return, listening to the reunion recital of the exploits that resulted in his prison term. Her attitude toward life, her relation to the family circle are both defined by a description of butterflies that hover around her throughout the scene: "Out there with her flew the yellow butterflies of August—as wild and bright as people's notions and dreams, but filled with a dream of their own; in one bright body, as though against a headwind, they were flying toward the east."[13] And the scene in which Judge Moody reads Miss Mortimer's letter to the reunion is juxtaposed with this account of the twilight hour: "The moon did not yet give off light— it was only turned to the light, like a human head" (LB, 299).

In *Losing Battles*, then, the act of focusing most important to the

---

12. Charles T. Bunting, "'The Interior World': An Interview with Eudora Welty," *Southern Review*, VIII (Autumn, 1972), 720.
13. Eudora Welty, *Losing Battles* (New York, 1970), 39.

development of the characters in relation to their world is an act that is cinematic; we are offered pictures in motion directed over a richly varied surface of natural images which have special illuminating power when associated with the poses or gestures of certain characters. "I see things in pictures," Welty once explained, and since her own eye is the key focusing agent in *Losing Battles*, the novel itself becomes a remarkable panorama of open spaces and figures who expose themselves freely and fully through words and actions.[14]

Welty's experimental technique works well in *Losing Battles* partly because of the qualities of the particular place that she creates in this novel. Banner offers an environment in which nature itself is such a powerful force that it permeates every aspect of the lives of the characters who abide in it. The family that gathers at the Renfro homestead is an extension of the land itself; these folk feel their roots in this gathering spot as a physical force. The changing patterns of weather, seasons, sunlight, and moonlight are the guideposts of their tribal existence. Like the land, they have nothing to depend on but themselves.

The situation is quite different in *The Optimist's Daughter* where there is no one stable pastoral landscape to provide a fixed point of illumination for the characters. *The Optimist's Daughter* deals in part with the breakup of traditional values and easy associations between person and place; this, perhaps, is one reason why it has a strong seer figure to provide focus. Laurel McKelva is a character very much like Virgie Rainey of *The Golden Apples*, as Mount Salus is a place very much like Morgana. The chief difference between the two novels is that in the later work time has made more definite inroads into the insular community.

The fact that in *The Optimist's Daughter* a sense of fragmentation is stronger than in the earlier works can be seen by a new treatment of the fourth type of character, the insider, a standard in all of the works. Insider figures play dominant roles in *Delta Wedding*, in *The Golden Apples*, and in *Losing Battles*, but this dominance is seriously challenged in *The Optimist's Daughter*. The insider is traditionally the spokesman for place and is secure only when firmly entrenched in place. And since the family circle is the mainstay of a reverent sense

14. Bunting, "'The Interior World,'" 725.

of place, the insider character is always found thriving within that circle, often as its strongest link. The Fairchild aunts at Shellmound, the ladies of Morgana, and the Beechum sisters and brothers are all insiders; their main function, as well as the exalted purpose of their lives, is to preserve the fabric of their place against outsiders, against change, against time.

It is significant that in *The Optimist's Daughter* the strongest proponent of place lives only as a sharp yet distanced memory. Becky McKelva, the judge's first wife and Laurel's mother, exercises her power over the lives of her family only as a reminder, though a keen one, of something lost. The "bridesmaids," Laurel's Mount Salus friends, also function as insider figures who promote place, but here again their label reveals the limitations of their usefulness, the narrowness of their capacities. The bride herself lives now in Chicago; her father, once so much a part of Mount Salus, marries a second wife so completely the antithesis of everything that his community stands for that her presence causes a rupture. The second wife's family is an example of a new rootless world in which the need for place has been supplanted by a culture whose trademarks are her mother's trailer and her brother's wrecking business.

Relationships among the four types of characters—the objects, insiders, outsiders, and seers—develop solidly within the definitive place in which they are fixed, temporarily or permanently, as their stories progress. The patterns these relationships take differ for each book, yet all take their shape primarily from one locale, the "gathering spot," as Welty has called it, "for all that has been felt, is about to be experienced, in the novel's progress." Each work develops one type of character to a higher degree than the rest in order to evolve some special insight important to the novel's overall meaning. In *Delta Wedding*, an object figure is the dominant factor involved in dramatizing the act of focusing; in *Losing Battles* an outsider figure becomes the chief catalyst of vision; in *The Golden Apples* and *The Optimist's Daughter*, the seer figures develop to the fullest the dramatic possibilities of Welty's ideas concerning living relationships between character and place in fiction.

George Fairchild holds the key to insight in *Delta Wedding*. None of the seer figures is used fully or consistently to provide a unified vision for this novel. Nonetheless, a measure of unity is achieved by the fact that the focus of all the characters returns again and again to the same fixed point, to George, as though everyone senses instinctively that he is the only one capable of revealing the meanings they seek. As Ellen Fairchild perceives, "everything he did meant something." [15]

The family at Shellmound looks to George. In this charmed, perfectly pastoral little world, he offers hope for the continuance of the past because he alone seems unthreatened by the present. If he marries a modern town girl it is to bring her into their circle, not to take them out of it; if he moves to Memphis, still he will come back to fish, to smoke his pipe, to reassure them all that nothing has changed. It is important that he has married an outsider, that he does live in a large city. By performing these gestures of separation but remaining still a Fairchild, George seems proof that Shellmound itself can endure against time, that the values it stands for can be submitted to any kind of test, as George is, and still survive. For George is not afraid of the present; he will even stand down a speeding train on a railroad trestle. If the present cannot harm George, the Fairchild hero and, as one seer recognized, its "sacrificial beast" (DW, 63) as well, then Shellmound is safe.

George's distinctiveness is defined well by Dabney, the Fairchild daughter who will soon marry an outsider too. She recalls a moment which revealed to her "a curious division between George and the rest," and finally puts her finger on the difference: "And George loved the *world*, something told her suddenly. Not them! Not them in particular" (DW, 37). George's detachment allows him to become a kind of mirroring device through which his personality reflects back to each seer that looks to him an image of that character's own deepest concerns. Robbie takes note of this: "George was not the one they all looked at, she thought at that moment, as he was always declared to be, but the eye that saw them, from right in their midst" (DW, 212).

For young Laura McRaven, so conscious herself of belonging yet not belonging to Shellmound, George represents a way to cope with her peculiar position as city cousin. She is made sensitive, out of her

15. Eudora Welty, *Delta Wedding* (New York, 1945), 222.

special need for acceptance, to George's gift for staying separate while accepting all the demands of his family: "Something told her . . . that it was right for him to stand apart" (DW, 75). Shelley Fairchild is another seer figure whose perceptions of Shellmound are not totally those of an insider and who thus can find personal revelations in focusing on George. Shelley seems to have a quality that the other Fairchilds, as a group, lack—a sense of fear of an encroaching world beyond their gates, a sense of its inevitability as well: "what was going to happen was going to happen" (DW, 196). She is at one point "sickeningly afraid of life, life itself, afraid for life" (DW, 197), yet through an identification with George is able to learn to anticipate the unknown. With George's special "vision of choice" in mind, Shelley is able to make a commitment: her "desire fled, or danced seriously, to an open place—not from one room to another room with its door, but to an opening wood, with weather—with change, beauty" (DW, 220).

It is this recognition of the necessity of change, of opening doors, of knowing about "geography" that the seers of *Delta Wedding* achieve through their focus on George Fairchild. The character for whom this recognition is most meaningful is Ellen Fairchild, whose focus vacillates between her needs as an individual for change and growth and her obligation and instincts as the Fairchild mother to hold her children's world intact and secure.

The dual motion involved in the act of focusing is held in balance in Welty's conception of this character: Ellen wants life to "stand still," an order she often gives her children, yet she also recognizes that a frozen surface does not reveal truth, that existence for all at Shellmound is only temporarily "a charmed life," and so she finds herself "wishing worse predicaments, darker passion, upon all their lives" (DW, 166). The threats to Ellen's pastoral kingdom are there as surely and unavoidably as time, and her ability to focus on George as a being "infinitely simple and infinitely complex, stretching the opposite ways the self stretches" (DW, 222) seems her greatest aid in coming to terms with those threats.

Dabney's wedding to Troy has been only one of many events to challenge Shellmound's serenity. To be sure, the wedding itself is securely encased in a timeless ritual. Likewise, all other threats have seemed to dissolve before the "charmed life" at Shellmound, as Ellen

Fairchild notes: "The Yellow Dog had not run down George and Maureen; Robbie had not stayed away too long; Battle had not driven Troy out of the Delta" (DW, 166). Yet the illusion of perfect peace within the plantation's borders is no more than that, an illusion doomed to be broken not by events as dramatic as a train accident (though the Yellow Dog does hit a beautiful young girl walking on the tracks on the day of the wedding) but by the sheer force of life going on its forward course. The photographer is unable to get the family group to hold still for a wedding portrait: "You all moved," he laments.

That things will change is brought home to all the Fairchilds in the last scene of the novel. In a gentle yet almost deliberately disruptive fashion, George injects a definitely threatening note into the idyllic setting of a family picnic by talking of a scheme to turn his Delta home, "The Grove," into a progressive farm. The Fairchilds cope with this new threat largely by ignoring it or writing it off as one of George's passing fancies. The perfect stillness of this evening with its family ritual allows them to hide together from a truth they would all have to acknowledge separately.

In *Delta Wedding* it is ritual that dominates even George, yet he seems best equipped to handle the knowledge that rituals celebrate ending as well as beginning over. So it is with this picnic occasioned by the return of Dabney and Troy but also by the projected leave-taking of George and Robbie. The family circle remains full and complete, yet is itself propelled in new directions by each new quest for life going on within it. The last act pictured in the novel is an act of focusing on a changing world, as the family watches stars falling through the September night and one of the children looks into the river that flows by at their feet "as if she saw some certain thing, neither marvelous nor terrible, but simply certain, come by in the Yazoo River" (DW, 247).

Delta Wedding takes place in a year (1923) which Miss Welty chose from an almanac as being one in which there were no wars or floods or other outside forces to act on this region and its people; her purpose in choosing such a time, she has explained, was to allow the Fairchild family to develop as though its life could truly go on "on a small scale in a world of its own." For *Losing Battles*, she chose a very different time, having in mind for this novel a different purpose: "I wanted to get a year in which I could show people at the rock bottom of their whole lives, which meant the Depression." These would be people who had "no props to their lives, had only themselves, plus an indomitable will to live even with losing battles."[16]

Delta Wedding and *Losing Battles* have many striking similarities as well as differences which make them interesting to examine side by side, particularly with regard to their handling of the idea of focus. The surface parallels are numerous: in both, one large family meets in an insular, ritualistic gathering to celebrate a custom which is of religious significance to the members, who see themselves self-consciously as a kind of closed tribe grouped together for survival. In both novels, favored male members have married outsiders who are held within the tribe, regarded uneasily but tolerated for the sake of tribal unity. In both, the outside world encroaches; there are threats of disruption from several directions; the families might hide themselves from reality but the great world looks in on them easily, imperturbably—theirs is a losing battle.

Still, a key difference is pointed up by Miss Welty's choice of a dominant character type to act as catalyst in each novel. In *Delta Wedding* an object figure is the center of focus who stimulates the others into the acts of contemplation that are essential to the novel's progress. In *Losing Battles* an outsider is the catalyst who reveals the nature of the struggle going on. George, the key object figure of the earlier novel, protects his family even while exposing them to necessary glimpses of the outside; Miss Julia Mortimer is unkind enough to die on the day of the Beechum-Vaughn-Renfro reunion, sparking conversations and insights very untypical for the day's usual program.

Miss Julia's way is not to give gentle doses of eye-openers as George does. As an outsider she has no family ties to induce her to be tender or even courteous concerning the Beechums' ignorance of what the world demands: "All my life I've fought a hard war with ignorance," she writes to Judge Moody (LB, 298). For her it is total war, involving for both sides "the survival instinct": "It's the desperation of staying alive against all odds that keeps both sides encouraged" (LB, 298). The nature of Miss Julia's "enemy" is perhaps best exemplified in

16. Bunting, "'The Interior World,'" 721, 722.

the novel by Miss Beulah, the most indomitable Beechum of all. When a new relative sees that a family story she is being told is about to get back to where it first started, she asks, "Are we back around to that?" Miss Beulah haughtily replies, "It's the same gold ring, and all the one sad story" (LB, 219). The Beechums and Renfros, with Beulah in the lead, revel in the retellings of their story, in finding ways to fit all the happenings of the world around them into the tightly woven, immovable framework of their past.

Nothing would keep "the one sad story" from being told and re-told on this reunion day as it has been on all the others if it were not for a set of comically intricate circumstances that bring Judge Oscar Moody into the center of the family circle bearing what has turned out to be a deathbed mandate from Miss Julia Mortimer. Judge Moody's presence only causes the family to draw their wagons closer together to turn away the challenge he represents, yet for once the reunion is moved off its established ground. The feeling is an unsettling one, and Judge Moody is told, "We don't appreciate a comer like you getting up in our midst and making us listen to ourselves being criticized" (LB, 302).

At the beginning of Part Four, the reunion hears the news that Miss Mortimer has died. From this point on in the novel, the family's focus is diverted from a self-congratulatory rehearsal of its own private history to an uncomfortable encounter with an unwelcome ghost. There are four different renditions of Miss Julia's struggles; all of them tend to confirm the schoolteacher's own assessment that "except in those cases that you can count off on your fingers, I lost every battle" (LB, 298) in the war she fought to change the Banner citizens' concept of themselves.

The Beechum aunts and uncles who were her students begin the recital, smug enough in their belief that though "she had designs on everybody," they escaped her influence. A dimension of powerful irony is added to the picture the Beechums sketch of Miss Julia by the fact that they know her lessons by heart and repeat them word for word, but without understanding or even curiosity. We find that what they most resented was not her own differences from them—her red sweater, her habit of reading books in the daytime—but the fact that she wanted to make *them* different: "She thought if she mortified you long enough, you might have hope of turning out something you wasn't!" (LB, 236). Their indomitable attachment to the sameness of their lives keeps Miss Julia from winning any total victories over the Beechums.

Lexie Renfro recites a second segment of Miss Julia's story, one that adds the dimension of tragedy to the tale. In her last months, Miss Julia had been left totally alone in the care of Lexie, a shrewish spinster who is repulsive even to her own family. Lexie's horrifying story of Miss Julia's final battles against ignorance and apathy and, finally, death, is too much for all of them. The full measure of the horror is communicated best through Miss Welty's description of Granny's growing consternation as Lexie talks. Granny has Miss Julia's last losing battle soon to face, and at the end of Lexie's gruesome account of Miss Julia's desperate situation, she only says, "I'm ready to go home now."

Gloria and Judge Moody add crucial pieces to the puzzle in their accounts of relationships with Miss Julia. These two, as outsiders, can supply touches of sensitivity and sympathy that are lacking in other descriptions, yet their final effect is only to give more weight to the sense of failure and frustration that surrounds the picture of the schoolteacher, since they, too, have proven unequal to her hopes for them. Gloria's recitative functions as well to spark the family's acknowledgment of Miss Julia's more personal ties to them, ties going far beyond the schoolhouse where she tried to badger them into learning who they really were. It is discovered that she possessed greater knowledge of certain private identities among them than they themselves knew. Their fight to keep her out of their lives has been a losing battle too.

If Gloria's account of Miss Mortimer functions to show the schoolteacher in intimate, private relationship to the Beechum clan, then Judge Moody's does the converse, demonstrating her effect on the world beyond Banner, Boone County, and even Mississippi: "She's made her a Superior Court judge, the best eye, ear, nose, and throat specialist in Kansas City, and a history professor somewhere—they're all scattered wide, of course" (LB, 305).

More importantly, however, Judge Moody is willing to reveal her effect on the course of his own life, and in the process to show both her and himself in their full humanity. He is her only success, the only example we are given, at any rate, of a character who honestly takes up her charge of self-discovery and faces who he really is. The effect on him of having to focus on Miss Julia's failures, of being "maneuvered" into the "root of it all . . . the very pocket of ignorance" that the reunion represents, is a thoroughly disheartening one. "Nothing wrong," he answers when his wife asks. "Only I don't care quite the same about living as I did this morning" (LB, 307).

Judge Moody would be a crucial character even without these self-revelations because of the deathbed letter that he carries from Miss Julia and reads to the reunion. At the end of the novel, Gloria tells Jack that Miss Mortimer "wanted everything brought out in the wide open, to see and be known. She wanted people to spread out their minds and their hearts to other people, so they could be read like books" (LB, 432). Miss Julia's letter to Judge Moody indicates her own willingness to be read in this way. It also acts as counterpoint to the reunion's way of life, as she defines the battle that all of them were involved in and brings to them a consciousness of time and its consequences of knowledge and change, a consciousness that has been their life work to avoid.

The principal factor in Miss Mortimer's defeat has been not dragons of ignorance in the shape of the children of Banner School, but time. Time made her too old to fight, but only by bringing death could it remove her from the struggle. "Mostly I lost, they won," she writes. "But as long as I was still young, I always thought if I could marshal strength enough of body and spirit and push with it, every ounce, I could change the future" (LB, 298).

Miss Julia's letter expresses her feeling that both her way of taking on the future in deliberate, forward-looking steps and the Beechums' way of circling around the past have, in the final analysis, "the same force" behind them, "the survival instinct." Both are ways of fighting to perpetuate cherished values. Miss Julia's way, because it leads more directly to confrontations with time, seems to be the surer way to defeat. There is a compensation to this, however: "But the side that gets licked gets to the truth first," she discovered, and truth is the "one reliable thing" (LB, 298).

The Beechums and Renfros are doomed to "get licked" eventually themselves and will have to meet truth privately, without the protection of the family circle drawn in around them. Granny's separateness from her family and her last cry of "Don't leave me!" to the departing reunion symbolize the nearness for her of the battle that only

Miss Julia has faced squarely and openly. The focus on Miss Julia shows that she alone discovered the kind of value in truth that compensates for losing battles or perhaps even turns them into victory.

In *Losing Battles* the act of focusing, as applied by the reunion figures, centers most intensely on Miss Julia. Thus the Beechums and Renfros, willingly or not, are made participants in the battle with time and change as she herself defined it and set the rules. In *The Golden Apples* there is a character of the same mold who draws a reluctant, closed community into a similar battle. Miss Eckhart, like Miss Julia, is an outsider who is never given a word to speak directly and who is the center of the focus of others. As in the portrayal of Miss Julia in *Losing Battles*, Miss Welty's depiction of Miss Eckhart solely through the eyes and opinions of other characters accomplishes the purpose of setting her squarely within an enemy camp.

Like Miss Julia in her jousts with the Banner community, Miss Eckhart will seem to lose every battle with Morgana. There is, however, one element in *The Golden Apples* that is not applied consistently in *Losing Battles*, one that will allow Miss Eckhart a more positive final victory than Miss Julia is allowed within the framework of her novel. That element is a seer figure who operates within *The Golden Apples* to vindicate the position against Morgana taken by Miss Eckhart.

Virgie Rainey, in the last story of *The Golden Apples*, "The Wanderers," gives to the collection as a whole a single unifying vision. The concerns of all the other stories are filtered through her consciousness as "The Wanderers" progresses; those concerns are shown to have a common theme involving the relations between insiders and outsiders, between those who cling to concepts associated with a single, certain place and those who see the larger world pressing in.

"The Wanderers" gathers all the chief actors and actresses of the collection together in the performance of a ritual, a device of the earlier *Delta Wedding* that would be used again in both *Losing Battles* and *The Optimist's Daughter*. In "The Wanderers" the occasion is a funeral, a time like weddings and reunions for summing up, for reexamining the past and putting it into perspective. Only a seer figure can perform such functions fully and relate them as well to a necessary contemplation of the future. Virgie Rainey is the first really dynamic figure in Miss Welty's fiction to show herself equal to the task.

While Morgana's citizens gather in the Raineys' parlor for the "laying out" of Miss Katie (Virgie's mother), Virgie herself begins her role as seer: "When she opened her eyes, she watched and listened to the even fuller roomful as carefully, and as carelessly, as vacillating as though she were on the point of departure" (GA, 237). Again we see the quality of double vision in Virgie's focus; she is both "careful" and "careless," both "at home" and "on the point of departure." It is her special power of vision that allows her a number of revelations as the story progresses.

Virgie's first visions involve focusing on Morgana as a social structure, one called out upon this occasion of death to engage its system of checks and balances in summing up and fitting in this new development. The dead fit easily enough into Morgana's scheme: "Attrition was their wisdom . . . this was the past now" (GA, 263), and with the past, Morgana's people are comfortable. It is the living who must be held in check in Morgana. Throughout the story the old ladies' hands are always on Virgie, pushing her into the bedroom to view her mother's body, pulling her to the table to eat, guiding her into the car for the ride to the cemetery. When they finally leave her alone, "they seemed to drag some mythical gates and barriers away from her view" (GA, 247).

Yet the imprisoning power of a place is something to be sought out, as Virgie has learned through a dream: "And if, as she dreamed one winter night, a new piano she touched had turned, after one pristine moment, into a calling cow, it was by her own desire" (GA, 266). This dream represents, by the metamorphosis of piano into cow, the life choice that Virgie has made. She has traded the piano, which represented her chance for an escape from the prison of Morgana, for the duties of service to place: milking cows, typing for Mr. Nesbitt, nursing her mother. Only by such an apprenticeship can she learn the value of time: "as if she would hunt, hunt, hunt daily for the blindness that lay inside the beast, inside where she could have a real and living wall for beating on, a solid prison to get out of" (GA, 266).

Virgie's relation to all that Morgana represents is made clearer to her by her vision of King MacLain, another wanderer, like herself returned to this place to face its definitions of his own possibilities. In King the wild urge for freedom from place has resulted in years of traveling away from Morgana. Still he has found himself trapped there in the end, as though he had never left: "I'd come and I'd go again, only I ended up at the wrong end, wouldn't you say?" (GA, 253). Yet he is not defeated; as the funeral service goes on in the Rainey parlor, King makes a "hideous face" at Virgie which looks to her like "a silent yell . . . a yell at everything—including death, not leaving it out" (GA, 257). Later Virgie is able to turn this feeling into a perception of life's power over place: "But Mr. King MacLain, an old man, had butted like a goat against the wall he wouldn't agree to himself or recognize. What fortress indeed would ever come down, except before hard little horns, a rush and a stampede of the pure wish to live?" (GA, 264).

It is significant that two cemeteries appear in "The Wanderers." In the Morgana cemetery are those who lived and died by Morgana's rules—the Raineys, Starks, Carmichaels, Morgans, even Miss Eckhart's sweetheart, Mr. Sissum—and also those who beat their heads against Morgana's walls but found the struggle not worth the effort and so committed suicide—Cassie Morrison's mother and the "little country girl" who had an affair with Ran MacLain. Yet Miss Eckhart is not buried in the Morgana cemetery, nor will King MacLain himself be. Their resting place is the MacLain cemetery, where other fighters are buried—Eugene MacLain and a grandfather MacLain who killed a man and so left "a long story behind [his grave], the vaunting and wandering from it" (GA, 274).

Virgie Rainey's last act of focusing is a trip to MacLain where she sits in the rain and looks upon this cemetery, thinking of the dead and the living who have entered her life and left impressions. What she sees most clearly, though, is a picture from her past, the picture in Miss Eckhart's studio of Perseus with the head of Medusa. The picture of Perseus cutting off the Medusa's head makes "visible" for Virgie "a horror in life, that was at once the horror in love" (GA, 275). The horror is "separateness," the necessary revelation that one is all to oneself and apart from everything else. Yet on this last day, as Virgie is about to affirm her own separateness by leaving Morgana, she is aware of a deeper meaning to life than just its "horror": "beyond the beauty and the sword's stroke and the terror lay their existence in time—far out and endless, a constellation which the heart could read over many a night" (GA, 276).

Miss Welty explains why Virgie is able to reach a recognition of her full humanity as she is about to leave Morgana: it is "because Virgie saw things in their time, like hearing them" (GA, 275). For Morgana's proper citizens, things find acceptable existence only when they are seen in their place; place is used to fix things in a way that ignores time. Thus these people's vision of life lacks continuity; they are left open to an unrelieved "horror" of separateness. Virgie sees separate people and their places wrapped together in a "constellation" held together by the common bond that all things share through their existence in time: "Every time Perseus struck off the Medusa's head, there was the beat of time, and the melody. Endless the Medusa, and Perseus endless" (GA, 276).

Virgie's perception of the existence of things in time does not motivate her to deny the value of place but allows her to open Morgana's windows to the world, to measure it in terms of larger possibilities and realities, such as time, history, the arts, and death. Miss Welty, with her penchant for pictures, ends *The Golden Apples* with one that shows forth the full possibilities of Virgie's vision of things in their time:

> Then she and the old beggar woman, the old black thief, were there alone and together in the shelter of the big public tree, listening to the magical percussion, the world beating in their ears. They heard through falling rain the running of the horse and bear, the stroke of the leopard, the dragon's crusty slither, and the glimmer and the trumpet of the swan. (GA, 277)

If Virgie Rainey's focus at the end of "The Wanderers" provides, for *The Golden Apples* as a whole, a vision of the possibilities inherent in seeing things in their time, then Laurel McKelva's focus in *The Optimist's Daughter* adds an important corollary, that of accepting the full consequences that a commitment to the dimension of time demands. We witness Virgie at the beginning of such a commitment, as if she has just learned how to focus the lens of a camera on some truly valuable subject and is ready to click the shutter.

Life's achievements and limitations are both ahead of Virgie, so her task as seer is quite different from Laurel McKelva's. Laurel returns to her home of Mount Salus to develop a completed roll of film, as it were, to provide the light and skill by which the lives of her parents and herself might be wisely interpreted. Discussing her own photographs (and by simple extension, the art of seeing itself) in *One Time, One Place,* Miss Welty tells us, "It was after I got home, had made my prints in the kitchen and dried them overnight and looked at them in the morning by myself, that I began to see objectively what I had there." Later she adds, "If exposure is essential, still more so is the reflection." [17]

Laurel McKelva in *The Optimist's Daughter* develops the reflective side of the seer most fully for Miss Welty's fiction as she sifts through all the testimony compiled concerning her family and the places and experiences which have defined them. From its opening chapter, set in the office of a noted eye specialist, *The Optimist's Daughter* takes as its fundamental concern the problems of seeing, in the literal, but of course more importantly in the symbolic, sense of that act. For both of Laurel's parents, a losing battle with death begins with eye problems, and in the course of the novel it is shown that in their private, separate lives, Judge and Becky McKelva each suffered from a sort of imperfect inner vision. The first personal note given in the description of Laurel herself is that "her dark blue eyes looked sleepless." [18] The closing sentence speaks of "the last thing Laurel saw."

In *The Optimist's Daughter* the ability to see and the ability to belong to place are correlated, and this relationship is borne out by the descriptions of things as Laurel sees them in Mt. Salus after her father's death. New Orleans, even during the vividly localized carnival season, is a "nowhere," while Mt. Salus, Laurel's birthplace, is a definite, solid "somewhere," in which everything can be seen because it is intimately *known,* in which everything is familiar, no room or chair or house "anonymous." Every object is visible to Laurel's mind as well as her eyes in Mt. Salus. Each one can be described not only in terms of how it looks but what it means.

In the world of Mt. Salus, only Judge McKelva's second wife, Fay, remains an enigma; as Laurel says, "I don't think I can safely predict about Fay." The reason, of course, is that nothing is known about Fay. She has no roots, no sense of place, no one to count on but "me, myself, and I" (OD, 54). And in order to understand herself, her world, or the meaning of all that has happened to her life, it is finally with Fay that Laurel must contend, without the aid to vision that might

17. Welty, *One Time, One Place,* 7–8.
18. Eudora Welty, *The Optimist's Daughter* (New York, 1972), 3.

be supplied by a sense of the familiar. Having to "see" Fay fully and deeply poses a terrifying challenge to Laurel, since "where there was no intimacy, Laurel shrank from contact" (OD, 18).

Fay is, quite simply, the future, the unknown factor of life that only time can bring into focus and the factor that changes all known, fixed quantities such as place. *The Optimist's Daughter* becomes a battle-ground between future and past, the past represented by Becky McKelva, or more correctly by the memories and mementos of Becky McKelva that keep the past in the present. Becky belonged to Mount Salus even though she was reared in the mountains of West Virginia. She fits into Mount Salus through her reverence for things in their place, for naming and knowing and fixing all the things that are part of her life—from rose bushes to college notes on *Paradise Lost*.

Thus Becky and Fay are well-matched opponents. Laurel returns to Mount Salus to vindicate the past as Becky represents it and to set it into an order that will allow it to endure against the future. Having buried her father and recommitted her mother's values to memory by sorting over, then burning, her letters and keepsakes, Laurel thinks she has accomplished all she needs to do for herself or her family: "There was nothing she was leaving in the whole shining and quiet house now to show for her mother's life and her mother's happiness and suffering, and nothing to show for Fay's harm; her father's turning between them, holding onto them both, then letting them go, was without any sign" (OD, 170).

Yet Laurel is not allowed off the hook so easily; Fay's essential threat lies not in her relation to Becky or to the judge but in her relation to Laurel's living sense of values. Laurel alone of her family remains to face the future, and it is a confrontation that she is not permitted to avoid. She must fight her own special "losing battle" with the Fay who can say nonchalantly, "The past isn't a thing to me. I belong to the future, didn't you know that?" Laurel must realize that she belongs to the future too, and her final revelation, that "the past is no more open to help or hurt than was Father in his coffin" (OD, 179), marks the essential turning point in her ability to place her own life in proper perspective.

Laurel is "the optimist's daughter." The stress of the title is that she has something to inherit from her father, the optimist. Her father's vision, as the story opens, has been "dislocated"; ever since her mother's death he has been an "optimist," a man who can look at the future unflinchingly, who accepts it, as he accepted Fay after Becky, with hope.

Judge McKelva is the figure of the novel who adds a sense of the dimension of time to the proceedings. He has had a vital relation to both past and future, "holding onto them both, then letting them go" (OD, 170). It is this sense of time that he bequeaths to his daughter. Laurel, watching him in the hospital, becomes aware that "what occupied his full mind was time itself"; she "was conscious of time along with him, setting her inner chronology with his, more or less as if they needed to keep in step for a long walk ahead of them" (OD, 19–20).

Time stops for the judge, but Laurel has the long walk ahead and will need a consciousness of time particularly in Mount Salus. Time seems to have stopped there, as the mantel clock in the McKelvas' house has stopped; Laurel supposes that it "had not been wound . . . since the last time her father had done duty by it" (OD, 73). The "bridesmaids" of Mount Salus, like the Fairchilds in *Delta Wedding* or the Beechums of *Losing Battles* or the citizens of Morgana in *The Golden Apples*, have structured their world so that the future is withheld for as long as possible. Whenever anything threatens, it is the bridesmaids' symbolic policy to shut one eye in a wink: "this was the . . . automatic signal in moments of acute joy or distress, to show solidarity" (OD, 50).

Laurel is not able to "wink" at the threat posed by Fay. She must be willing to wind the mantel clock, her duty as it was her father's; she must leave her parents' house to Fay and leave the past to itself with the recognition that she is nothing to it, "although it has been everything and done everything to me, everything for me" (OD, 179). Such a leave-taking is not a denial of the usefulness of the past, however. What makes Laurel a true seer is her ability to fuse past and future, the pull of place and the power of time, by her trust in the validity of memory. Memory, she acknowledges fairly early in the novel, "had the character of spring" (OD, 115). This revelation has practical application at the end when Laurel must acknowledge the inevitability of Fay as future: "You *are* the weather, thought Laurel. And the weather to come: there'll be many a one more like you, in this life" (OD, 173). Such an admission might constitute a total capitulation before the force of time if it were not for memory, "the somnambulist," as Laurel recognizes it.

The past itself "can never be awakened"; herein lies the folly of the closed circles of talk about the people and places of former times that occur at Miss Welty's reunions and funerals. There is no provision for renewal in the way her insiders cling to the past; in them there is no understanding of the part memory might play not simply in rehashing but in revitalizing what is forever out of reach by any other means. "The memory can be hurt, time and again—but in that may lie its final mercy. As long as it's vulnerable to the living moment, it lives for us, and while it lives, and while we are able, we can give up its due" (OD, 179). With this vision Laurel can return to Chicago and a life that is not trapped in a futile attempt to protect the cherished past from the future.

All of Miss Welty's seers are called upon by the demands of their worlds to put place into the context of time, to put the past in juxtaposition with the future. Such acts are essentially acts of focusing, seeing things in their time, and the art of such an endeavor involves both reverence for the stability of place and past and acceptance of time and future. And for Miss Welty the vulnerability of memory "to the living moment" is cause for celebration. The sense of place that endows her works with the charm of the personal and the particular loses nothing by being exposed, through the reflective light of a seer's focus, to more universal realities governing all life. There is the gain of what Miss Welty calls "human vision"; "and that," as she says in *One Time, One Place*, "is of course a gift."

TEN

The South Beyond Arcady

Eudora Welty published her first short story, "Death of a Traveling Salesman," in 1936. It was, no less than her most recent novel, a work in which both technique and theme relate to the act of focusing. The story closes in on the failures of perception of Mr. R. J. Bowman, who "for fourteen years had traveled for a shoe company through Mississippi." Mr. Bowman, as we meet him, has just recovered from an illness that suggests the weakness of vision and spirit that plagues him, a weakness caused primarily by his rootlessness. He is modern man, cut off from the world of human ties and the land which nurtures them. As he nears death, his lost opportunities for relationship make their way into his consciousness with a vibrancy that constitutes a stunning revelation. He is a man of time who measures himself only in terms of his years on the road until his own heart, and the rural land itself that he has always passed through, rebel. Forced to witness the deep, elemental life of a young farm couple, whose relationship he for a long time misconstrues as that of mother and son instead of husband and pregnant wife, Bowman is finally submitted to his heart's aching awareness, "protesting against emptiness." These folk live the life of the land, their actions riveted to archetypal patterns that shine through such gestures as cleaning a lamp or going to a nearby homestead to "borry some fire" even after Bowman has offered his matches. In this story the deeply rooted rural life achieves a simple yet eloquent moment of triumph over the barren disconnection of the modern man who lives out of his suitcase in a series of hotels in towns whose increasing size is his only standard of his own progress. Bowman's final perception is as much a judgment of his circumstances as it is a comprehension of the scene he has intruded upon:

> There was nothing remote or mysterious here—only something private. The only secret was the ancient communication between two people. But the memory of the woman's waiting silently by the cold hearth, of the man's stubborn journey a mile away to get fire, and how they finally brought out their food and drink and filled the room proudly with all they had to show, was suddenly too clear and too enormous within him for response.[1]

For "Death of a Traveling Salesman" a pastoral world is invoked as a tangible, enduring reality, and it is positioned both to balance and to contain the alien vision of the shoe salesman. Cut off completely from the mode of "ancient communication" he witnesses, his thought ("A marriage, a fruitful marriage. That simple thing. Anyone could have that.") might only emphasize the irony of his exclusion; still, the idyll of simple things that Sonny and his wife's world represents is, as rendered in this story at least, a vital, accessible "gathering spot" for acts of life as well as acts of focusing. The availability of such a world will recede in later Welty works, as *The Optimist's Daughter* demonstrates, but here it is a fruitful place to be.

The husband-wife relationship, the affirmation of a dynamic rural mode over the empty existence of the modern exile from it, makes "Death of a Traveling Salesman" an interesting work to compare to another story of roughly the same time and place which applies a similar balance of worlds with a decidedly agrarian bias. In Robert Penn Warren's "The Patented Gate and the Mean Hamburger," the hill-town hamburger stand that is "built like a railway coach" symbolizes, like Bowman's sample case in Welty's story, a mobile, sterile way of life that is balanced in Warren's sketch by Jeff York's farm, the sixty acres and a barn whose possession York proudly declares by the white patented gate that opens into his place. The farm is Jeff York's dream, fulfilled by years of "sweat and rejection"; the "dogwagon" is his wife's dream, nurtured by her desire for city ways and city talk,

---

1. Eudora Welty, "Death of a Traveling Salesman," in *A Curtain of Green and Other Stories* (New York, 1941), 251.

for a relief from the isolation and monotony of her husband's circumscribed life in the hill country. Mrs. York applies the kind of pressure that makes it impossible for her husband to refuse her; the farm is, in effect, traded for the hamburger stand; and Jeff York, shortly thereafter, hangs himself from the crossbeam of the patented gate, the symbol finally of a way of life betrayed. And while this story might seem to mark the triumph of the world of the "mean hamburger" that is Mrs. York's and modern man's material specialty, Jeff York's dream, like that of Cousin Lucius in John Donald Wade's *I'll Take My Stand* essay, has an integrity about it that, in the balance of ideals, weighs far more heavily; the agrarian dream itself resembles the tenant farmers who come to town on Saturdays to stand on the corner and watch the city life go by: "They are past many things," says Warren. "They have endured and will endure in their silence and wisdom. They will stand on the street corner and reject the world which passes under their level gaze as a rabble passes under the guns of a rocky citadel around whose base a slatternly town has assembled." [2]

Jeff York's farm and Sonny's cabin are citadels built around a silent, simple flow of life. The mood and light of these places belong to the same world as that portrayed in an album of pictures that Eudora Welty collected, as a hobby, while traveling through rural Mississippi on W.P.A. projects during the depression years of the 1930s. In 1971 the collection, entitled *One Time, One Place*, was published with a fascinating preface by Miss Welty. In her pictures, the faces make more of an impression than the settings, but the remarkable thing is how they go together—the faces with their settings; they belong to each other in a reassuring way. "It is trust that dates the pictures now," comments Miss Welty, "more than the vanished years." [3] The titles of some of the photographs indicate that this was a rural world, indelibly a southern world, but that for a later time it represents by and large a lost world. "Chopping in the field," "Making cane syrup," "Washwoman carrying the clothes," "Saturday in town," "Watermelon on the courthouse grounds," "Carrying the ice for Sunday dinner" are as foreign to the eye trained on the modern southern city as Sonny's going to "borry fire" is foreign to Bowman's.

2. Robert Penn Warren, "The Patented Gate and the Mean Hamburger," in *The Circus in the Attic and Other Stories*, 121.
3. Welty, *One Time, One Place*, 6.

It is in large degree the pastoral sense of abiding community recorded in Miss Welty's pictures that has given the South's literature its historic distinctiveness. The subjects of this study, although their ideologies and evaluations of the South's pastoral tendencies differ radically, share a basic assumption: the South itself has been distinguishable from the rest of the nation primarily because it offered, often insisted upon, a hereditable structure of values that could function as a pastoral rebuke to other systems and standards. The value or validity of using the image of some southern scene as a dream of Arcady to make such a rebuke has been criticized and questioned, as often as it has been upheld, by southern writers themselves. We have seen, in addition to the faith of Page and the nostalgic retreat of Harris, the denial of Charles Chesnutt, the ambiguity of Jean Toomer, and the irony of William Faulkner as responses to the kind of values available within the southern world.

The twentieth-century southern writer, in particular, has been compelled by the circumstances of modern life as well as by his artistic integrity to seek more complex functions for the basic pastoral strategy of measuring a corrupt or diminished present by some vital image of the past which was often employed uncritically by the nineteenth-century writers. Still, as modern southern writers have come to new terms with the fact of change, and as they have taken their own individual stands against the disruptions that accompany it, their responses have often involved the creation of some very tangible, and viably pastoral, community to symbolize the threatened world. Considering such works as *Cane, Absalom, Absalom!, The Golden Apples,* or *I'll Take My Stand,* we see in all of them a communal experience of traditional values through which or against which an individual struggles to search out and maintain his sense of himself. The literature of the South has generally assumed the importance, for good or ill, of the essentially rural, inheritable way of living and the necessity of man's connections to it.

For this reason, two stories by southern writers, Jean Toomer and William Faulkner, are significant as instances of a progression, or perhaps more aptly a procession, away from fictional dreams of southern arcadies that, even from squarely within the same period of pastoral concern that produced the stories of Warren and Welty, indicates a new and different ordering of responses to modernity in more recent times. Each of these writers created a character in a relatively late work who illustrates a kind of imperviousness to the whole concept of a community of shared values and who consequently must be measured by a different standard than pastorally oriented rules of conduct supply. Faulkner's *The Hamlet* contains, in the character of Flem Snopes, the terrifying portrait of modern man totally isolated from community, in fact completely oblivious to, more than even contemptuous of, the kind of force that community traditionally played in the life of an individual. And Jean Toomer's little-known but fascinating story "Mr. Costyve Duditch," published in the *Dial* in 1928, gives us a comparable study. Mr. Duditch would seem on the surface the antithesis of Flem Snopes, but both men illustrate what the individual becomes as the availability of and the accountability to a traditional society recede.

Flem Snopes is so completely alien to the world of Frenchman's Bend that, while he is constantly watched and analyzed by the people who make up the community, he remains totally undefined by it. He is an inscrutable mystery who changes the course of everything connected with the community he inhabits, seemingly without being aware or interested in his impact other than in purely economic terms. When Faulkner relates Flem's early entrance into the Varners' economic monopoly in Frenchman's Bend, he makes this point as he describes Flem's shirt and the way it dirties as the week progresses: "It was as though its wearer, entering though he had into a new life and milieu already channelled to compulsions and customs fixed long before his advent, had nevertheless established in it even on that first day his own particular soiling groove."[4] Flem has an inexhaustible supply of "cousins" but no real family; his kinfolk, his wife, his daughter, in fact all of his social relationships attest to an identity in which the traditional function of marriage, family, parenthood, and neighbors is unrecognizable. After one particularly grim instance of Flem's rapacity, it is said of him by an onlooker, "By God . . . you can't beat him." And that is all that can be said of Flem, whose undeviating attention to wealth without care for comfort and to position without concern for respect cannot be judged, condemned, or forgiven because there is missing in his makeup any moral faculty that

4. William Faulkner, *The Hamlet* (New York, 1940), 58.

might be assailed. The community's function shrinks from that of providing a system of values against which man might be measured to that of providing a gaping, gawking audience for a demon who establishes from the first "his own particular soiling groove."

The image that ends *The Hamlet* is a chilling one in terms of its suggestion concerning the role of the community and the motivations which have replaced the ones that traditionally operated through interaction with a community. The townspeople come to watch the maddened Henry Armstid digging for gold on land that Flem Snopes has sold him after duping him about a supposed buried treasure. They watch "with the decorum of a formal reception, the rapt interest of a crowd watching a magician at a fair." Ritual has degenerated into this sort of mindless curiosity, and Flem Snopes has become a kind of monster-god. When he too comes to watch the frantic digging by Armstid, "the heads of the women holding the nursing children turned to look at him and the heads of the men along the fence turned to watch him pass." It is as if the whole citizenry has been mechanized as Henry has been, who works on, "spading himself into the waxing twilight with the regularity of a mechanical toy." Flem Snopes, the victor, chewing his tobacco "with that steady and measured thrust," has succeeded so thoroughly in outwitting the community because he is the most mechanized of all, like a slot machine incapable of operating without coin, impervious to any other stimulus, measurable in terms of no other compulsion.

Jean Toomer's "Mr. Costyve Duditch," which appeared six years after *Cane*, seems to present a different world and a different species of man from Flem Snopes and Frenchman's Bend. The story is set in Chicago and concerns a sophisticated, sensitive world traveler who has come "home" to this windy metropolis for a brief rest between voyages. Duditch is, the narrator tells us, "a sort of aimless globetrotter"; he has no vocation, no family, no loyalties, no roots. If *Cane* gives us, in Blyden Jackson's words, people who share attitudes, values, and a sense of the past that make them "into a coherent body of people," then "Mr. Costyve Duditch" shows us the void that results when these factors are withdrawn and the individual exists in a kind of cell of self.[5] *Cane* on one level is about the necessity of roots and even Kabnis,

5. Blyden Jackson, in *Southern Literary Study: Problems and Possibilities*, ed. Louis D. Rubin and C. Hugh Holman (Chapel Hill, 1975), 162.

"suspended from the soil," is aware of the value of renewal through connection with the folk community he has come to know in Georgia. Duditch, like Flem Snopes in *The Hamlet*, has gone beyond the point at which he would be able even to recognize what a community is, much less what it might mean: "For his purposes, Peking was just as good as Moscow, Moscow just as good as Paris, London, New York, or Chicago."[6] Like Flem, Duditch is sexless, sterile, "a gelding" as his narrator puts it.

In Costyve Duditch we can see some agonizing self-mockery on the part of Toomer, who, after his exhilarating experience with self-discovery through an association with the black rural South, seems to have propelled himself far beyond what he records in *Cane* and into many other searches, most of them unproductive, for a way to define himself apart from either race or community. Toomer identifies with Costyve Duditch in ways that Faulkner certainly did not identify with Flem Snopes; the disease of these two characters is similar but the presentations differ dramatically. Ironies and confusions surround Duditch who, unlike Flem, is very much aware of a void in his life. Duditch gives the impression "that he was in urgent search of some special something which was nowhere to be found." Duditch's trouble is somewhat comparable to Thomas Sutpen's: he is so completely dislocated that he can define himself only in terms of abstractions. Duditch is in the process of writing three "books": one on "How Travel Grooms the Person," another on "love affairs of great men," and a third on "the creative processes as they are manifest in life and art." The ironies of these studies in relation to Duditch's own supremely disconnected, uncreative life are obvious. At one point, at a cocktail party, he holds forth on "how one never caught the true spirit of El Greco's genius until one had seen his art in the midst of the very conditions, physical and spiritual, which had given it birth and form." While he believes in the value of place and community in forming genius, Duditch himself has no ties to any physical or spiritual community and thus no identity, no sources for genius; even his voice, as he lectures, seems "disembodied," "strangely unrelated not only to the subjects but to Costyve himself." The climax of Toomer's story comes when Duditch appalls the guests at the cocktail party given in his honor

6. Jean Toomer, "Costyve Duditch," in *Dial*, LXXXV (December, 1928), 467.

by nonchalantly discussing his own death. He is able to remark casually, "I have no doubt but what some fine morning a strange person using a foreign tongue will enter my room, cast one frightened glance at my body lying there, and say, 'He's dead.'" The partygoers are dismayed that Duditch can be so calm, that he can even have considered, in so impersonal a fashion, the intimate details of the discovery of his corpse in a foreign land by strangers. Their difference from him resides in their feeling that they belong somewhere and that particularly in death they should be identifiable in terms of specific, familiar places and people. As the guests awkwardly take their leave, Duditch is aware only that he has said some "impolite and terrifying thing," and his response is a usual one for him—he catches the first train out of the city with the wish "to see no human being on earth." In a beautifully understated denouement, Toomer describes how Duditch's "spirit hugged itself in loneliness" and then with gentle irony shows how the world traveler's depression will not last, how speed and motion have become substitutes in his life for love and commitment: "For on awaking in the morning to find himself speeding over some southwest section of the American wilderness, he would bounce from berth, bowl up the aisle, and out-beam all the men in the shaving-room."

"Mr. Costyve Duditch," although appearing only six years after *Cane*, is different enough from the earlier work to seem to belong to a different generation. Toomer's intense quest for identity seems to have led him in a short span of years from the dramatic double sense of belonging and alienation out of which *Cane* was created to the feeling of permanent homelessness and racelessness that resulted in "Mr. Costyve Duditch" and two years later motivated his refusal to allow his work to be included in an anthology of Negro writings. Part Two of *Cane*, the last section of the book to be written, gives some indications of Toomer's feeling of dislocation; the last story of the group, "Bona and Paul," suggests in its treatment of Paul the problems that are chronic in Costyve Duditch: an unrelieved restlessness, an inability to become attached to people or places, a habit of abstraction that dehumanizes. Flem Snopes, even with his total disregard for the concept of community, is set squarely within the context of a definite social milieu which, while it cannot modify or judge him, still provides important values and meanings. On the other hand,

Costyve Duditch is the product of a fragmented, desensitized urban environment which has become almost a staple of American fiction only since World War II.

In these two "late" portraits by Faulkner and Toomer, the emphasis has shifted from the portrayal of characters within a compelling social system to an interest in what happens when people have no meaningful relation to a tradition or community, when traditions and communities in fact no longer provide any stimulus for the establishment of human bonds. This very definite shift indicates a different strain of thought for recent southern literature. The southern writers who molded structures for a southern dream of Arcady based on a pastoral ideal were attempting to deal imaginatively with a series of explosive tensions contained in their culture. However, the oppositions out of which southern literature of pastoral intent has been written—town versus wilderness, Old South versus New South, past versus progress, man in nature versus man in science—no longer seem to provide quite the same essential friction because the victory of town over wilderness, progress over past, new over old has been accomplished in recent years so thoroughly. The opposition between man in nature and man in science goes on in ideological battles in and outside literature, but the question now seems to be the one that Walker Percy says he applies in his novels: "What is it like to be a man in a world transformed by science?"[7]

Much of the literature of the South that has emerged in recent times has gone on to a new territory. There seems to be a void even where memory might be considered available to fix an image of the kind of community Eudora Welty has kept alive in her fiction. Walker Percy's *The Last Gentleman* (1966) is fascinating to consider as an elegy to the southern dream of Arcady—even the book's title reflects the nuances of nostalgia, inevitable decline, and faded chivalry inherent in the South's version of pastoral. Its protagonist, Williston Bibb Barrett, is the scion of an old southern family who has attended Princeton, knows the right people, and is yet a classic example of the "displaced person."

With a short family history Percy manages to condense within Barrett's genealogy a somewhat parodical summary of the whole

---

7. Ashley Brown, "An Interview with Walker Percy," *Shenandoah*, XVIII (Spring, 1967), 6.

southern literary tradition. Barrett's family, in the finest manner of Compson and Sartoris, was "honorable and violent," but "gradually the violence had been deflected and turned inward."[8] From a great-grandfather who knew "what was what" with such certitude that he challenged the grand wizard of the Ku Klux Klan to a duel, the Barrett family sense of noblesse oblige has dwindled down to Will Barrett's father, who committed suicide because, rather like Quentin Compson, he could not bear "the strain of living out an ordinary day in a perfect dance of honor." For Will himself, "life was a gap." He wanders around old Civil War battlegrounds; he works as a janitor in a department store in New York City; when he meets a Negro, they have nothing to say. But "their fathers would have had much to say."

Percy once explained that Will Barrett is on "a passionate pilgrimage that he must follow, and he is looking for a father figure."[9] He is, then, by the familiar southern implications of fatherhood, looking for a way to inherit his tradition. His pilgrimage takes him from New York City back home to Mississippi and beyond, to a confrontation with a southern past which should mean something but doesn't. He is looking for answers—"a watcher and a listener and a wanderer"—and the motivations for his pilgrimage come from the southern community and what it has symbolized to past generations of Barretts, but the answers must be found elsewhere. For in Will's "homeland" his aunts have put a television on the front porch so they can watch enraptured as Bill Cullen gives away cabin cruisers on "Strike It Rich." Will's uncle returns from quail hunting to sit with his black servant and revel in the televised exploits of Chester and Matt Dillon in "Gunsmoke."

In *All the King's Men* Jack Burden goes home to a town named for his ancestors to find and take up the "burden" of answers provided by past and place. Like Will Barrett he has been a watcher, a listener, and a wanderer; he too is looking for a father figure and must cope with his actual father's suicide. Yet Burden can come to terms with his knowledge, his ancestry, and his guilt within an environment which offers standards, responsibilities, obligations. Thus *All the King's Men* provides a touchstone for gauging the distance that *The Last Gentleman* has come from the literature of the period of the southern renascence. It is a distance measurable in terms of the technological ad-

8. Walker Percy, *The Last Gentleman* (New York, 1966), 9.
9. Brown, "Interview with Walker Percy," 7.

vances that have overtaken the rurally ordered southern community. Jack Burden discovered that he was accountable to a world that, while it was in the throes of dramatic, often violent changes, still meant enough to enlist men of conscience in a quest to maintain its values. Will Barrett finds in his South no moral distinctions that matter. Watching his aunts as they hypnotize themselves with the television give-away show, Barrett muses: "The TV studio audience laughed with its quick, obedient, and above all grateful Los Angeles laughter—once we were lonesome back home, the old sad home of our fathers, and here we are together and happy at last." Jack Burden returns to Louisiana from California and learns to abandon to the western land his philosophy of "the Great Twitch." In *The Last Gentleman*, California and the twitch have come to stay in Mississippi.

Walker Percy's Will Barrett, as the comic hero of a new kind of southern fiction, illustrates the problems of lost community and isolation as he struggles against the disintegration of communication in a traditionless society. As a wanderer in a strange land he is not like the wanderers that Toomer shows with Kabnis, or Faulkner with Ike McCaslin, or Welty with Virgie Rainey. The earlier figures, while they might not have the reality of the pastoral community to cling to, are goaded, or tortured, or even sustained by the power of memory to reproduce the "lost forest," a relevant society that, for good or ill, demands attention.

Walker Percy has noted that the South is now "almost as broken a world as the North, and we must learn to live in it."[10] Like writers outside of the South, the southern writer today finds perhaps his greatest challenge in involving his characters in quests for a way to live actively and responsibly within a broken world. The pastoral mode requires a viable myth of the past; southern literature has had such a myth in the dream of Arcady. The pastorally grounded image of a South of old as an Arcadian community represents for most writers today perhaps a garden left too far behind, to use John Crowe Ransom's image.[11] Yet for roughly one hundred years that garden and the southerner's reponse to the loss of it have provided an astonishingly fertile field for artistic response.

10. *Ibid.*, 9.
11. John Crowe Ransom, "Art and the Human Economy," *Kenyon Review* (Autumn, 1945), 687.

Bibliography

Blotner, Joseph. *Faulkner: A Biography.* Vol. I. New York: Random House, 1974.

Bone, Robert. *Down Home: A History of Afro-American Short Fiction from Its Beginnings to the End of the Harlem Renaissance.* New York: G. P. Putnam's Sons, 1975.

Brooks, Cleanth. *Toward Yoknapatawpha and Beyond.* New Haven: Yale University Press, 1978.

———. *William Faulkner: The Yoknapatawpha Country.* New Haven: Yale University Press, 1963.

Brown, Ashley. "An Interview with Walker Percy." *Shenandoah,* XVIII (Spring, 1967), 3–10.

Buck, Paul. *The Road to Reunion, 1865–1900.* Boston: Little, Brown, 1937.

Buckley, William F. "The Southern Imagination: An Interview with Eudora Welty and Walker Percy." *Mississippi Quarterly,* XXVI (Fall, 1972), 493–516.

Bunting, Charles T. "'The Interior World': An Interview with Eudora Welty." *Southern Review,* VIII (Autumn, 1972), 711–35.

Cardwell, Guy. "The Plantation House, An Analogical Image." *Southern Literary Journal,* II (Fall, 1969), 3–21.

Chase, Patricia. "The Women in *Cane.*" *CLA Journal,* XIV (March, 1971), 259–73.

Chesnutt, Charles W. *The Colonel's Dream.* Upper Saddle River, N.J.: Gregg Press, 1968.

———. *The Conjure Woman.* Ann Arbor: University of Michigan Press, 1968.

———. "Dave's Neckliss." *Atlantic Monthly,* LXIV (October, 1889), 500–508.

219

———. "Post-Bellum—Pre-Harlem." In *Breaking into Print*. Ed. Elmer Adler. New York: Simon & Schuster, 1937.

———. *The Wife of His Youth*. Ann Arbor: University of Michigan Press, 1968.

Chesnutt, Helen M. *Charles Waddell Chesnutt: Pioneer of the Color Line*. Chapel Hill: University of North Carolina Press, 1952.

Cousins, Paul M. *Joel Chandler Harris*. Baton Rouge: Louisiana State University Press, 1968.

Cowley, Malcolm. *The Faulkner-Cowley File*. New York: Viking Press, 1966.

———, ed. "Robert Penn Warren." In *Writers at Work: The "Paris Review" Interviews*. New York: Viking Press, 1959.

Davidson, Donald. *Southern Writers in the Modern World*. Athens: University of Georgia Press, 1957.

Davis, Charles T. "Jean Toomer and the South: Region and Race as Elements Within a Literary Imagination." *Studies in the Literary Imagination*, VII (Fall, 1974), 23–37.

Durham, Frank, ed. *Studies in Cane*. Columbus, Ohio: Charles E. Merrill, 1971.

Empson, William. *Some Versions of Pastoral*. Norfolk, Conn.: New Directions, 1950.

Fain, John Tyree, and Thomas Daniel Young, eds. *The Literary Correspondence of Donald Davidson and Allen Tate*. Athens: University of Georgia Press, 1974.

Faulkner, William. *Absalom, Absalom!* New York: Random House, 1936.

———. *Go Down, Moses*. New York: Random House, 1942.

———. *The Hamlet*. New York: Random House, 1940.

———. *Sartoris*. New York: Harcourt, Brace, 1929.

———. *The Sound and the Fury*. New York: Random House, 1946.

———. *The Unvanquished*. New York: Random House, 1934.

Gaines, Francis Pendleton. *The Southern Plantation: A Study in the Development and the Accuracy of a Tradition*. New York: Columbia University Press, 1924.

Gelfant, Blanche H. "Faulkner and Keats: The Ideality of Art in 'The Bear.'" *Southern Literary Journal*, II (Fall, 1969), 43–65.

Greg, Walter W. *Pastoral Poetry and Pastoral Drama*. New York: Russel and Russel, 1959.

Gwynn, Frederick L., and Joseph Blotner, eds. *Faulkner in the University*. New York: Random House, 1959.

Harris, Joel Chandler. *The Complete Tales of Uncle Remus*. Boston: Houghton Mifflin, 1955.

————. *Life of Henry Grady, Including His Writings and Speeches.* New York: Cassell, 1890.

————. *Nights with Uncle Remus.* Boston: James R. Osgood, 1883.

————. *Told by Uncle Remus: New Stories of the Old Plantation.* New York: Grosset and Dunlap, 1905.

————. *Uncle Remus and His Friends: Old Plantation Stories, Songs, and Ballads with Sketches of Negro Character.* Boston: Houghton Mifflin, 1892.

————. *Uncle Remus: His Songs and His Sayings.* New York: Grosset and Dunlap, 1908.

Harris, Julia Collier. *Joel Chandler Harris: Editor and Essayist.* Chapel Hill: University of North Carolina Press, 1931.

————. *The Life and Letters of Joel Chandler Harris.* Boston: Houghton Mifflin, 1918.

Hoffman, Frederick J. "Sense of Place." In *South: Modern Southern Literature in Its Cultural Setting.* Eds. Louis D. Rubin, Jr., and Robert D. Jacobs. New York: Doubleday, 1961.

Howells, William Dean. "Mr. Charles W. Chesnutt's Stories." *Atlantic Monthly,* LXXV (May, 1900), 699–701.

————. "A Psychological Counter-Current in Recent Fiction." *North American Review,* CLXXIII (December, 1901), 881–83.

I'll Take My Stand: The South and the Agrarian Tradition by Twelve Southerners. New York: Harper & Row, 1930. Reprint 1962 with intro. by Louis D. Rubin, Jr.

Jackson, Blyden. "The Negro's Image of the Universe as Reflected in His Fiction." In *Black Voices: An Anthology of Afro-American Literature.* New York: New American Library, 1968, pp.623–61.

Kennedy, John Pendleton. *Swallow Barn: A Sojourn in the Old Dominion.* Ed. Jay B. Hubbell. New York: Harcourt, Brace, 1929.

Kermode, Frank, ed. *English Pastoral Poetry.* London: George G. Garrup, 1952.

Korenman, Joan S. "Faulkner's Grecian Urn." *Southern Literary Journal,* VII (Fall, 1974), 3–23.

King, Grace Elizabeth. *Memoirs of a Southern Woman of Letters.* New York: Macmillan, 1932.

Lanier, Sidney. *The Centennial Edition of the Works of Sidney Lanier.* 10 Vols. Baltimore: Johns Hopkins Press, 1945.

Lewis, R. W. B. "William Faulkner: The Hero in the New World." In *Faulkner: A Collection of Critical Essays.* Englewood Cliffs, N.J.: Prentice-Hall, 1966.

Locke, Alain. *The New Negro.* New York: Albert and Charles Boni, 1925.

Lynen, John F. *The Pastoral Art of Robert Frost*. New Haven, Conn.: Yale University Press, 1960.

Marx, Leo. *The Machine in the Garden*. New York: Oxford University Press, 1964.

Nelson, John Herbert. *The Negro Character in American Literature*. Lawrence, Kansas: Department of Journalism Press, 1926.

Page, Rosewell. *Thomas Nelson Page: A Memoir of a Virginia Gentleman*. New York: Charles Scribner's Sons, 1923.

Page, Thomas Nelson. *Gordon Keith*. New York: Charles Scribner's Sons, 1903.

———. *In Ole Virginia*. Chapel Hill: University of North Carolina Press, 1969.

———. *The Negro: The Southerner's Problem*. New York: Charles Scribner's Sons, 1904.

———. *The Old South*. New York: Charles Scribner's Sons, 1894.

———. *Red Rock: A Chronicle of Reconstruction*. Ridgewood, N.J.: Gregg Press, 1967.

———. *Two Little Confederates*. New York: Charles Scribner's Sons, 1916.

Percy, Walker. *The Last Gentleman*. New York: Farrar, Straus and Giroux, 1966.

Pratt, William, ed. *The Fugitive Poets: Modern Southern Poetry in Perspective*. New York: E. P. Dutton, 1965.

Price, Reynolds. "The Onlooker, Smiling: An Early Reading of *The Optimist's Daughter*." *Shenandoah*, XX (Spring, 1969), 58–72.

Ransom, John Crowe. "Art and the Human Economy." *Kenyon Review*, VII (Autumn, 1945), 683–88.

Redding, J. Saunders. *To Make a Poet Black*. Chapel Hill: University of North Carolina Press, 1939.

Rubin, Louis D., Jr. "Southern Local Color and the Black Man." *Southern Review*, VI (Autumn, 1970), 1011–30.

———. *The Wary Fugitives: Four Poets and the South*. Baton Rouge: Louisiana State University Press, 1978.

———. *Writers of the Modern South*. Seattle: University of Washington Press, 1966.

———, and C. Hugh Holman, eds. *Southern Literary Study: Problems and Possibilities*. Chapel Hill: University of North Carolina Press, 1975.

Starke, Aubrey Harrison. *Sidney Lanier: A Biographical and Critical Study*. Chapel Hill: University of North Carolina Press, 1933.

Tate, Allen. *Collected Essays*. Denver: Alan Swallow, 1959.

———. *The Fathers*. Baton Rouge: Louisiana State University Press, 1977.

———. Letter to the Editors. *Partisan Review*, VI (Winter, 1939), 125–26.

Toomer, Jean. *Cane*. New York: Harper & Row, 1969.

———. "Mr. Costyve Duditch." *The Dial*, LXXXV (December, 1928), 460–76.

Toomer Collection. Fisk University, Nashville, Tennessee.

Tourgée, Albion. "The South as a Field for Fiction." *Forum*, VI (February, 1888), 404–13.

Turner, Darwin. *In a Minor Chord*. Carbondale: Southern Illinois University Press, 1971.

Wade, John Donald. *Selected Essays and Other Writings of John Donald Wade*. Athens: University of Georgia Press, 1966.

Wagner, Jean. *Black Poets of the United States*. Urbana: University of Illinois Press, 1973.

Warren, Robert Penn. *The Circus in the Attic and Other Stories*. New York: Harcourt, Brace, 1947.

Weaver, Richard M. *The Southern Tradition at Bay: A History of Postbellum Thought*. New Rochelle, N.Y.: Arlington House Publishers, 1968.

Welty, Eudora. *A Curtain of Green and Other Stories*. New York: Harcourt, Brace, 1941.

———. *Delta Wedding*. New York: Harcourt, Brace, 1945.

———. *The Golden Apples*. New York: Harcourt, Brace, 1947.

———. *Losing Battles*. New York: Random House, 1970.

———. *One Time, One Place*. New York: Random House, 1971.

———. *The Optimist's Daughter*. New York: Random House, 1972.

———. "Place in Fiction." *South Atlantic Quarterly*, LV (January, 1956), 57–72.

———. "Some Notes on River Country." *Harper's Bazaar*, No. 2786 (February, 1944), 150–56.

———. "Some Notes on Time in Fiction." *Mississippi Quarterly*, XXVI (Fall, 1972), 483–92.

———. *The Wide Net and Other Stories*. New York: Harcourt, Brace, 1943.

Williams, Raymond. *The Country and the City*. New York: Oxford University Press, 1973.

Wilson, Edmund. *Patriotic Gore: Studies in the Literature of the American Civil War*. New York: Oxford University Press, 1962.

Woodward, C. Vann. *Origins of the New South, 1877–1913*. Baton Rouge: Louisiana State University Press, 1951.

Index

225

Walden. *See* Thoreau, Henry David
Warren, Robert Penn: involvement in
"I'll Take My Stand, 134–36;
criticism of Sidney Lanier, 33
—Writings: *All the King's Men*, 216;
"Blackberry Winter," 154–55; "The
Patented Gate and the Mean
Hamburger," 208–209
Washington, Booker T., 104
Washington College, 41
Wasson, Ben, 157
Weaver, Richard, 15–16
Welty, Eudora: 7–8, 133, 180,
181–206, 215, 217; place in,
183–84, 200–201, 209; time in,
198–99; relationship of place and
time, 181–82, 202–206; compared
to Faulkner, 183; use of past, 199ff;
object figures, 184–85, 191–92, 195;
outsiders, 184, 185–86, 191, 196,
199; insiders, 184, 190–91, 206;
seers (onlookers), 184, 187–90,
191–92, 199–206

—Writings: "Death of a Traveling
Salesman," 207–208; *Delta Wedding*,
184–88, 191–95, 199; *The Golden
Apples*, 181, 184, 185, 188–89, 191,
199–202; *Losing Battles*, 184, 185,
189–90, 191, 194–99; *One Time,
One Place*, 183–84, 202–203, 206,
209; *The Optimist's Daughter*,
184–87, 190–91, 199, 202–206;
"Place in Fiction," 182, 184; "A Still
Moment," 180
Whitman, Walt, 21
Williams, Raymond, 4–6, 29
Wilson, Edmund, 37
Wirt, William, 9
Wolfe, Thomas, 33
Woodward, C. Vann, 8, 9, 13
World War I, 132
World War II, 215

Yeats, William Butler, 146
Young, Stark, 136; "Not in Memoriam,
But in Defense," 143